IT HAPPENED TO ME

Series Editor: Arlene Hirschfelder

Books in the It Happened to Me series are designed for inquisitive teens digging for answers about certain illnesses, social issues, or lifestyle interests. Whether you are deep into your teen years or just entering them, these books are gold mines of up-to-date information, riveting teen views, and great visuals to help you figure out stuff. Besides special boxes highlighting singular facts, each book is enhanced with the latest reading lists, websites, and an index. Perfect for browsing, there are loads of expert information by acclaimed writers to help parents, guardians, and librarians understand teen illness, tough situations, and lifestyle choices.

1. *Epilepsy: The Ultimate Teen Guide,* by Kathlyn Gay and Sean McGarrahan, 2002.
2. *Stress Relief: The Ultimate Teen Guide,* by Mark Powell, 2002.
3. *Learning Disabilities: The Ultimate Teen Guide,* by Penny Hutchins Paquette and Cheryl Gerson Tuttle, 2003.
4. *Making Sexual Decisions: The Ultimate Teen Guide,* by L. Kris Gowen, 2003.
5. *Asthma: The Ultimate Teen Guide,* by Penny Hutchins Paquette, 2003.
6. *Cultural Diversity—Conflicts and Challenges: The Ultimate Teen Guide,* by Kathlyn Gay, 2003.
7. *Diabetes: The Ultimate Teen Guide,* by Katherine J. Moran, 2004.
8. *When Will I Stop Hurting? Teens, Loss, and Grief: The Ultimate Teen Guide to Dealing with Grief,* by Ed Myers, 2004.
9. *Volunteering: The Ultimate Teen Guide,* by Kathlyn Gay, 2004.
10. *Organ Transplants—A Survival Guide for the Entire Family: The Ultimate Teen Guide,* by Tina P. Schwartz, 2005.
11. *Medications: The Ultimate Teen Guide,* by Cheryl Gerson Tuttle, 2005.
12. *Image and Identity—Becoming the Person You Are: The Ultimate Teen Guide,* by L. Kris Gowen and Molly C. McKenna, 2005.
13. *Apprenticeship: The Ultimate Teen Guide,* by Penny Hutchins Paquette, 2005.
14. *Cystic Fibrosis: The Ultimate Teen Guide,* by Melanie Ann Apel, 2006.
15. *Religion and Spirituality in America: The Ultimate Teen Guide,* by Kathlyn Gay, 2006.
16. *Gender Identity: The Ultimate Teen Guide,* by Cynthia L. Winfield, 2007.

17. *Physical Disabilities: The Ultimate Teen Guide,* by Denise Thornton, 2007.

18. *Money—Getting It, Using It, and Avoiding the Traps: The Ultimate Teen Guide,* by Robin F. Brancato, 2007.

19. *Self-Advocacy: The Ultimate Teen Guide,* by Cheryl Gerson Tuttle and JoAnn Augeri Silva, 2007.

20. *Adopted: The Ultimate Teen Guide,* by Suzanne Buckingham Slade, 2007.

21. *The Military and Teens: The Ultimate Teen Guide,* by Kathlyn Gay, 2008.

22. *Animals and Teens: The Ultimate Teen Guide,* by Gail Green, 2009.

23. *Reaching Your Goals: The Ultimate Teen Guide,* by Anne Courtright, 2009.

24. *Juvenile Arthritis: The Ultimate Teen Guide,* by Kelly Rouba, 2009.

25. *Obsessive-Compulsive Disorder: The Ultimate Teen Guide,* by Natalie Rompella, 2009.

26. *Body Image and Appearance: The Ultimate Teen Guide,* by Kathlyn Gay, 2009.

27. *Writing and Publishing: The Ultimate Teen Guide,* by Tina P. Schwartz, 2010.

28. *Food Choices: The Ultimate Teen Guide,* by Robin F. Brancato, 2010.

29. *Immigration: The Ultimate Teen Guide,* by Tatyana Kleyn, 2011.

30. *Living with Cancer: The Ultimate Teen Guide,* by Denise Thornton, 2011.

31. *Living Green: The Ultimate Teen Guide,* by Kathlyn Gay, 2012.

32. *Social Networking: The Ultimate Teen Guide,* by Jenna Obee, 2012.

33. *Sports: The Ultimate Teen Guide,* by Gail Fay, 2013.

34. *Adopted: The Ultimate Teen Guide, Revised Edition,* by Suzanne Buckingham Slade, 2013.

35. *Bigotry and Intolerance: The Ultimate Teen Guide,* by Kathlyn Gay, 2013.

36. *Substance Abuse: The Ultimate Teen Guide,* by Sheri Bestor, 2013.

37. *LGBTQ Families: The Ultimate Teen Guide,* by Eva Apelqvist, 2013.

38. *Bullying: The Ultimate Teen Guide,* by Mathangi Subramanian, 2014.

39. *Eating Disorders: The Ultimate Teen Guide,* by Jessica R. Greene, 2014.

40. *Speech and Language Challenges: The Ultimate Teen Guide,* by Marlene Targ Brill, 2014.

41. *Divorce: The Ultimate Teen Guide,* by Kathlyn Gay, 2014.

DIVORCE

THE ULTIMATE TEEN GUIDE

KATHLYN GAY

IT HAPPENED TO ME, NO. 41

ROWMAN & LITTLEFIELD
Lanham • Boulder • New York • Toronto • Plymouth, UK

Published by Rowman & Littlefield
4501 Forbes Boulevard, Suite 200, Lanham, Maryland 20706
www.rowman.com

10 Thornbury Road, Plymouth PL6 7PP, United Kingdom

British Library Cataloguing in Publication Information Available

Library of Congress Cataloging-in-Publication Data

Gay, Kathlyn.
    Divorce : the ultimate teen guide / Kathlyn Gay.
        pages cm. — (It happened to me ; No. 41)
    Includes bibliographical references and index.
    ISBN 978-0-8108-9238-5 (cloth : alk. paper) — ISBN 978-0-8108-9239-2 (ebook)
    1. Children of divorced parents—Psychology—Juvenile literature. 2. Divorce—Juvenile literature. 3. Divorced parents—Juvenile literature. 4. Stepfamilies—Juvenile literature. I. Title.
    HQ777.5.G39 2014
    306.89—dc23
                                                                            2014007662

Contents

1 Dealing with Parental Separation and Divorce 1

2 Divorcing in the Past 17

3 Breaking Up 31

4 Struggling and Hurting 47

5 Placing Blame and Taking Sides 61

6 Being in the Middle 75

7 Worrying about Money 91

8 Coping with Addiction, Depression, and Jailed Parents 107

9 Learning to Cope with Divorce 121

10 Living in a Stepfamily 135

11 Staying Connected and Communicating after Divorce 149

12 Planning for a Future Marriage—or Not 163

Appendix: Sample Nonmarital Cohabitation Agreement 181

Helpful Resources 183

Notes 187

Selected Bibliography 207

Index 209

About the Author 213

1

DEALING WITH PARENTAL SEPARATION AND DIVORCE

....

"I had just come home from the last day of school in my 10th grade. I checked the answering machine for new messages and I found what I had least expected—a message from my mother's divorce lawyer. Even though all the warning signs had been there, I was still surprised. . . . I thought my family was completely normal. One of my friends had even commented that my family was perfect. It turns out, not so much."
—Creigh, writing for the website Divorce and Teens[1]

Like Creigh, many young people are completely surprised when it happens—they probably thought it would never happen to them. Still others expect it. "It" is parental divorce. As Ryan from the Chicago suburbs noted in 2011 when he was sixteen,

[In] November . . . my father announced he and my mom are splitting up and getting a divorce. I foresaw this years ago when I was in 8th grade, but ever since then it just sat in the back of my mind and would only manifest whenever they argued. Arguments escalated; verbally not physically, dad came home from work later, mom stuck to doing the laundry and complaining. Everyone in the house was sucked into an unhappy routine, my sister and twin brother also just seem to get used to the fights and the awkward living conditions. It was like we were all waiting for one of them to make a serious move, and one day it happened.[2]

A twenty-one-year-old male from the Philippines now living in California was taken aback to learn about his parents' breakup. He explained that his mom moved to the United States in 2003 and his father stayed in the Philippines. The first time his mom went back home was around 2010. He said,

> I never saw it [the divorce] coming, they only told me on my eighteenth birthday. Their divorce was the year before they told me. I tried to not think about it. It is as if they decided to get a divorce over the phone or through email. My mom was the one who sat me down and told me. I was shocked. First, I was surprised and a little upset and all I was thinking of was my younger sister; she was ten at the time.[3]

When divorce happens, an entire family is affected. In some cases, the breakup of a family can be one of the most devastating life experiences for all involved. Katie, a Michigan teenager, responded to a poem about divorce on FamilyFriend Poems.com. She wrote,

> When my mom was pregnant with me my dad cheated on her then decided he didn't want a family and left with hardly a goodbye. He visited when I was 2. Then I didn't see him again until I was 5. Then he disappeared. I turned 16 in April [2011] and felt like something was missing so I looked him up and found him. Finally getting to know the man that helped bring me into the world is rough. I'm getting so many of my questions answered though and I found out that he regrets every day what he did. I have two little brothers too! No it's not perfect now and I've spent many days crying. It's not an easy road but I'm willing to do this so maybe one day I won't have to wonder about him and we can finally be a family.[4]

Yet, there are also situations where parental divorce or separation can bring some measure of relief, particularly if children and teenagers fear a parent because of threatened or actual physical, mental, or sexual abuse. One teenager in Waukegan, Illinois, said that he was relieved when his parents divorced. His father once threw a knife at him, and that left the teenager afraid for his life. When asked the whereabouts of his father, the boy merely shrugged and reported matter-of-factly that his father steals cars and drives them south. The teenager had no desire to see his father again.

Effects of Divorce

The effects on broken families can take many forms, depending on numerous factors such as age, financial and social status, personalities, and religious beliefs. Some offspring of divorcing parents fear they will be abandoned. Many young

Watch It!

Torn Apart (2009) is a documentary produced by an Australian youth known as bigmiki139 and produced as part of a course at the Gap State High School's Film and Television department. Uploaded to YouTube, the documentary opens with angry parents arguing, accusing, and threatening each other. Their conflicts dramatize the prelude to separation and divorce, setting the stage for teenagers to comment on the fallout from family breakups. One teen girl recalled her father leaving; another remembered the "fighting and yelling and stuff" at home; a male youth said, "I've been disadvantaged by not having a father in my childhood . . . especially one with such talent that could have helped me."

Feeling abandoned, angry, used, and manipulated and having trouble with relationships are all effects of divorce that the teenagers express. But some noted that they became more independent and grew up earlier than their peers and gained a realistic perspective on life. The documentary ends with counsel to other teens. As one girl advised, "Be strong and be yourself."[a]

people exhibit anger when their parents divorce. Often that anger is directed at the parent thought to be responsible for the family breakup. Sometimes youth vent their anger on classmates or act out by destroying property. Teenagers' reactions can range from shame and embarrassment to conflicts over whose side to take—mom's or dad's. Instability, depression, loneliness, and longing for the way things used to be are other common teen reactions to their parents' divorce.

Children and teens who have been adopted are especially fearful and vulnerable when parents divorce. Debbie B. Riley wrote about this on Adoptive Families.com. She explained,

During adolescence, many adoptees begin to ask harder questions about their birth families, and why they were relinquished; and they may feel sad or angry about their adoption. They may feel as though they had been rejected by their birthparents, that the adoption was somehow their fault, or that they had no control over the decisions made by the adults in their lives. When adoptive parents divorce, many of these feelings are rekindled: A teen may feel rejected by the parent who "leaves" her, at fault for her parents' split, or angry that she has no control over her family situation. She may also feel a keen sense of loss over the fracture in her adoptive family.

On the same website, an adoptee in her twenties who was a teenager when her parents divorced, noted, "At the time, I remember thinking, 'Why do people keep leaving me?' It was the saddest time of my life. As I watched my dad move out, I felt utterly alone."[5]

When adoptive parents divorce, adoptees often believe they face parental loss twice. In other words, the adoptees may feel biological parents gave them away and then adoptive parents abandoned them. Adoptees may also worry that when their parents divorce, their adoption will be terminated, which legally is not the case unless the adoption was not finalized before the divorce. In addition, they may feel isolated from others around them if, for example, their skin color or culture differs from their adoptive family members.

Even within intact families, many young people fear that their parents *might* separate or divorce, and that fear can last a lifetime. For instance, one middle-age father says that even though his parents stayed married for decades, he knew as a teenager that his parents were miserable together. But he was glad his mother and father stayed married; he had a great fear about the family breaking up and did not want to go through that. When he thinks back, he still remembers the fear of having a broken family.

A Widely Publicized Topic

The fear of a family breakup can be heightened by the media. The topic of divorce is often discussed on TV shows, portrayed in movies and videos, and written about in newspapers and magazines. News media convey numerous stories (sometimes called scandals) about the breakups of politicians such as former South Carolina governor Mark Sanford, whose wife divorced him. While he was in office, Sanford disappeared for six days saying he was "hiking the Appalachian trail," but he was actually visiting his mistress (now fiancée) Maria Belen Chapu in Argentina.

Yet, in April 2013, Sanford won the Republican nomination for South Carolina's seat in the U.S. House of Representatives. Political pundits suggest that in current times divorce is not a major factor in politics as it was in the 1960s, say, when Nelson Rockefeller hoped to be the Republican nominee for the U.S. presidential race. He lost to Barry Goldwater, in part because he was divorced. On the other hand, Ronald Reagan won the presidency for two terms, even though he was the first (and only) divorcee to be elected president, serving two terms (1981–1989).

Other political divorce stories or scandals (depending on one's point of view) that have made news include those of

- former U.S. House speaker (1995–1999) Newt Gingrich, who divorced his first wife in 1981, discussing the settlement while she was in the hospital recovering from tumor surgery; he and his second wife divorced in 1999 after she refused Gingrich's request to have an "open marriage" so he could carry on his relationship with his mistress, now his wife, Callista.
- former 2008 presidential candidate and former New York City mayor (1994–2001) Rudi Giuliani, who announced at a 2000 press conference that he was divorcing his second wife, Donna Hanover. This was news to Hanover, and she refused to leave the governor's mansion. She also tried to prevent Giuliani's mistress from living in the place.
- former Nevada governor Jim Gibbons, the state's first incumbent governor to lose his party's primary in 2008, which many believe was due to his nasty divorce.
- former vice president (1993–2001) and later presidential candidate Al Gore and his wife, Tipper, who divorced in 2010 after decades of marriage.

Divorces of movie stars, sports figures, and other celebrities also make news, such as the breakups of actors Tom Cruise and Katie Holmes; TV personality Kim Kardashian and basketball player Kris Humphries; comedian Russell Brand and recording artist and songwriter Katy Perry; professional golfer Tiger Woods and former Swedish model Elin Nordegren; actress Olivia Wilde and Italian filmmaker Tao Ruspoli; film luminaries Jennifer Aniston and Brad Pitt; singers Jennifer Lopez and Marc Anthony; actor Orlando Bloom and model Miranda Kerr—plus many others.

On the popular *Dr. Phil* TV show, married or divorcing couples are frequent guests who air their grievances with each other. In addition, *Oprah* and other reality TV programs like *Divorce Court* have long dealt with unhappy married couples and marriage dissolution (the legal term for divorce). *Happily Divorced*, a weekly TV comedy whose second season ended in February 2013, centered on a Los Angeles florist played by Fran Drescher. She dealt with the aftermath of divorcing her realtor husband, who she unexpectedly discovered is gay, and many of the episodes involved Fran's new relationships and humorous encounters with suitors. All the while her ex-husband, played by John Michael Higgins, still lived under the same roof. Viewers have petitioned for a third season of the series that is based on experiences of Dresher and her real-life ex-husband Peter Marc Jacobson.

Even *Sesame Street* has a segment on divorce, although the first attempt in the early 1990s failed miserably. Preschool viewers were devastated when the character Snuffy (Mr. Snuffleupagus) tearfully tells Big Bird, "My dad is moving out of our cave." Big Bird wants to know why and learns from Snuffy that it's "because of something called divorce." Youngsters watching the trial show worried about where Snuffy and his sister Alice would live, whether they would be loved, and whether their own parents would divorce. While viewing the show, youngsters were crying. That segment was cancelled, but in December 2012 another version was ready to be shown.[6]

The new video is part of a multimedia kit called *Little Children, Big Challenges* presented only online. Divorced or separated parents can view it with their children. In the video, preschooler Abby Cadabby, a magical Muppet, talks about her parents' divorce, which has already happened, and she shows crayon pictures that she has drawn of her two houses. As she says, "This one is where I live with my mommy and this one is where I live with my daddy." When the other Muppets ask Gordon why Abby has two houses, he explains some of the reasons people divorce.[7]

Along with all the media hype about marital breakups are numerous statistics on U.S. marriages and divorces. For example, the U.S. Centers for Disease Control and Prevention (CDC) reported in 2012 that based on data from the 2010 census the U.S. divorce rate was 3.6 per 1,000 population, with forty-four states and the District of Columbia reporting. California, Georgia, Hawaii, Indiana, Louisiana, and Minnesota do not gather such data, so the CDC can only project the divorce rate for the nation.[8] Various studies show that at least 50 percent of first marriages and up to 75 percent of second marriages in the United States will end in divorce. That means large numbers of children, teenagers, and young adults feel the effects of broken families.

Other statistics indicate that couples who marry in their early teens are more likely to divorce than those who marry in their twenties or thirties. If married teenagers have dropped out of high school, their chances of marital breakup increase. Married couples who have a college education have a higher probability of keeping their marriages intact. The U.S. Bureau of Labor Statistics issued a report in 2013 that points out that about 30 percent of married college graduates divorced compared to half of the couples that did not complete high school.[9]

The *HuffingtonPost.com* also published a report in 2013, stating, "In states with high shares of college-educated adults, men and women marry at older ages. . . . In states with low shares of college-educated adults, adults are more likely than average to marry three or more times. In states with low income levels, men are more likely than average to have been married three or more times."[10]

In spite of statistics, TV portrayals, and news stories on divorce, most Americans view marriage positively and see it as a union that lasts "until death do us part." In an article for Disney World's Family.com, Carma Haley pointed out that teenagers "still hold the union of marriage sacred and in high regard." Seventeen-

> ## ! Access This!
>
> Literally millions of Internet sites contain advice for parents who are divorcing and for children of divorce. They include psychology blogs, newspaper and magazine articles, medical and counseling guidance, religious views, workshops, family resource centers, support groups, and published academic studies. Some sites are especially for teenagers, such as DivorceandTeens.weebly.com, and SafeTeens.org. Others are aimed at both teens and parents such as Divorce360.com and ChildrenandDivorce.com.

year-old Mallory of Illinois thought that "people get divorced because they try to rush into things . . . so many people are getting married so young, that they don't know what they want. The first person that comes along, they automatically think that he/she is the 'right' person for them." Mallory told reporter Haley that she does not plan to marry early: "I think that if I marry the first guy I 'fall in love with' I will only become a statistic. I think I will reduce my risk of becoming a divorce statistic by not rushing into things and by knowing that it is right."[11]

Causes of Divorce

As divorce rates have increased over the past decades, more and more studies and surveys have been conducted to try to determine the causes. Many personal factors and conditions may determine whether couples will stay together. Some researchers suggest that major events in the nation's history, such as wars and the state of the economy, affect both marriage and divorce.

During World War II (1939–1945), for example, there was a great increase in marriages. Thousands of the wartime marriages were likely based on the idea that the present was all that counted because the future held the probability of a loved one's death. Immediately after the war, divorces skyrocketed, too. Many couples who had been apart for long terms during the war found they were not well matched after they were reunited. For them, the only alternative seemed to be divorce.

More recent wars in Iraq and Afghanistan have had similar effects on military couples. Some veterans of these wars have had difficulties trying to make the transition to civilian life. Both veterans and spouses change during the time they are apart. Frequently, when veterans return to civilian life, they discover that their marital relationships are not what they used to be, and sometimes they have to adjust to new and different roles in the family. The same is true for civilian spouses. If couples are unable to cope, particularly if a veteran suffers from post-traumatic stress disorder or returns with physical injuries, the marriage may be headed toward a breakup.

In 2012, the overall military (Army, Navy, Air Force, and Marine Corps) divorce rate was 3.5 percent—about the same as the U.S. civilian population and down slightly from 3.7 percent of military divorces in 2011. "Enlisted female soldiers and Marines, however, continue to experience the highest rate of divorce—9.4 percent and 9.3 percent respectively," reported Amy Bushatz on Military.com. Nevertheless, Bushatz also noted that the military divorce rate has remained fairly steady for decades.[12]

Generally, some groups or categories of people may be "divorce prone." Age and education, as statistics show, are factors in marital breakup. Divorce may occur if one or both of the partners come from a split family. Interfaith couples with children may also be likely to divorce *if* they cannot agree on how to raise their offspring. Hollywood celebrities Tom Cruise, a Scientologist, and Katie Holmes, a former Catholic, are examples. The religious upbringing of their daughter was a source of conflict that finally resulted in divorce.

Financial difficulties can lead to conflicts and stresses that trigger separations or divorce proceedings. Some experts even contend that money problems top the

Divorcing parents in a lawyer's office.

reasons couples divorce. Suppose, for example, a couple has limited income and each partner has conflicting attitudes about how to spend money. One spouse is a spender and likes to buy nonessential items (like video games) while the other is thrifty and believes that the couple's priority should be using earnings for basics like food, clothes, and housing. But there is not enough income to cover both nonessentials and basics. The practical spouse might frequently express resentment toward the free spender who in turn might respond with accusations that the frugal person is a "spoilsport" and doesn't want to have fun. Eventually such arguments over money can contribute to other disagreements that trigger divorce proceedings.

There are many other factors that lead to breakups. For example, some couples cannot agree on marital roles—who should care for the children, who should handle the money, and so forth. Differences in political views can create conflicts that become so heated that they prompt couples to separate. If one partner's family disapproves of a marriage, that situation can have a negative effect on a couple. Alcohol and other drug addiction, obsessive gambling, and physical and mental abuse can destroy families as well as individuals. Then there are those who say they no longer love their spouse. They want a divorce so they can date, cohabit with, or marry someone else.

In the opinion of Cathy Meyer, who has worked for years with divorcing couples, there are three major causes of divorce: (1) laziness—couples do not want to work at saving their marriage; (2) lack of communication—people don't talk or listen to each other; (3) unrealistic expectations about marriage.[13] But whatever the causes, they are not legal grounds (reasons allowed by a court) for granting a divorce. The statutes for dissolution of marriage are set by each state.

Legal Grounds

Before a divorce is granted, a spouse (petitioner) files a Petition for Dissolution of Marriage in the county court where he or she lives. "This document states that one or both parties seek to dissolve the marriage; it then lists the legal grounds for the request," explained Jennifer Bender on LegalZoom.com. "One or both parties may sign the petition. If only one party signs the petition, that party must serve the other party with the petition and a summons. If both parties sign the petition, the court deems the parties in agreement and no trial is scheduled. If one party serves a petition and the other party fails to respond within the state statutory time limits, the filing party can submit a signed divorce decree for the approval of the court. The divorce decree is the formal court order setting forth the terms and conditions ending the marriage," such as how property will be divided and who will have custody of the children.[14]

For years in the United States, one party petitioning for divorce has had to prove according to the law that the other spouse was responsible (at fault) for breaking up the marriage. In a fault divorce the grounds include adultery, physical abuse, desertion, alcohol or other drug addiction, imprisonment, or severe mental illness of the person accused of being at fault. Even if neither party was at fault, couples had to place blame for marital breakups. For example, a couple might agree between them that their marriage is not working, but in court a wife or husband would charge the other spouse with, say, "mental cruelty" or "mean and violent behavior." Such charges could cause the accused person to become bitter and angry.

However, U.S. divorce laws have altered over the years, in part because they reflect the changing attitudes of the population and the lawmakers who represent them. Currently every state has passed some form of no-fault divorce laws, which means neither spouse has to prove that the other one is responsible for the breakup. Either spouse can sue for divorce because of irreconcilable differences or incompatibility—they simply cannot get along.

States have different regulations for no-fault divorce, and frequently require that one of the spouses live in the state for a certain amount of time before filing for divorce. For example, at the end of 2013, the residence requirement was six months in Alabama, ninety days in Colorado, twelve consecutive months in New Jersey, six months in Texas (as well as ninety days in the county where the filing takes place), and sixty days in Wyoming. As of 2013 in Washington State, a person simply has to live in the state at the time he or she files for divorce, and in New Hampshire there is no residency requirement.

In some cases couples agree to a "collaborative divorce." This means lawyers and other professionals like accountants and psychologists help a couple come to mutual agreements regarding their divorce. Rather than engaging in court fights, all involved work together to end a marriage peacefully, without rancor, which is especially beneficial if there are children. A family law judge in Florida noted that collaborative divorce takes "the decision away from the person sitting in a robe in the courtroom, who's a stranger to [the couple's] children." Instead, parents with professional assistance, make the arrangements regarding custody, visitation, and so forth.[15]

When couples consider a divorce, the question sometimes arises, "Do we need a lawyer?" The answer is not necessarily. If couples agree on conditions of the dissolution, they may opt for a pro se or do-it-yourself divorce, completing the paperwork, filing it with the court, and attending a hearing without the aid of an attorney. Most states have websites that provide links to free online divorce forms that can be downloaded. The documents have the required legal language and space to fill in details. A court clerk's office also may provide the needed forms.

What Is Custody?

When there are minor children of a marriage, divorce settlements often include custody—provisions to determine where children will live and who will care for them on a daily basis. Custodial arrangements also establish religious training and medical care of children, schools they will attend, and other matters. In some cases, a parent may have sole custody, meaning that children live with only one parent and visit the other.

If joint custody is allowed by the court, it can mean parenting is shared and that a child takes turns living with each of the parents. But that does not necessarily mean there is an equal arrangement for child care. For example, a mother may have sole custody but both mother and father have a say in decisions about their offspring's activities. Sometimes, parents are unable to care for their children, so the court selects a guardian (a close relative or perhaps foster parents) to make decisions about children's welfare and provide a home.

Whatever the custody arrangements, lawyers, judges, psychologists, counselors, and others say they try to make judgments based on the best interests of the children, although no one can be sure exactly what "best interests" are since most people agree that an intact family is "best." Perhaps in custody arrangements the decisions should be based on what is "least likely to harm" the children.

In recent years, there has been a trend among wealthy couples who divorce to arrange a different type of custody for their children. It is sometimes called "nesting." Instead of the offspring moving back and forth from one parent's house to the other's, the progeny stay put and the parents move out. Some people suggest this is a formula for disaster. But in these instances, each parent takes a turn at caregiving and running the household. In other words, when mom is in charge, dad moves out, and when dad comes back to take over, mom moves out. "There are no reliable figures on how widespread nesting is, maybe because it's often a temporary arrangement," writes Belinda Luscombe in *Time* magazine, adding, "it's still unconventional enough that many people who do it aren't eager to talk about it. Those who are willing say that for their kids, not having to shuttle between parents or leave the home they've always known provides stability and continuity at a time of turmoil." Luscombe includes a comment from Kamaria, who "was 14 when her parents split and was finishing high school by the time they gave up their 3 1/2-year [nesting] experiment. 'I think it made my experience of the separation a little easier,' Kamaria told Luscombe. 'I'm very close to both my parents now.'"[16]

Teenagers frequently ask, "Why can't we make decisions about where to live and go to school?" They want a choice in custody arrangements, and that is taken into consideration if a judge deems the teenagers are mature enough to contribute to the decision. For example, a judge would take into account whether a teen is afraid of physical abuse from one parent; whether a teen believes a parent needs her or his help; or whether a teen fears rejection by a parent who has no custody rights.

Religious Views

Religious faith can play a major role in both marriage and divorce. Although some Americans view marriage as a social contract, theologians, clergy, and traditional religious individuals see marriage as a sacred promise; thus, divorce usually is prohibited or severely condemned. Attorney Bari Zell Weinberger explained how religion may affect views on divorce, noting on *HuffingtonPost.com*, "In general, most religious denominations look upon marriage not just as a covenant between two people, but also between the couple and God, as in 'What God has joined together, let no man put asunder.' This seems to be where the spiritual conflict arises."[17]

Religious doctrine varies on the matter, as preachers, elders, rabbis, priests, imams, gurus, and clergy of varied faiths have made clear in their online and in-person messages. Here are some examples:

From the United States Conference of Catholic Bishops:

> The Church believes that God, the author of marriage, established it as a permanent union. When two people marry, they form an unbreakable bond. Jesus himself taught that marriage is permanent (Matthew 19:3–6), and St. Paul reinforced this teaching (see 1 Cor 7:10–11 and Eph 5:31–32). The Church does not recognize a civil divorce because the State cannot dissolve what is indissoluble.[18]

From a Resurrection Life Church (Christian) pastor:

> God joins man and woman in marriage when they say their marital vows, but soon crises arise when poor communication flows from their hidden childhood hurts. If marriage vows are then broken through infidelity, harm or abandonment, divorce will be an option that is often avoidable.[19]

From an Islamic leader:

> [Divorce] is allowed in Islam as the last resort of non-reconciliation (Quran states that the most hated allowable practice to God is divorce). A couple could remarry after divorce. This, however, should be taken very

seriously and not to be abused. Islam considers the institution of marriage as the most sacred and most important unit for a strong healthy society.[20]

From a Jewish leader:

There is no basis in the Hebrew Bible to forbid divorce. "A man takes a wife . . . she fails to please him because he finds something obnoxious about her, and he writes her a bill of divorcement." The Biblical grounds for divorce are vague, resulting in a broad range of reasons for divorce. Later Rabbinic law decreed that a man may not divorce a woman against her will, and that under certain circumstances, a Rabbinic court may compel a man to give his wife a divorce.[21]

From the Book of Mormon:

Verily, verily, I say unto you, that whosoever shall put away his wife, saving for the cause of fornication, causeth her to commit adultery; and whoso shall marry her who is divorced committeth adultery.[22]

From a Hindu leader:

Hindu civil law permits divorce on certain grounds. But the religion as such does not approve divorce, because the concept is alien to Hinduism.[23]

From an Amish ("Plain People") website:

Amish take their wedding vows seriously. Divorce is not sanctioned in the Amish church, though may occur in rare cases. Divorce is seen as reason for excommunication. Separations, however, do occasionally occur among Amish.[24]

From a Bahá'í international website:

If a Bahá'í marriage fails, divorce is permitted, although it is strongly discouraged. If Bahá'ís choose to seek a divorce, they must spend at least one year living apart and attempting to reconcile. If a divorce is still desired after that year, it is then granted, dependent on the requirements of civil law.[25]

Young people whose parents have divorced often face concerns and sometimes problems related to religion. So wrote Ann Kass, a district judge in the Second

---

It's a Fact

A married couple cannot get a divorce in Vatican City, an ecclesiastical Catholic state in Italy. The Vatican has no provisions for divorce. In the Philippines, primarily a Catholic country, divorce is illegal, although there are exceptions for Muslims. The exception is called the Code of Muslim Personal Law of the Philippines (1977). In 2013 two distinctly different divorce bills were presented to the Philippine House of Representatives. One was the Anti-Divorce and Unlawful Dissolution of Marriage Act, which sought to guarantee a ban on any law facilitating or recognizing divorce. Another bill would amend the Family Code to include a divorce provision. Neither proposal passed.[b]

Judicial District of New Mexico. A common question is, What religion should youth follow after their parents divorce? In the state of New Mexico, if parents had no specific religion when they were married, "neither parent may then enroll the children in any specific denomination without the other parent's agreement," the judge stated in her undated article on AllLaw.com. "If one parent changes religion after the divorce, and it is relatively common for a change in religion to accompany a divorce, that is fine, for each of the parents. But, when a divorced parent attempts to impose his or her change of faith on the children, trouble erupts. To avoid that trouble, the law in New Mexico, recognizing that religion is a major issue, prohibits one parent changing the children's religion."[26]

Off the Bookshelf

Divorce (Greenhaven, 2012), a young adult book in the Opposing Viewpoints series, covers numerous pro and con issues about parental divorce. Edited by Jacqueline Langwith, the book includes topics such as whether or not there is a divorce epidemic in the United States, whether divorce harms or is beneficial to children, and what laws should govern divorce proceedings. The book also includes "Facts about Divorce," organizations to contact, and a list of printed and website sources. Photographs, sidebars, charts, and a glossary help make this a helpful book for teenagers in the midst of parental divorce.

State laws on religious issues differ and can change at any time. But, "[w]hen courts are asked to answer the question of what religion a child should follow after a separation or divorce, they often balance two competing interests, the best interests of the child, and the rights of the parents," according to FindLaw.com. "On one side, courts routinely answer questions about what is in the best interests of a child and have become quite proficient with these types of issues. On the other hand, the First Amendment of the United States Constitution protects the parents' freedom of religion as well as their right to raise their child under the religion of their choosing."[27] State courts, however, do not usually allow parents to impose their religion on a child if the religious practices harm their offspring. Legal experts advise parents to try to reach agreement about religious upbringing outside of court, if possible.

2

DIVORCING
IN THE PAST

··

"My stepfather has been generally drunk since he married my mother.
When drunk he is very cross and cross when sober."—teenager Nellie Bly testifying
in 1881 when her mother filed for divorce from her abusive husband.[1]

Because of the numerous current discussions about divorce, many people think it is a recent phenomenon. But the practice goes back thousands of years, and for the most part husbands divorced wives; wives seldom were allowed to divorce husbands. In ancient Israel, for example, there were explicit rules and procedures to dissolve a marriage, as described in the biblical book of Deuteronomy 24:1–4 (New King James Version):

> When a man takes a wife and marries her, and it happens that she finds no favor in his eyes because he has found some uncleanness in her, and he writes her a certificate of divorce, puts *it* in her hand, and sends her out of his house, when she has departed from his house, and goes and becomes another man's *wife, if* the latter husband detests her and writes her a certificate of divorce, puts *it* in her hand, and sends her out of his house, or if the latter husband dies who took her as his wife, *then* her former husband who divorced her must not take her back to be his wife after she has been defiled; for that *is* an abomination before the LORD, and you shall not bring sin on the land which the LORD your God is giving you *as* an inheritance.[2]

In early Europe, laws regarding divorce were based on religious doctrine—beliefs of Catholic, Anglican (Church of England), or Protestant (Lutheran, for example) churches. When the British founded American colonies, they continued practices of England's legal system, which in the case of divorce meant that the colony's court had to approve dissolution of marriage. For instance, Mrs. James Luxford in 1639 petitioned the Massachusetts Bay Colony's Court of Assistants, requesting a divorce because her husband "already had a wife." Almost a decade later in 1643, "[a]n unidentified magistrate [on the court] granted the divorce and took this hapless woman and her children under the court's protective wing by seizing Luxford's property and transferring it to her," writes Glenda Riley in her book *Divorce: An American Tradition.* The court also fined the husband, sentenced him to be put in the stocks, and then banished him to England. Massachusetts Bay became the first colony to issue a legal divorce.[3] But that did not mean dissolving a marriage became common in Massachusetts or other colonies.

From colonial times until the American Revolutionary period, few colonies had laws regarding marital breakup, and if such legislation existed it was based on Christian religious beliefs, usually those brought with British colonists. "Colonies like New York and Virginia followed the English tradition where full divorce was an ecclesiastical affair and only rarely granted. English law, until 1753, retained the principle of canon law that no marriage can be destroyed. In those states following English tradition, divorce could be obtained only by a private bill in the legislature," according to the *Encyclopedia of Children and Childhood in History and Society.* "Following what they believed to be the laws of God, states granted divorce (with the right to remarry) when either party to a marriage could prove that the other had neglected a fundamental duty. The usual grounds for divorce were adultery, desertion, and absence for a length of time determined by the government."[4]

Runaways

During the 1700s, one way some wives and husbands escaped from unhappy marriages was to elope from (meaning abandon) their spouses. Some mothers were so miserable in their marriage that they left not only their husbands but also their children. As a result it was common to see so-called runaway advertisements in various newspapers. Some ads were published along with notices about runaway slaves, servants, and farm animals. Ads placed in New York newspapers were compiled by Clare Lyons, associate professor of history, University of Maryland, for her History 210 course, such as these examples:

New York Mercury
February 11, 1754
Whereas Anne, the wife of Alexander Ross, of this city, hath eloped from her said husband, and run him considerably in debt; these are therefore to warn all persons from trusting her on my account, as I will not pay any debt she shall contract from the date hereof. February 8th, 1754.
Alexander Ross.

New York Gazette
April 12, 1762
Whereas Mary, the wife of Charles Prosser, of this city, has eloped from his bed and board, and since had been found naked in bed with one Edward Painter, who was immediately confined in gaol [jail]: He therefore gives public notice that no person shall credit the said Mary, as he is determined to pay no debts of her contracting from this date. April 5, 1762. Charles Prosser.

While forsaken husbands placed most of the ads, wives also had their say:

New York Gazette
July 25, 1757
Whereas Thomas Johnson, of the city of New-York, Mariner, hath been pleased very scandalously to advertise me, his wife, as having eloped from his bed and board without any provocation, and that I was endeavoring to run him in debt: ———— be it known, that on Monday evening last, without any least provocation, be basely, cruelly, and inhumanly barred his doors against me, forced me to take refuge in a neighbor's house, and other ways so basely carried himself towards me, that I was obliged on Thursday last to have him bound over before authority: in consequence of which he issued advertisements against me without any regard to truth or decency, as I did not elope from his bed nor board (other than obliged to by him) nor never attempted to run him in debt, since his ill-treatment: I therefore hope my friends will regard the advertisement as false and scandalous in itself, and him as a base and cruel man.
Ruth Johnson.

New York Gazette
February 13, 1764
Whereas Oliver Loshier, on Friday last the 10th instant, very falsely advertised me as having eloped from his bed and board; that I had not only run him in debt, but was continuing to do so; and afterwards forewarns all persons either to credit or harbor me.—The public may be assured, that he very shamefully and abusively turned me out of his house on occasion of only a single and most trifling family occurrence which his impatience, (through liquor) could not overlook, when a more considerate person would.—I also declare, I have neither run him, or attempted to run him in debt: nor do I intend it: —It is therefore a false and malicious advertisement.
Elizabeth Loshier.[5]

It Happened to Nellie Bly

Nellie Bly (1867–1922) is a pseudonym for Elizabeth Cochrane or Cochran, who became well-known as an investigative reporter. Her mother, Mary, had been married to a wealthy widower, Michael Cochran, of Pennsylvania; he died when Elizabeth was six years old, leaving Mary with fifteen children to raise. Because Cochran's property had to be sold in order to divide funds equally among the children and the widow, the family was left with little money. Seeking financial security, Mary soon remarried. Her second husband was John Jackson Ford, who before long revealed his nasty temper. Ford was abusive and after five years of marriage, Mary divorced him.

At the time Elizabeth was fourteen years old and testified in court that her stepfather "threatened to do mother harm. Mother was afraid of him."[a] After the divorce, Elizabeth tried to help her mother financially, and in 1885 at eighteen years old became a columnist for the *Pittsburgh Dispatch*. Under the pen name Nellie Bly, one of her first articles was about the need to reform the state's divorce laws. Later, in 1887, she was hired by the *New York World*, which published Nellie's exposé on the horrific conditions in a New York insane asylum. Her article helped bring about reforms in patient care. Nellie also suggested to the *New York World* that she could break the record of the fictional character in *Around the World in Eighty Days* by Jules Verne. The newspaper used the 1889 trip for publicity purposes and asked readers to guess how long it would take Nellie to make the trip. "Traveling by ship, train and burro, she returned back to New York in 72 days, 6 hours and 11 minutes as a celebrity, cheered by crowds of men as well as women."[b]

Divorces were still rare in the early 1800s, primarily because women had few rights and usually were financially dependent on their husbands. When a woman married, she had no legal right to own property or a business nor could she sign contracts. A woman's husband became the owner of all his wife's assets. Thus for survival most women needed to stay in a marriage, even if it was unhappy or abusive. In addition, a wife and mother had little choice regarding children of the marriage. The husband/father had complete control of his family during the marriage, and if a divorce occurred, the father had legal custody of the children. Emily Collins, who lived in a remote area of western New York, recalled,

In those early days a husband's supremacy was often enforced in the rural districts by corporeal chastisement [beatings], and it was considered by most people as quite right and proper. . . . I remember in my own neighborhood a man who was a Methodist class-leader and exhorter, and one who was esteemed a worthy citizen, who, every few weeks, gave his wife a beating with his horsewhip. He said it was necessary, in order to keep her in subjection, and because she scolded so much. Now this wife, surrounded by six or seven little children, whom she must wash, dress, feed, and attend to day and night, was obliged to spin and weave cloth for all the garments of the family. She had to milk the cows, make butter and cheese, do all the cooking, washing, making, and mending for the family, and, with the pains of maternity forced upon her every eighteen months, was whipped by her pious husband, "because she scolded." . . . The laws made it his privilege—and the Bible, as interpreted, made it his duty . . . thought to be fixed by a divine decree. . . . "Wives be subject to your husbands," and "Wives, submit yourselves unto your husbands as unto the Lord." caused them [the wives] to consider their fate inevitable."[6]

A Nineteenth-Century Custody Battle

An extreme instance of an abused mother who attempted to maintain custody of her children occurred around the time of the War of 1812, often called America's second war for independence from Britain. Author Ilyon Woo tells the true story of Eunice, wife of James Chapman, and their three children, George, Susan, and Julia, in *The Great Divorce: A Nineteenth-Century Mother's Extraordinary Fight against Her Husband, the Shakers, and Her Times*. According to Woo, who spent more than a decade researching Eunice's life, the Chapmans had marital problems for years because of James's alcoholism, womanizing, joblessness, and physical attacks on his wife. Strife between them worsened when James joined the community of Shakers, a celibate commune of religious zealots with settlements in New England, Ohio, and Kentucky.

Like most other communal societies of the time, Shakers held their property in common and depended on agriculture and some small industries to maintain their lifestyle. Almost every detail of a Shaker's existence was covered by a rule that had to be followed precisely. There was, for example, an exact time to rise in the morning (4:30 in the summer and 5:30 in the winter) and a strict schedule for the day's activities. Men and women were separated; they were not allowed to even touch in a handshake. Boys and girls also were kept apart and overseen by an adult of their gender. The Shakers demanded conformity in clothing—bonnets, long dresses, and cloaks for girls and women; baggy pants, long overcoats, and broad-brimmed black or straw hats for boys and men.

When James joined the Shakers in upstate New York, he claimed he had forsaken his previous ways, had a religious conversion, and wanted Eunice and his three children to also become members of the Shaker commune. Eunice tried to be open-minded and went to see for herself what the commune was all about, but she could not tolerate their oppressiveness, celibacy, and religious beliefs. She refused to join the Shakers and struggled to care for her children without any help from James. She visited the community again, leaving her children with her sister, but without Eunice's knowledge, James appeared at his sister-in-law's home and took custody of the children, which he had the legal right to do. He then put George, ten; Susan, eight; and Julia, four in the care of the Shakers.

For more than five years, Eunice fought in every way possible to regain her children and her maternal rights, formidable tasks in the early 1800s. When Eunice was able to visit her children, a Shaker member always stood guard. The children were not allowed to receive gifts from their mother and were taught to be wary of her and to keep their distance. In fact, they addressed Eunice by her first name and according to Shaker rules the only Mother (always capitalized) was Mother Lucy Wright, the supreme head of the commune.

Eunice wrote letters to the Shaker authorities, consulted lawyers, lobbied the legislature, attended trials, wrote a book and articles attacking the Shakers, and in desperation stirred up mob action against the commune. When she finally won the right to her children, George at age sixteen, was fearful and tried to escape. But eventually he was reconciled with his mother and embraced the "outside world" as did his sisters.

It Happened to Edna St. Vincent Millay

Poet, playwright, and Pulitzer Prize–winner Edna St. Vincent Millay (1892–1950) was the daughter of Cora Lounella Millay, a nurse, and Henry Tollman Millay, an educator. When Millay was eight years old, Cora divorced her husband for "financial irresponsibility"—apparently for excessive gambling. Cora raised Edna and two younger daughters, Norma and Kathleen, earning the family's paltry income by nursing. Mother and daughters moved frequently and eventually settled in Camden, Maine, living in a small house on a relative's property.

Edna dealt with her parents' divorce in a variety of ways. Partly due to her mother's struggle to earn a living, money worries plagued Edna for most of her life. However, Cora encouraged her daughters to read literature (including Shakespeare) and strongly supported Edna's talent for writing poetry. Edna often recited her poetry for her family's enjoyment. In 1912, with her mother's urging, Edna entered her poem "Renascence" into a contest and won fourth place and a scholarship to Vassar. After graduation, Edna moved to New York's Greenwich Village, where she became part of a Bohemian lifestyle and wrote poetry in spite of abject poverty. She went on to publish volumes of poetry and was awarded the Pulitzer Prize for poetry in 1923. That year she also married Eugen Boissevain, who managed Millay's literary career over the twenty-six years they were together. He died in 1949; Edna died of a heart attack in 1950.

U.S. Divorces in the Early Twentieth Century

As Americans moved West, they found that divorces were much easier to obtain. States such as the Dakotas, Indiana, Nevada, and Utah were noted for allowing "quickie" divorces. It was common to be of service to people wanting to divorce. Restaurant and hotel owners and lawyers found that divorce was a profitable business.

After a women's rights convention in 1848 at Seneca Falls, New York, women in some areas of the United States began to assert and win their independence. They organized in many states to try to obtain suffrage and property rights. Women established and joined antislavery groups.

Following the American Civil War (1861–1865), industrialization and urbanization increased, and women marched in protest against child labor and advocated for better working conditions in crowded, unsafe factories, particularly textile mills where the majority of employees were women and children. Over the decades, women gained more and more civil rights and independence. At the same time, an increasing number of divorces occurred. In 1900 there were 55,751 recorded divorces. By 1910, divorces had increased to 83,401. So how did families handle their breakups? Since those divorces occurred well over a century ago, information about them usually comes from written materials—autobiographies, biographies, diaries, journals, and family records.

Novels also informed readers how divorce affected families. Consider *Mary Marie* (1920) by Eleanor H. Porter (1868–1920). It is a fictional account of parental divorce and is a fairly accurate portrayal of how a family breakup affects a child—this one in an affluent family. Porter is better known for her book *Pollyanna* and the character by that name who always finds something to be glad about no matter what the difficulties. (*Pollyanna* was such a success, a series of "glad books" followed.) In somewhat the same style, *Mary Marie*, digitalized for free download on Gutenberg.org, is a teenage story (written as a diary) that began in a rather light-hearted fashion:

I'm thirteen years old, and I'm a cross-current and a contradiction. That is, Sarah says I'm that. (Sarah is my old nurse.) She says she read it once—that the children of unlikes were always a cross-current and a contradiction. And my father and mother are unlikes, and I'm the children. That is, I'm the child. I'm all there is. And now I'm going to be a bigger cross-current and contradiction than ever, for I'm going to live half the time with Mother and the other half with Father. Mother will go to Boston to live, and Father will stay here [in a small town]—a divorce, you know.

I'm terribly excited over it. None of the other girls have got a divorce in their families, and I always did like to be different. Besides, it ought to be awfully interesting, more so than just living along, common, with your father and mother in the same house all the time—especially if it's been anything like my house with my father and mother in it!

That's why I've decided to make a book of it—that is, it really will be a book, only I shall have to call it a diary, on account of Father, you know. Won't it be funny when I don't have to do things on account of Father? And I won't, of course, the six months I'm living with Mother in Boston. But, oh, my!—the six months I'm living here with him—whew! But, then, I can stand it. I may even like it—some. Anyhow, it'll be *different*. And that's something.

Well, about making this into a book. As I started to say, he wouldn't let me. I know he wouldn't. He says novels are a silly waste of time, if not absolutely wicked. But, a diary—oh, he loves diaries! He keeps one himself, and he told me it would be an excellent and instructive discipline for me to do it, too—set down the weather and what I did every day. The weather and what I did every day, indeed! Lovely reading that would make, wouldn't it?

As the story continued, Mary Marie experienced the turmoil of going back and forth from one parent's home to the other's, changing her behavior and what she calls herself—she is Mary when with her prim, scholarly father and is Marie when with her fun-loving mother. At times she feels "specially lonesome and homesick, and not-belonging-anywhere like." She also encounters girls in her school who shun her because her parents are divorced. By the age of sixteen, she learns that her parents really do love each other and she creates a plan to bring about a reunion, which results in her parents remarrying and both of them calling her "the whole name now, Mary Marie."[7]

One real-life account of parental divorce in the past is from a family historian and retired teacher, Shirley Blackburn, who has lived in a Chicago suburb for years. She described incidents from her family history surrounding her divorced grandparents and the effects on their children.

Blackburn's grandmother Mary Sollers married George Washington Corbin "around 1898" and the couple had two children, Charles (Chuck) and Alma, Blackburn's mother. Mary and George Corbin divorced in 1910. Blackburn wrote, "I don't know for sure why my grandparents divorced. I know Gram *hated* Gramps. I think there may have been physical abuse."[8] George Corbin also was an alcoholic, and the addiction eventually killed him.

After her grandparents divorced, Blackburn's grandmother Mary Corbin moved from Pennsylvania to Chicago "around 1912" and "spent her years working and caring for Chuck and Alma." George Corbin also migrated to Chicago, and although Mary refused to see her ex-husband, "she didn't deny him the right to spend time with the children." The Corbin children "maintained healthy and loving relationships with both their parents."

The family story continues, with Blackburn relating that her mother, Alma, was in her preteens, when "Gram remarried a railroad man, Samuel Gingrich, from Elkhart, Indiana." There were some "very happy years" for the family in Indiana. But once again, Mary Corbin Gingrich divorced, although Mary kept in touch with Sam as did the Corbin children.

Alma and Charles eventually lived once again in Chicago. Grandmother Mary also moved back to Chicago and remarried in the late 1930s, but "it only lasted a short time," Blackburn noted, adding, "Gram finally found security when she went to stay with her great uncle in Altoona, Pennsylvania. Uncle John was in his 80s, was a bachelor, and promised Gram he would leave his estate to her if she would take care of him. He kept his promise and after Uncle John's death Gram

TV's "Ideal" Family

During the 1950s and 1960s, most Americans were influenced by the "ideal family" as exemplified by the Nelsons in the *Ozzie and Harriet* TV show (1952–1966) with the intact nuclear family (husband, wife, and kids). If the couple ever argued, "they resolved the tiff in thirty minutes, with time for commercials," as Bruce Bower wrote in *ScienceNews.org*.[c] Other near "perfect" families included the Andersons of *Father Knows Best* (1954–1960); the "all-American" suburban Cleavers in *Leave It to Beaver* (1957–1963); and the upper middle-class family with teenage children in *The Donna Reed Show* (1958–1966).

Perhaps some of the most influential images in the shows just described were the adults' immaculate dress, the happy smiles of family members, and close relationships portrayed on the TV screen. In these "ideal" family representations, problems were solved; conflicts were resolved; dads had jobs; moms were housewives and caregivers; racial discrimination rarely existed; crimes were not seen.

was finally financially secure. Then she met Sherman Forney, a widower, and they married and had a good life" well into the late 1940s.

The point of this account, according to Blackburn, is that her grandmother's divorces did not adversely affect her children. Blackburn does not explain what the legal grounds were for the divorces, but credits her grandmother with positive outcomes, calling her a loving and compassionate person. "Nothing got her down. She didn't complain. She enjoyed life" and passed those qualities on to her daughter, and thus to her granddaughter. Although Blackburn reports no adverse effects of divorce in her family, dissolution of marriage can create long-lasting negative impacts, according to numerous adults who themselves were or are children of divorce.

Changing Times

By the 1960s, the nation was undergoing widespread social changes. The African American civil rights movement was well underway and many groups were de-

Hippies of the 1960s often wore colorful clothing and demonstrated for peace, using this symbol.

manding the end of racial discrimination. Women's organizations were seeking the same opportunities as men for education, jobs, and equal pay for equal work. College students and other groups across the United States were protesting the war in Vietnam. Hippies—rebellious teens and young adults—were staging counterculture concerts with songs about sex and drugs, living in communes, demonstrating for peace as well as advocating for preservation of the environment, and touting sexual freedom and doing their "own thing."

The decade also brought great tragedies. President John F. Kennedy was assassinated in 1963. Civil rights leader Martin Luther King Jr. was shot and killed in 1968. That same year, Robert Kennedy, the president's brother who was campaigning for his party's nomination for president, was killed. Riots erupted in cities because of the murders and also because of continued racial discrimination and police violence against people of color.

Whether all the social turmoil of the decade had an impact on marriage breakups is debatable. But changes in divorce laws from 1969 through the next two decades certainly influenced the rate of divorces. In late 1969, then California governor Ronald Reagan signed the first *modern* no-fault divorce law that became effective January 1, 1970. (Oklahoma passed such a state law in 1953, but it was complex and often required litigation.) The California law replaced its seven grounds for divorce with simply two provisions: "irreconcilable differences which have caused the irremediable breakdown of the marriage or incurable insanity," according to California Family Code Section 2310.[9] Other states then took similar actions over the next decades. Along with no-fault provisions, the laws required a certain period of residency in the state granting the divorce.

With no-fault divorce laws, what followed appeared to be a "divorce revolution" as numerous writers labeled the increase in divorces throughout the 1970s and 1980s. One sociologist predicted that "no-fault divorce would remove the last vestiges of stigma from divorce."[10] That has not proven to be the case, however. Consider some public figures who may be stigmatized by the media if they happen to be divorced; the conjecture sometimes is that a failed marriage is akin to a character flaw. Yet, the new laws have been widely praised for reducing hostility between divorcing couples. No spouse has to accuse the other of wrongdoing. The cost of divorce has also decreased with no-fault laws.

W. Bradford Wilcox, who is director of the National Marriage Project at the University of Virginia and a senior fellow at the Institute for American Values, notes,

> The nearly universal introduction of no-fault divorce helped to open the floodgates, especially because these laws facilitated unilateral divorce and lent moral legitimacy to the dissolution of marriages. The sexual revolution, too, fueled the marital tumult of the times: Spouses found it easier in the Swinging Seventies to find extramarital partners, and came to have higher, and often unrealistic, expectations of their marital relationships. Increases in women's employment as well as feminist consciousness-raising also did their part to drive up the divorce rate, as wives felt freer in the late '60s and '70s to leave marriages that were abusive or that they found unsatisfying.[11]

The divorce rate, which according to the Centers for Disease Control and Prevention is the number of divorces per 1,000 population, slowed in the 1980s and remained fairly steady, then began to slowly decline. Some researchers attribute the lower rate to the fact that marriages have decreased also. Couples are marrying and having children when they are more mature—in their mid-twenties or early thirties rather than in their late teens. And fewer marriages are taking place. Some people prefer to stay single and cohabit—live together but not marry.

See This Flick!

The film *Kramer vs. Kramer* (1979) was an adaptation of Avery Corman's best-selling novel by the same title. Robert Benton adapted Corman's book for the movie, which won five Academy Awards and is now on video disc. Although the film was released years ago, it depicts problems of a divorcing couple and their young son. Housewife Joanna Kramer (Meryl Streep) leaves her husband Ted Kramer (Dustin Hoffman), an advertising designer, and their son Billy (Justin Henry), a first-grader. Joanna is determined to be liberated and sets out to "find herself." Ted has to learn how to care for Billy and keep up with his work load. He fails at the latter and loses his job. Joanna meantime has found well-paying employment and she returns eighteen months later to take custody of Billy. Even though Ted found a job that allows him time to care for Billy, the court grants his ex-wife custody. But Joanna finally begins to realize that Ted and Billy have become very close, and she tells Ted that she won't take Billy with her. After a tearful goodbye to her son and ex-husband, Joanna leaves; the couple do not reunite.

"Far-Reaching Effects"

Whatever the reasons for fewer divorces, many adults whose parents divorced in the 1970s and 1980s have vivid recollections of their family breakups and attest to their far-reaching effects, according to Stephanie Staal, author of *The Love They Lost: Living with the Legacy of Our Parents' Divorce*. Staal's parents divorced when she was thirteen years old, and she writes, "For my generation, divorce has taken on the social proportions of a Great Depression, a World War II, or a Vietnam in influencing our lives. Divorce struck in the privacy of our own homes, shaking our beliefs about family to the core. We saw affection wither into nasty words, kisses replaced by custody battles. We knew too much about how relationships end before our own relationships even started."[12]

Staal interviewed or surveyed 120 adults for her book and includes their recollections of parental divorce when they were youngsters or teenagers. One example is a report from twenty-five-year-old Brent—his name, like all participants', was changed to protect his privacy. Brent's parents split up when he was sixteen years old:

I knew enough of the family secrets to understand why they divorced. Heck, I knew more than they did since they talked to me and not each other. I also came to the conclusion that they probably should have divorced sooner and save me a lot of the annoyance of living in a dysfunctional household—like maybe when I was twelve or so.

"Staying together for the sake of the children" just messes with their heads. Better a healthy divorce with closure so people can get on with their lives than a hostile household filled with bitterness and resentment. If both parties consent to a divorce, why not?[13]

Author Elizabeth Marquardt, a scholar with the Institute for American Values, has a different view about a "healthy divorce." Between 2001 and 2003, Marquardt, herself a child of divorce, and sociology Professor Norval Glenn conducted a national study of 1,500 young adults from both divorced and intact families. In her book *Between Two Worlds: The Inner Lives of Children of Divorce*, Marquardt presents findings from the study along with stories from adults (between the ages of eighteen and thirty-five) whose parents divorced when they were young children or teenagers. The stories reveal that years after their parents' divorce, many young people grew up with inner conflicts and feeling like "chameleons" as they moved back and forth from one parent's home to the other's and tried to adapt to beliefs and values of each parent (rather like the 1800s fictional account of *Mary Marie*). As Marquardt notes, divorce leaves children "struggling with divided selves."[14]

Marquardt acknowledges that divorce is sometimes necessary because of violence or abuse in a family, but she rejects the idea of a "good" or "healthy divorce." She writes,

When Dr. Norval Glenn and I compared young adult children of divorce with their peers from intact families, we found that for children a "good divorce" often compares poorly even to an unhappy marriage, so long as that marriage is low-conflict (as approximately two-thirds of marriages that end in divorce are). Increasingly, too, many people think that a "good divorce" and a happy intact marriage are about the same for kids. . . . But our research demonstrates strongly that, without question, a "good divorce" is far worse for children than a happy marriage. Of course, any child could tell you the same thing. No child thinks a "good divorce" is as good as the happy marriage of his or her own two parents.[15]

While Marquardt and other authors focus on the long-term effects of divorce on children and teenagers, events before the family breakup also haunt many young people. As young people of divorce note, breaking up is hard, very hard.

3

BREAKING UP

....

"When my parents told me that they were getting divorced, it felt like my heart was ripped out of my chest. I cried for days. I mean, come on. They were married for twenty five years! They had four kids! And now, it's all 'Oh, we don't love each other anymore.' What the hell happened?!?!"—anonymous teenage girl writing for TeenInk.com[1]

When young people talk and write about their family breakups, their words often describe how agonizing the whole process is. In 2011, a young woman identifying herself as DesolationRow noted that she was "completely blindsided" when her parents announced the possibility of a divorce. She posted this on the website ExperienceProject.com:

If you had asked me even just a week ago how likely I thought it was that my parents would ever get divorced, I would have told you that it was completely inconceivable to me, it would never happen. . . . I have no idea what this is going to mean. We were always a really tight-knit family, went through a lot [of] different medical and financial problems. . . . I look back and I can see where and how they would have frustrated each other, and I feel like I should have just called them on it, and maybe they would have toned it down. But I just thought that was between them and I shouldn't interfere. They'd hung on for 30 years, right? Even then, I never in a million years would have guessed that it would kill the marriage.[2]

The teenager DesolationRow was not alone. Another teenage girl who called herself blairwardolf posted on the same website in 2012:

I feel like I have nothing left going for me. My parents are divorcing, all my 'friends' hate me and my grades are not how they should be. This isn't fair. Why me? It's been about a month since my parents first told me and I know they're both happy but me . . . not so much. I'm miserable to say the least. . . . This all stresses me out beyond belief. I've gotten a headache

Places to Vent

Numerous websites offer places for people to share life experiences and often to vent frustrations, anger, fear, or loneliness. Some are sites where young people and adults can express their feelings about parental divorce. One is ExperienceProject.com (http://www.experienceproject.com/stories/Have-Divorced-Parents/1058443) where many posts are from teenagers who use fictitious names as they write about trying to deal with the emotional effects of their family breakups.

almost everyday the past week. I hate talking about this. I hate crying. I hate it. I think I've cried more this past month than I have my entire life.[3]

In 2013 a seventeen-year-old wrote on ExperienceProject.com how she learned about her family's breakup:

[M]om sat me, my sister who is 21, and my brother who is 18, down to tell us she had found a house and plans to move out. . . . I didn't really do anything, I just sat there and basically didn't let myself feel anything. I ignored the fact that it was really happening and I just went on with life for a few days. I guess this is the "denial" stage of the grieving process. Well yesterday night it really hit me and I felt absolutely awful. I felt so depressed, I felt like somebody I loved just died. I guess if you look at it in a symbolic way, "my parents" died, and now I have "mom" and "dad." They are no longer a unit.[4]

In an online forum called "Any Late Teens with Divorcing Parents?" Rareyes3 reported,

My mom and dad are divorcing and I can't seem to find a way to reconcile them before things get finalized. I still wish them to be together because I want to live a normal, whole and happy family. But I just realized, If they really don't want each other anymore, then maybe I just have to let them do what they want. But really, at this point, I need some teenage help on how to deal with this matter. I'm only 16 and I am actually having difficulty thinking of many things from school, friends, activities and home. I'm having so much confusions.[5]

Other young people have reported their feelings in print. High school senior Esi of Maryland told *Scholastic Choices* what a shock it was to learn that her parents were breaking up. She was only ten years old at that time, but as a teenager she recalled her reaction: "I cried a lot. I asked a lot of questions. I wanted to fully understand why my family was ending. My parents tried to make it seem as though we would still be one big family, but I knew deep down that it wouldn't."[6]

In *YourTeenMag.com*, an online magazine for parents, teenager Annie wrote,

It was a beautiful Saturday afternoon, and I was about to go over to a friend's house when my parents sat my siblings and me down at the kitchen table. They seemed uncomfortable, and I knew something wasn't right, but I tried to stay optimistic. Hesitantly, they announced that they were getting a divorce and that at the end of the school year, my mom would move out. I was shocked; I hadn't seen it coming. Sure, they fought sometimes, but I knew most parents fought one time or another. I managed to keep it together downstairs, but when I was back in my room the tears came like a flood.[7]

Sixteen-year-old Lara G. of Massachusetts wrote in *Teen Ink*,

I grew up in a small hick town. . . . I had everything I needed (I thought) and was content. Then suddenly, everything changed. Mom and Dad stopped talking and started yelling and I said to myself, "Mom and Dad would never get a divorce." One morning Mom suddenly left and Dad looked unhappy. Then he told me. I didn't know what to do; I just sat there, watching cartoons. After that moment, my life slowly underwent major changes.[8]

In another *Teen Ink* article, Joanne H. of Massachusetts wrote,

For some kids, the death of a parent or even a close relative is enough to turn their world upside down. They go through withdrawal, denial, depression and sometimes make themselves sick (either physically or mentally). They will never be the same. For me these feelings came as a result of my parents sitting me down one day to tell me the big news—DIVORCE! . . . My parents called me at a friend's house and said that they wanted to talk to me. So I came home. My mother started to tell me about how she hadn't been happy with the marriage for 10 years but that she had stuck with it for me. I laughed and said, "Are you guys getting a divorce or something?" I expected them to tell me that they were going to go to a marriage counselor, but they confirmed that they were, in fact, getting a divorce.[9]

The reactions to parental divorce just described are echoed in Britain, as BBC filmmaker Olly Lambert reveals in his documentary *Mum and Dad Are Splitting Up* (2013). In the film, Lambert interviews teenagers, asking them about their parents' breakup when they were youngsters. The teens tell of the tremendous pain and desperation they felt, and some of them say they still feel that way as young adults. During some interviews, the teenagers' parents are also present, and the young people say in varied ways that their emotional lives would have been better if their parents had talked about what was going on.

Filmmaker Lambert told Joanna Moorhead of the *Guardian*,

> Each story started in an identical way. . . . It began with the parents calling the child in, sitting him or her down and saying: "You know we've not been getting on very well together, don't you?" Then the parents would say they were separating, and the child would cry and run out of the room in tears, knowing their world had just fallen in and that life would never be the same again. . . . You get the feeling in so many cases that it was easier [for the parents] to pack their bags and split up than to sit down and have a conversation with their children, leaving young people with many unanswered questions.[10]

The full documentary can be accessed and seen on YouTube.com.

Although most young people who have experienced parental divorce share their hurt, on occasion there are some positive reactions. Max Sindell, who wrote *The Bright Side: Surviving Your Parents' Divorce* (2007), had a lot to share about his parents' multiple divorces during his growing-up years, but he also pointed out a "bright side." He gained independence as he traveled between parents: "Life became enormously exciting because I was allowed to do things like fly halfway across the country by myself. My father moved to a small town, gave me free rein, and I put four hundred miles on my bike that first summer."[11]

Upside Down World

As noted, most teenagers' reactions to their parents' imminent breakup can be devastating. Many youth "just want normal" and have problems facing the reality of divorce. As a divorced mother of two daughters, Laura Andrzejewski noted, "I can tell you as a parent that the children of divorce have a lot of pressure. It doesn't make any difference if the divorce is civil or not."[12]

Kids struggle and hurt. They often put on a "game face," but "despite the air of nonchalance, or even indifference . . . there is a lot going on inside them, and it is anything but serene," according to clinical psychologist Joseph Nowinski. On *HuffingtonPost.com*, he wrote,

> Regardless of how "mature" a teen may want to appear, he or she is still a work in progress. . . . Beneath the veneer lies an intense internal struggle to define who we are and who we will be. A parental decision to divorce at this point represents a monumental disruption and a very unwanted distraction. Very simply, it can throw a wrench into this process of identity development. It can literally turn a teen's world upside down.[13]

David Royko, a marriage and family counselor in Illinois, would agree. He has interviewed "well over a thousand" children of divorce as a mediator for the Cook County Court. He also conducted dozens of voluntary interviews for his book *Voices of Children of Divorce* (1999). Although the book was written years ago, the contents still reflect what current young people experience when parents divorce. Chapters in the book provide clues as to the contents: "Divorce: The Big Event"; "Putting the Child in the Middle: Caught in the Web"; "Custody and Custody Wars: Where Are We Going?"; "Siblings: We're All in It Together, Aren't We?"; "Coping: How Do I Handle This?" and many others. In the twelve-page introduction Royko noted, "[W]hen parents divorce, it is the child in his or her late teens or early twenties who tends to be overlooked by parents, friends, relatives, and society in general. Because children are usually becoming independent at that age, parents assume they will not be affected by the event as much as younger children. . . . Older children may have a different perspective on and reaction to a divorce, but they are still deeply affected by it."[14]

Royko cited numerous examples, among them an eighteen-year-old called Charlotte (all of the names he used are changed to protect the participants' identities). Charlotte noted that before her parents divorce, it was "really upsetting to know now that they've contacted attorneys. It's not so much that it surprises me, because it doesn't. But it's still upsetting. You don't want to know that that's true, even though it seems like it is."[15]

Not only is a child's world upset and upended, the memories can last well into adulthood, as Susan Gregory Thomas, author of *In Spite of Everything: A Memoir* (2011), recalled. She wrote about her experiences in a 2011 *Wall Street Journal* article:

> When my dad left in the spring of 1981 and moved five states away with his executive assistant and her four kids, the world as I had known it came to an end. In my 12-year-old eyes, my mother, formerly a regal, erudite figure, was transformed into a phantom in a sweaty nightgown and matted

A teenager listens as parents argue, a common prelude to a family breakup.

hair, howling on the floor of our gray-carpeted playroom. My brother, a sweet, goofy boy, grew into a sad, glowering giant, barricaded in his room with dark graphic novels and computer games.

I spent the rest of middle and high school getting into trouble in suburban Philadelphia: chain-smoking, doing drugs, getting kicked out of schools, spending a good part of my senior year in a psychiatric ward. Whenever I saw my father, which was rarely, he grew more and more to embody Darth Vader: a brutal machine encasing raw human guts.[16]

Can Parental Breakups Be Prevented?

It depends, might be the response. In some cases, divorce is unavoidable, especially if there is abuse. In other instances there may be opportunities to save marriages. Sometimes divorce education, counseling, and waiting periods can help prevent breakups.

A group called the Coalition for Divorce Reform (CDR), founded in 2011, hopes to reduce family breakups and the resulting negative impacts on children. The nonpartisan coalition includes "divorce reform leaders, marriage educators, domestic violence experts, scholars, and concerned citizens dedicated to supporting efforts to reduce unnecessary divorce and promote healthy marriages," ac-

> ### Listen Up!
>
> "Breaking Up Is Hard to Do," a popular song for decades, was cowritten in the 1960s by singer/songwriter Neil Sedaka and Howard Greenfield. Sedaka's renditions of the song have been recorded on vinyl records and CDs, uploaded to YouTube, and downloaded as a ring tone for cell phones. The name of the song is frequently used as a title for books, articles, news stories, and other published materials on families broken by divorce. It is also the title of a film released in 2010, starring Demetria McKinney and Kendrick Cross. The movie, produced on DVD in 2011, is set in Atlanta, Georgia, and tells the story of what happens when a couple's relationship is failing and how they attempt to save it through therapy.

cording to its website. Co-chairs Chris Gersten and Beverly Willett note that the CDR's main effort is "supporting the Parental Divorce Reduction Act (PDRA) and exploring ways to improve the proposed legislation."[17]

The legislation has been created as a model and, according to Gersten,

The PDRA is designed to reduce unnecessary divorce where minor children are involved. Approximately two-thirds of all divorces involve low-conflict marriages. These are marriages where one spouse or both spouses feel frustrated or bored, can't communicate effectively with his/her spouse, or feel the romance has left the relationship and that life would be better by divorcing.

Our current marriage laws have made it easier in the US than in any other industrial nation to get out of such a marriage. One spouse only needs to simply state under oath that the marriage is irretrievably broken and, except for dividing up the property and the children, that's pretty much the end of the discussion. Many of these divorces, however, need not happen. Research shows that at least one in three divorcing people are open to reconciliation. The PDRA provides the mechanics for finding them, and giving them the tools they need to work on saving their marriage. If there is physical violence in the relationship, the victim will not be required to participate in this process.[18]

The coalition has persuaded lawmakers in a number of states (Colorado, Louisiana, New Mexico, and Texas are among them) to take action. Legislators have proposed bills based on PDRA, which is aimed at parents with minor children. Parents contemplating divorce are required to attend marriage education classes, and must also wait eight months—a period for possible reconciliation—before filing for divorce.

Other model state legislation to prevent "unnecessary divorce" has been written by Professor William J. Doherty of the University of Minnesota's College of Education and Human Development and retired Georgia Supreme Court Chief Justice Leah Ward Sears. The co-authors have proposed Second Chances Act (SCA), which is similar to the Parental Divorce Reduction Act. SCA would require a waiting period—in this case, one year—before parents could divorce. It also calls for "high-quality education about the option of reconciliation" and creation of "university-based centers of excellence to improve the education available to couples at risk of divorce."[19]

A "surprising number" of parents who are on the brink of divorce, pull back and are open to reconciliation, according to a study conducted by Doherty. Working in collaboration with Hennepin County (Minnesota) District Court Judge Bruce Peterson, Doherty surveyed 2,500 parents who had filed for divorce to learn how they decide whether to end the marriage or try again. The study, "Interest in Marital Reconciliation among Divorcing Parents," was published in an April 2011 issue of *Family Court Review*, the leading academic journal for professionals who work in family courts. For the study, parents were asked if they would be seriously interested in obtaining reconciliation services, and "about three in 10 individuals expressed openness to receiving help. . . . Overall, in about 45 percent of couples, one or both of the partners reported holding hopes for the marriage and a possible interest in reconciliation. Males were more interested than females in reconciliation," according to a news release.[20]

Second Chance, the act and organization, contends that "[a] modest reduction in divorce would benefit more than 400,000 U.S. children each year" and "would produce significant savings for U.S. taxpayers." The organization makes the case that taxpayer funds would be saved because the number of school suspensions and juvenile delinquencies would drop, fewer children would need therapy, and teenage pregnancies would be reduced.[21]

Opponents of Proposed Laws

Even though most people support reduction of parental divorce, there are opponents to the proposed laws. For example, attorney Robert Franklin posted his arguments on FathersandFamilies.org (now nationalparentsorganization.org). He stated,

> I'm all for the institution of marriage. There's little doubt that children raised in a marital household with two biological parents tend to do better

than any of their peers raised in other situations. . . . I know people are dissatisfied with the state of marital breakdown, but that doesn't mean they want *their* freedom to divorce impaired. And it's anything but certain that more restrictive laws will actually cut the divorce rate. Gersten's group's model legislation calls for education and a period of "reflection." I don't see that stopping many divorces, although I'd be happy to be proven wrong.[22]

An outspoken opponent of PDRA is journalist Vicki Larson, who writes about marriage and divorce. She took part in a debate with CDR cochair Willett about the divorce legislation. Their arguments were published in the *New York Times* Room for Debate section. The exchange can be accessed online at http://www.nytimes.com/roomfordebate/2013/02/13/when-divorce-is-a-family-affair.

Larson questioned wording in PDRA that would consider some divorces unnecessary. "It's that word—'unnecessary'—that's disturbing. Who decides whether a divorce is 'unnecessary'? . . . The only people who can decide whether a divorce is necessary or not are the people in the marriage—no one else," Larson wrote.

In one of Willett's counterpoints, she noted, "No-fault [divorce] is an on-demand system with 'me' at its core, permitting one 'person' to decide for all. Children, divvied up like chattel, get no vote in the dismantling of their families. That sounds harsh, but it's true. Marriage protects men, women and children, emotionally, physically and economically."

Larson argued, "Our limited resources and energy would be better spent helping people marry—or partner—smarter, creating policies that support fragile families, and educating divorcing couples about how to co-parent apart in healthy, collaborative ways." In the debate, one of Larson's final reasons was, "Make divorce harder and people may choose to opt out of marriage altogether and cohabit instead, which . . . is worse for children."[23]

Other Efforts to Prevent Divorce

Other efforts to prevent divorce include some lawmakers' proposals to overturn no-fault divorce laws, which are in effect in all fifty states. In March 2013, Radio-Iowa.com reported that "[s]even Republicans in the Iowa House [were] pushing a bill to prohibit parents of minor children from getting a 'no fault' divorce. . . . Under the proposed legislation, parents with kids under the age of 18 could not get a no-fault divorce. Instead, they'd have to show a spouse was guilty of adultery, had been sent to prison on a felony conviction, had physically or sexually abused someone in the family, or had abandoned the family for at least a year."[24]

Some Iowa representatives opposed the bill. A Democrat from Des Moines cited her experience before no-fault was passed. Then a couple had to prove a spouse was guilty of wrongdoing. "The stay-together time was very, very damaging to my family," the representative (the oldest of four children) told RadioIowa, "and although we're all adults now, I'm not sure any of us have ever really gotten past that."[25]

In California, John Marcotte has been heading a grassroots effort to legally ban all divorces. He began his effort after Proposition 8 (Prop 8) passed in 2008; the law banned gay marriage in the state. In Marcotte's opinion that measure was not enough to protect traditional marriage; he said divorce is a sin. So Marcotte proposed an amendment to the state constitution called the California Marriage Protection Act that bans married couples from divorcing during their lifetime. However, it is doubtful that a bill will be presented for a vote in the California legislature, because on June 26, 2013, the U.S. Supreme Court ruled that same-sex marriage should be allowed in California, thus Prop 8 was no longer in force.

It Happened in Utah

Co-authors Alan J. Hawkins, a member of the faculty in the School of Family Life at Brigham Young University, and Utah attorney mediator Tamara A. Fackrell wrote a booklet—*Should I Keep Trying to Work It Out? A Guidebook for Individuals and Couples at the Crossroads of Divorce (and Before)*—for divorce education classes in Utah. According to an introduction to the lessons, "In 2007, the Utah Legislature passed a first-of-its-kind law to require individuals who file for a separation or divorce and who have children under 18 years old to participate in a divorce orientation education class. The purpose of the class is to help individuals considering a divorce to think carefully about their options, including repairing problems in the marriage and keeping a family together, and to inform individuals of the potential consequences." Although the guidebook is offered primarily to Utah couples, the co-authors wrote it can be used by "Marriage counselors, religious leaders, and mediators who are working with couples facing a possible divorce. And because most people think that divorce is a serious problem in our society, this guidebook has general educational value; it is not limited just to those who are currently going through a divorce."[a]

The Court also struck down the Defense of Marriage Act (DOMA), which declared that the only legal marriages were those between a man and a woman. Justice Anthony Kennedy announced the High Court's decision to negate DOMA, noting that the law "humiliates tens of thousands of children now being raised by same-sex couples. The law in question makes it even more difficult for the children to understand the integrity and closeness of their own family and its concord with other families in their community and in their daily lives."[26]

Staying Together for the Kids

Just about anyone who has anything to do with marriage and divorce issues has an opinion about parents staying together for the sake of kids in the family, as is clear in the PDRA debate just described. Clergy, marriage counselors, psychologists, lawyers, TV show hosts, self-help websites, youth themselves, and countless others discuss the pros and cons of the issue. One minister declared, "[C]hildren don't ask to be born. Parents choose to create little carbon copies of themselves. Thus, I believe that parents should stay together for the sake of the children."[27]

Psychotherapist Tammy Gold, who practices in New York and New Jersey, explains some reasons why alienated couples decide to stay together:

> One may be that they are able to maintain normal family relations regardless of their martial state. In this instance, the parents might believe that since their issues are not harming their children, they will continue to maintain the family dynamic until they are no longer able to do so. . . . Monetary issues also play a role in whether couples stay together. If the couple deems that by separating they will be in great financial distress, they may wait until both parents will be stable enough on their own. These couples know that if they had to separate, both the parents and children would suffer due to the monetary loss. For example, a mother who had originally stayed at home might have to return to work. In turn, younger children might be forced into a childcare situation which would be a big change for them.[28]

Like other advisors, Gold acknowledged that breaking up is sometimes the best and perhaps the only course to take, "regardless of stress or financial situations. Issues such as domestic violence, abuse, neglect and severe parental fighting are instances when it would be more beneficial for a child to go through the divorce."[29]

When parental breakup is imminent, one spouse usually packs up to leave.

Rosalind Sedacca, founder of the Child-Centered Divorce Network, agreed. In 2013, she wrote for the *HuffingtonPost.com*,

Stay together for the sake of the kids? Generations of miserable parents followed that advice, hoping their sacrifices would pay off for their children in the end. Many still believe that it's the only option for parents stuck in a dead-end marriage.

Based on my own personal experience, I have another perspective. Having been raised by parents that chose to stay together in a miserable marriage, I opt in on the other side. For me, parental divorce is preferable to years of living in a home where parents fight, disrespect one another

? What Do You Think?

All the experts aside, what do young people have to say about "staying together for the kids"? On a CollegeNET forum, students competing for college scholarships responded with their opinions on the topic. Examples of their comments, published in 2011, follow:

- At all costs I would try to preserve the marriage for the children. To me my own children should be more important than my own happiness and that is something I am willing to sacrifice for.
- [I]f you have children, then you should make every effort to stay together. If a couple just can't get along though, they should definitely divorce. It isn't healthy for children to live in a home with constant tension and fighting.
- If there is no love between the mother and father anymore, the kids WILL know. Children have this knack for seeing right through their parents. They know when they're happy and when they're miserable. Staying in an unstable and loveless relationship for the kids will do nothing but harm the kids in the long run.
- I believe parents should stay together for the sake of the kids. My parents have the usual fights and it has come into subject a couple times, but luckily never happened. I think if it were to happen my grades would suffer because I would be experiencing something new and it would have an emotional effect on me.
- As an eighteen year old whose parents recently separated I am such a strong advocate for divorcing if you feel the need. The impact on children can sometimes be devastating but living in a dysfunctional atmosphere is often more detrimental.
- I came from a broken home [and] I want families to stay together, I believe its healthily [sic] for the family and the children that reside there as well.[b]

What do you think about this issue?

and children are surrounded by sadness and anger. That's the world I grew up in and the scars are still with me today, many decades later.[30]

What Marriage Counselors Do

Before a parental breakup, some young people urge or hope they can persuade their parents to consider getting help from a marriage counselor or therapist. They might let their parents know that watching and listening to them argue is difficult and stressful. Or parents themselves may seek professional advice to save their marriage. In some cases, social service agencies and mental health clinics can provide counseling. Or perhaps a counselor will provide therapy at the couple's home. Questions then arise: What does a counselor/therapist (sometimes called a "marriage coach") do? How much do sessions cost? Who offers advice? Some answers come from Kelli B. Grant on SmartMoney.com. She wrote,

> State-licensed psychologists, psychiatrists, mental health counselors and social workers can all offer sessions for couples, as can licensed marriage and family therapists. To earn the latter distinction, therapists are required by states to get at least a master's degree in the discipline and a passing score on a national licensing exam, followed by a set number of client hours—from 1,500 hours in New York to 3,000 in Texas—under the supervision of another fully licensed practitioner. But pretty much anyone can hang out a shingle as a marriage coach, relationship adviser or other uniquely labeled provider of "alternative marriage counseling"—they just can't call the services "therapy." License or no, experts say the risk

Did You Know?

There is a song with the title "Stay Together for the Kids" (2002) performed by Blink 182, an American rock band with vocalist Mark Hoppus, guitarist and vocalist Tom DeLonge, and drummer Travis Barker. DeLonge wrote this song when he was a teenager and his parents had announced they were divorcing. The song lyrics give the impression that he is hurting deeply and is bitter because of his parents' constant fighting. The singer is also angry that after twenty years of marriage his parents are breaking up. Many young people whose parents are in the process of divorcing say they can relate to the song and have posted their messages on a variety of websites.

for consumers is that it's so easy to pick a provider who doesn't have the education or skills to solve their problem.[31]

At the time Grant was writing, the cost was about $200 per hour with many couples attending anywhere from twelve to twenty sessions. Medical insurance seldom covers such expenses.

If parents do decide to see a marriage counselor, what happens during a session? Once again, the response might be "it depends"—on the issues and the couple. In general, though, the counselor begins by trying to determine a couple's needs, usually making that assessment by questioning each spouse alone and then as a couple: What are the disagreements? How much time do parents spend together? How well do they communicate with each other? What about the children? Is religion an issue? Are there financial difficulties? Do in-laws or friends create conflicts? A counselor is likely to ask many other questions, but all the probing is meant to identify basic problems and then try to help parents deal with them.

Finally, there is the question, Does counseling really work for parents? There are no statistics to support a definitive answer. Some say professional advisers

Off the Bookshelf

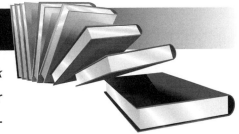

Broken Hearts . . . Healing: Young Poets Speak Out on Divorce (2001), edited by Professor Tom Worthen, is a collection of poems written by young people (primarily teenagers but also younger children) who have experienced parental separation or divorce. Worthen himself was divorced and has remarried. He dedicated the book to his and his first wife's three children. The titles of the chapters (in lowercase) indicate some of the poets' feelings: "divorce changes everything," "it happened to me," "my heart is broken," "i'm caught in the middle," "i want my family back." There are common expressions of emptiness, missing mom or dad, sadness and crying, pain and loneliness, and finally the realization "i'm still standing" and "lessons i've learned."

All of the poems were first submitted to a contest for young poets in grades 4–12. The poetry was published in a series of anthologies titled *A Celebration of Young Poets* published by Poet Tree Press in Utah. Worthen, an interpersonal communication specialist, selected the poems with the understanding from parents or guardians that the poets' works are originals.

can actually destroy a marriage because couples wait too long before they seek help; they are already inclined to get a divorce, or their practitioners do not take a strong stand for saving a marriage. But some experts are more positive and say counseling can be successful if couples seriously work at it and their practitioner is qualified.

STRUGGLING AND HURTING

....

"I believed that everything was just my fault. And keep in mind that much of
these feelings I had couldn't be expressed with words. I didn't truly feel the pain,
until I understood more about life and how different I was from other people. . . .
I thought nobody else could possibly understand."—Avaz, a teenager
writing in 2013 on ExperienceProject.com[1]

When parents divorce, offspring frequently struggle with emotional upheavals. Seventeen-year-old Mallory of Illinois expressed her opinion on the topic. She told a reporter for Family.com,

> Divorce causes a lot of unwanted arguments and disagreements between the divorced and the family members. I think that in some cases, kids get pulled into these arguments deliberately to hurt the accused parent. I think that teens that grow up without a mom or a dad miss out on a lot. I don't know what I would do without my mom there to discuss all of the problems I am having. I miss not having a dad around. I think divorce has a major affect [*sic*] on teens.[2]

Experts agree. Teenagers and preteens may suffer more than younger members of a split family, according to Marcia Polansky, a psychotherapist and professor at Drexel University in Philadelphia. She noted, teens are "at the point in their lives when they're starting to form their romantic views, having boyfriends and girlfriends, starting dating. They're wondering if their relationships are going to work out, because they see that their parents' didn't. . . . The question is, are they going to be like their parents or can they create a satisfying relationship?"[3]

Another expert, Daniel Pikar, PhD, of Sonoma County, California, wrote, "Adolescence is a period of substantial flux on all developmental fronts. Teenagers are dealing with their emerging sexuality, solidifying their identity, and pushing for increased autonomy, while also mourning the loss of childhood. When parents divorce, adolescents face the formidable task of adjusting to these changes while coping with their parents' divorce. More than ever, they need emotional support, love, and firm guidance from their parents."[4]

Besides the emotional reactions to divorce other negative factors affect the children of divorce. For example, a 2011 analysis by Hyun Sik Kim of the University of Wisconsin–Madison compared developmental skills of more than 3,500 students. The findings: "Children of divorced parents often fall behind their classmates in math and social skills and are more likely to suffer anxiety, stress and low self-esteem," according to a Reuters news report.[5]

A University of Toronto (Canada) analysis in 2013 of 19,000 American adults found that both sons and daughters who had experienced parental divorce in their youth were significantly more likely to initiate smoking in comparison to their peers from intact families. Smoking habits in turn create the risk of health problems. One researcher called the link "very disturbing."[6]

Youth Reactions

Individuals seldom have exactly the same reactions to divorce, but young people share common feelings. They are often anxious, sad, angry, embarrassed, and confused (in no particular order) when their parents are in the midst of breaking up or have divorced. In some cases, all of those emotions are experienced at different times and places.

College student Sandi Greene wrote in 2002 on the Christian website FocusontheFamily.com, "[A]fter 23 years of marriage, my parents were divorced. The people I had admired most throughout my life had broken my trust. As my life shattered to pieces, sorrow, anger, and a feeling of betrayal filled my heart." She noted that as a young adult at the time she "had enough to handle and adjust to . . . when abruptly you can be forced to deal with something you never expected, nor ever asked for. In my situation, I desired my reaction to be godly, but the divorce brought struggles I didn't know how to handle emotionally, socially, or spiritually."[7]

Bethany Jordan wrote about her reaction to the breakup of her family in 2007 when she was a high school sophomore. Her article appeared online in AZTeenMagazine.com. "How do you split a human being?" she asked and answered her rhetorical question:

> You can't, and this is where divorce gets tricky, and often takes an unpleasant toll on any teenager involved. For better or for worse, I have gone through not just one, but two divorces. The first was the divorce of my

parents when I was only seven years old. The second was far more recent and involved my father and his now ex-wife. The first time, it seemed like such a ludicrous idea that at the time didn't even occur to me as an option. Back then, divorce wasn't as common as it is now, so telling my friends about what my parent's divorce was like was traumatic, and made me feel like an outsider. Today, after I found out that my dad and his new wife were getting divorced, I didn't feel shocked like I did before. It wasn't because I had been through it before, but because divorce is so common now. I know a few parents that aren't divorced, and seeing them is awkward. It is like a spectacle, and I sometimes feel suspicious of their seemingly happy marriage.[8]

In another online article, twenty-one-year-old Tim shared his thoughts about his parents' divorce. In a 2011 article on Suite101.com he wrote,

There were four of us kids, two boys and two girls. I'm the youngest. I remember dad and mum arguing when we were little. Dad was having an affair, I found out later. When I was 12, he cleared off to be with his girlfriend and her children. It was horrible when my parents argued—but it was much worse when they divorced. I felt my father had betrayed us. He'd chosen another family, another man's kids over his own. I couldn't get my head round that at all. . . . Half the time I wonder if the majority of divorces are just because one partner in the marriage fancies having an affair. Unfortunately, it's other people in the family who get hurt.[9]

On the same website, Cheryl, fifteen, noted, "I know it's normal these days to have divorced parents but I think the one that breaks up the family is selfish. It screws kids up and makes them unhappy." She wished her parents had stayed together.[10]

In 2012, K. L. West, then a student at Robert Morris University in Coraopolis, Pennsylvania, a suburb of Pittsburgh, presented his reaction to his family breakup. West wrote,

I used to think my family was perfect and nothing bad would ever happen to us. I heard a lot about other kids' parents getting divorced and I always assured myself that it would never happen to me. My mom even told us that her and my dad loved each other too much to get a divorce. That all changed in seemingly a blink of an eye. My dad wasn't happy in the marriage anymore and wanted a divorce. I was shocked. I kept thinking about all the times I assured myself it would never happen and there I was, witnessing what I thought was my family falling apart.[11]

A teenager known as DesireeInWonderland posted her views on Experience Project.com in 2013. She explained that her parents' separation has "been hard . . . but I do my best not to show it. I've gotten to the point where I hold everything inside."[12]

Tyler Maffesoli of Michigan was ten years old when his parents divorced. As a sixteen-year-old in 2013, Tyler recalled, "[I] couldn't believe this would happen. I was very sad for the most part of the time they've been divorced. I was extremely upset—I was not okay with the separation." But he noted that he now lives part of the week with his mom and the rest of the week with his dad. And there is no more fighting and arguing. In retrospect he concluded, "I knew separating would be the best for them to do."[13]

Teenagers like this girl often struggle with the pain of parental divorce.

Megan, a California girl, told about her feelings when her parents separated and eventually divorced. In her 2013 article for *New Moon Girls*, she wrote, "I was upset, angry, sad, confused, depressed; I was feeling so many emotions! I had moved six times in three years, after never moving before. I also had to think of my parents as two people; not one unit—all this was new to me."[14]

Stages of Grief Related to Divorce

Attorneys, counselors, clergy, and others who advise teens and other family members experiencing divorce frequently cite stages of grief that may occur after a parental breakup. These stages are similar to *those that happen after* the death of a loved one, which were articulated years ago by the late Elisabeth Kübler-Ross in her book *On Death and Dying* (1969). Kübler-Ross was the medical director of the Family Service and Mental Health Center in Cook County, Illinois. Those five stages are part of the titles for five of her chapters: Denial and Isolation, Anger, Bargaining, Depression, and Acceptance.

For divorce, experts say, there are anywhere from five to seven stages of grief. After all, divorce is the death of a family. However, the actual number and severity of sorrow/anguish regarding divorce varies with each individual. These stages can include Shock or Disbelief, Denial, Anger, Bargaining, Guilt, Depression, Acceptance, and Hope.

Rob Callahan of Minneapolis, a journalist and editor of regional magazines, described the first stage: Shock or Disbelief. He wrote, "The initial realization that a marriage is or might be beyond any hope of saving will affect individual members of a family differently. Some may be emotionally stunned, unable to form or express strong feelings about the divorce or any other aspects of their life. Others may refuse to believe it, insisting instead that the process of divorce is simply a prolonged dispute. This stage may be brief, or may last several weeks."[15]

Anger is a common teen reaction when parents divorce. Some young people are irate because they think their parents should have made their marriage last. They may be so angry that they verbally attack one or both parents; they may try to injure themselves or take illegal drugs; they may run away from home. Or they may refuse to speak to a parent thought to be responsible for the divorce. Anger may also be mixed with other feelings, such as regretting the loss of the former family life or being unable to trust others. For example, in *Teen Ink* an Arizona teen wrote, "Anger and disappointment are like brother and sister. I resent the simplicity of life pre-divorce. One household, one schedule, and continual communication. I go to my father's for dinner three times a week, hating not the minor logistical complication, but what it belies: separation of what was a family unit."[16]

Bargaining after parents divorce is a stage in which children try to patch up their broken families, promising to do chores or get better grades in school or get a part-time job to help with finances. Along with trying to bargain may come feelings of guilt—believing that parental divorce is a child's fault (which it is not). Parents also have guilt feelings and worry that divorce will have a detrimental effect on their offspring.

One of the most difficult stages of grief related to divorce is depression. On Reddit.com, a teenager addressed his divorced parents: "Stupid. Stupid stupid stupid. I don't think you two realize how badly this had impacted me. It has thrown me in to a depression that *no matter how hard I try, it doesn't go away*" (writer's emphasis).[17] Another teenager, Leah, slipped into a depression when her parents divorced during her freshman year in high school. In a 2013 *HuffingtonPost.com* article, she explained that the divorce "wasn't really a surprise, but it made me feel so sad. Everything was changing." During the summer after tenth grade, she was in a deep depression. "Nothing felt right. I just wanted to stay in bed. I tried to get out of [doing] things as much as I could." She added, "I became closer to my boyfriend at the time, and we talked a lot about how I felt and everything I was going through. I spent more time with him because I didn't want to be home, and I kind of dropped my other friends. They knew something was wrong, they just didn't know how to approach me about it." Leah eventually told her parents about her feelings and they helped her find a therapist. She also was prescribed an antidepressant. She reported, "I noticed changes right off the bat. The medicine definitely helped, and the therapy let me talk out my feelings. I had been talking to my boyfriend, but the fact that the therapist was labeled 'therapist' helped me."[18]

When Same-Sex Couples with Children Divorce

In the United States an estimated 150,000 same-sex couples have married or legally registered as partners in civil unions, according to the 2010 U.S. Census report. An estimated one-quarter of all such households are raising children. Ironically, the largest percentage of couples of the same gender raising children is in states that ban the couples' marriages. However, there is no exact data nationwide because some couples do not reveal their sexual orientation in order to avoid harassment or discrimination.

Some of the children raised by two moms or two dads are adoptees. Some have been conceived by artificial insemination—donor semen and perhaps a donor egg are used to impregnate a lesbian woman, for example. Some children were conceived after heterosexual couples married and later divorced; some were borne by surrogate mothers.

About 1 percent "of the total number of currently-married or registered same-sex couples get divorced each year," reported the Williams Institute, which conducts independent research on sexual orientation and gender identity at the UCLA (University of California, Los Angeles) Law School.[19] Because most states still do not recognize or they ban same-sex unions, they will not grant a divorce. In those states, the marriage never happened so a divorce cannot happen.

When same-sex couples are legally divorced, children of those split couples react in the same way as that of children of divorced heterosexual couples. To repeat: They are often anxious, sad, angry, embarrassed, and confused.

Multiple Parental Divorces

"Multiple Divorces Strain Kids" was the headline for an article on Divorce360 .com. That seems like an understatement, especially when considering the many comments from young people who have felt the adverse effects of parental divorce or separation. Once is one time too many, they might say. In the guidebook *Should I Keep Trying to Work It Out?* the authors noted that "[i]n the United States, researchers estimate that 40%–50% of all first marriages, and 60% of second marriages, will end in divorce."[20] The divorce rate increases for third marriages to between 70 and 73 percent.[21]

When there are multiple parental divorces, the children involved have to deal with more than the breakup of their biological family. If parents remarry, the children must adapt to stepparents and stepsiblings. If they become attached to stepfamily members and another divorce occurs, additional emotional turmoil can result. Here is how Leslie Sheline, a young woman in her mid-twenties (now married with a family and living in Indiana), recounted her mother's two divorces and the consequences. She refers to her missing biological father as a "sperm donor" because he wasn't a "real father" to her. In her words,

> My mother and sperm donor procreated and married when my mother was 21 years old. A simple few years passed, and my mother [became part of] the world of single parenthood. It's a life I remember rather well for being so young myself. But, it was briefly lived. My mother then fell in love and married a man that became my younger sister's sperm donor. Another couple years passed and he too left, leaving my mother with two young girls to be mother/father/friend to.[22]

Leslie was only seven and a half when her little sister was born. "She was everything I dreamed of and more," she wrote. "However, never had I thought I would learn to be a parent before first learning how to be a child . . . unfortunately, it happens all too often during divorce. You see, my mother worked very hard for us kids. She kept a roof over our heads, food in our bellies, and clothes on our backs." The problem as Leslie saw it was the fact that even though her mom was being a responsible parent, she "was never quite there. I immediately took on the parental role with my sister. She seemed to be more like my own child than my sister. Our 'fathers' didn't come around and our mom worked hard and was tired when she was home." Continuing her story, Leslie wrote,

> I remember numerous nights of consoling my little sister after she got the call that her "dad" decided not to come get her. After she cried herself to sleep I then would go to my little hideaway and cry myself. "Doesn't anyone love us?" would be the first thing to pop into my head. I mean, I just witnessed two "dads" walk out on us. This is where it starts to get sticky. The man I considered "my dad" was in fact my sister's sperm donor [biological father]. We'll call him Rod. When I was around the age of 12, Rod became my role model. Though he wasn't any longer married to my mother, he at least tried to come and see us. He would treat me with as much love and respect as he treated his own blood.
>
> Boy, how I longed for that devotion from a father figure. The fact is, it was all a lie. When I was younger, he would use me as a babysitter for my sister (no big deal, right?). Then I started getting smart . . . and older. I started looking for my own sperm donor; still longing for my very own daddy to love. I couldn't find him. So I clung to Rod as tight as I could. He was the only man that made me feel like someone's little princess.
>
> Mom had a few boyfriends here and there but nothing too serious until Terry. He and I didn't see eye to eye real well in the beginning, which led me to demand that I be allowed to live with Rod and his wife. My wish was granted. There I went, right into the arms of a man that treated me like his very own. So much like his own that he wanted me around ALL OF THE TIME. Pretty soon my ties to the outside world were cut off. I had to live, breathe, and hail "King Rod." It was then I was introduced to my worst nightmare. This man who said he loved me like his very own child decided to take the level of his "love" to an all time new low . . . I became his house pet. After about a year of holding on to the idea of having a father in my life, I decided that being molested, raped, and abused just wasn't my gig and I got away, and took my sister with me!
>
> By this point in my life I was just 17 years old. I believed that men were scum. . . . Then I turned 18. I decided that I was tired of not knowing who I came from. I had many pictures from my first three years of life and I knew his name but, I didn't know him. So, with the help of the internet and a very special man in my life, by the age of 19 I got to meet

my sperm donor for the first memorable time in my life. It was beautiful. My OWN dad! My OWN blood hugging me . . . it was beautiful. That is, until four months later when he remarried and was told that he couldn't have a relationship with me.

Leslie acknowledged that she "just kinda gave up on" her biological father. "I was a lost soul for a little while. My entire life I always had my mother and my maternal grandparents, but I never really got to know the other part of me. I think that was the worst part of divorce."

Many adults carry the scars of multiple parental divorces. On the website Yahoo! Answers, a contributor named Pam.Bunnell responded to the question "How does parental divorce affect adult children's view of love and marriage?" This was her answer, in part:

It definitely has an affect [*sic*]. . . . In my case, my mother has been married 3 times, my Father was married and divorced 3 times by the time I was 12 years old. I learned you can not trust, when things get rough walk away. Parents when divorced become more selfish for they get lonely. The children seem to be put last. I wish I knew then what I know today for I would have done things differently. I would have not divorced my husband, I would have hung in there, yet watching my parents I did as they did. I suffered and my children suffered. They have a hard time with relationships and trust. When you have a positive childhood in which you live in an atmosphere of love and forgiveness, what a gift and a good start you will have in life. When, as I, brought up in a household of distrust, not able to commit, fighting, anger, confusion of rules it creates a low self esteem and you have to learn what love is by trial and error.[23]

Anxiety about relationships and difficulties in trusting others are not unusual among adult children of divorce. Some young adults worry that if they marry, they, too, will experience divorce. In addition, they may feel responsible for their siblings, or confused about changing rules in different households. Another common outcome is being protective of the custodial parent (or stepparent) and resentful of the other parent. Also they may dislike having to act like little adults because of the numerous responsibilities while they are still quite young.

Besides emotional upheavals in multiple divorces, there can be another "unfortunate dynamic," reported Geoff Williams for Reuters in 2012. Second divorces "compete for resources that the first divorce is still consuming. . . . Even after the $10,000 to $20,000 cost of a contested divorce, there are often lingering child-support costs and alimony." He added that finances are "especially tough for spouses who wind up paying child support for children from multiple marriages.

! It's a Fact

"Arkansas Leads Nation in Multiple Divorces." That was the title of an article on AllGov.com. According to the website, Arkansas and Oklahoma "lead the country in the highest number per capita of thrice-married men and women (10% for Arkansas, and just a tad below 10% for Oklahoma)." The statistics came from the 2008 American Community Survey conducted by the U.S. Census Bureau. The website further noted that "New York and Massachusetts have the lowest rates of multiple-married individuals (2%). These two states also have more people who wait longer to get married at all."[a]

Depending on the state, courts can look at what money is available for support without taking into consideration the adult's other financial obligations. A twice- or thrice-divorced individual could easily have very little left over, especially if they are also paying alimony to multiple ex-partners and splitting up the assets."[24]

If couples can collaborate during the divorce process, the costs can be fair and reasonable. Lawyers and counselors suggest that couples get help in determining how to choose compatible mates so that they will not repeat their mistakes and have multiple divorces. In the broader picture, that usually means a more positive outcome for children of divorce.

A Hopeful Future

In spite of all the negative reactions, comments, and statistics, most children of divorce eventually accept the reality of their parents' divorce and find hope for the future. Kevin, a California student, attested to the fact that there can be some positive outcomes. He was only seven years old when his parents divorced. As a sixteen-year-old, he wrote for DivorceWizards.com,

> I thought that my life was going to fall apart. To my surprise, my mother had planned for my sister and me to move, along with her, to Southern California. My dad, however, was going to remain in New Jersey because of his business. My family was splitting apart—what did this mean? Was I ever going to see my father again? Southern California? As my father backed down our long driveway, I refused to let go. I ran as fast as I could, crying hysterically, trying to get what I thought would be my last good-bye. . . . He gave me a hug and told me that everything was going to be

See This Flick!

In the film *The Squid and the Whale* (2005), released on DVD in 2006, sixteen-year-old Walt and his twelve-year-old brother, Frank, struggle in their attempts to cope with their parents' divorce. Their parents in the movie are Bernard and Joan Berkman, both writers. He is a creative writing teacher and literary novelist; she is just beginning a writing career that is commercially successful. When they divorce, they discuss their schedule for sharing custody of their two sons. The family home is in Park Slope, Brooklyn, but Bernard moves out and rents a house in another neighborhood.

Walt and Frank begin to take sides in their relationships with their parents. Walt wants to be an artist and songwriter and favors the parent he believes is the most artistic—his father. Frank prefers his mother, who supports his desire to become a professional tennis player. In fact, Joan dates and has an affair with Frank's upbeat and "cool" tennis instructor. Meanwhile, Bernard starts sharing his new house with Lili, one of his students, and both he and Walt become infatuated with the girl.

As the family conflicts become increasingly complex, Frank experiences his awakening sexuality and also begins a beer-drinking habit. Walt's inner turmoil leads him to perform at a school talent competition and claim he composed a song actually written by Pink Floyd. School officials and his parents determine Walt should see a psychologist to uncover the reasons for his lying. During sessions with the psychologist, Walt begins to realize that his father is not the idol of his childhood and was seldom around while he was growing up. He recalls how his mother cared for him and that they would go to the American Museum of Natural History to see the giant squid and whale exhibit. It always frightened him, so he would close his eyes whenever passing by the fabricated creatures. As the film ends, Walt stands in the museum looking at the squid and whale, apparently trying to come to terms with himself and his life.

okay. I didn't know then that a divorce and a cross-country move would change my life forever.[25]

Kevin explained that when living in a single-parent family he had to take on numerous responsibilities and he became "self-disciplined, and trustworthy" as a child and as a teenager. Those traits helped him excel in his studies and sports. In the end, he concluded, "My parents are happily remarried and have allowed me to maintain a loving relationship with both families. . . . At age seven, I struggled with the confusion and pain of coping with my parents' divorce. Today, at age sixteen, I understand that obstacles can result in opportunity and success. I learned that hard work, determination, and self-discipline can turn your worst time into your best time."[26]

Off the Bookshelf

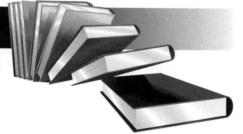

Surviving Divorce: Teens Talk about What Hurts and What Helps (2007) by Trudi Strain Trueit is a paperback easy to carry around and access for brief advice—from the author and teenagers. The book includes comments from young people like sixteen-year-old Paige, who reported that she "was all over the place emotionally" after learning that her parents were divorcing.[b] Jamie, another teen, put it this way: "Divorce stinks. Not having my dad around is tough, even though when he lived with us, he'd yell at us a lot. I wish he'd get his act together, but I know he won't." He wondered why his dad would leave and in an act of revenge not provide "enough money to get by?"[c] One teen complained of feeling rejected and abandoned; another felt anxious because he didn't know what to expect after his parents separated.

According to the author Trueit, "Dealing with the turmoil of divorce may mean confronting intense and ever-changing emotions. . . . Toss in the usual pressures that come with schoolwork, friendships, dating, and body image, and it isn't hard to see why teens trying to handle their parents' breakup may feel overwhelmed."[d] The titles of the six chapters provide clues on what to expect: "A Family Shattered," "Coming Undone," "The Course of Divorce," "Sea of Emotions," and the final chapter, "Divorce: A Survival Guide." The latter focuses on life after parental divorce and how to look positively toward the future.

Some other constructive outcomes for children of divorce include learning how to develop practical skills like problem solving or learning that all relationships require work. Some youth become more independent or take on more responsibility, such as helping care for young siblings in their families. Or they may try to help their peers who are experiencing parental divorce.

Whether children of divorce experience difficult emotional problems depends on the circumstances, as counselors, researchers, and children themselves have stated many times. In general, young people whose parents curb their arguments during and after the divorce process do better than children who are exposed to continual parental conflict. Parents, school personnel, friends, and others who provide positive support for children post-divorce also help protect young people from long-term negative effects of split families.

PLACING BLAME AND TAKING SIDES

"My parents are going through a divorce currently and I feel strongly that my dad has practically abandoned me. . . . I am 18 years old and I STILL can't understand how he can find it in himself to just up and leave."
—an unidentified male posting in 2011 on MedHelp.org[1]

A teenager calling himself lonesome_george commented about parental divorce on the community network Reddit.com. He noted, "I feel like my situation and my reaction [to parents' divorce] has left me emotionally stunted. I'm not the average high school kid. And I feel like my parents are to blame. *There must have been some way they could've worked things out better*" (teen's emphasis).[2]

Some teens feel their divorced parents have ruined their lives and take out their frustrations on one or both of their parents. They might rebel by refusing to clean up their room or to pick up their belongings scattered about the home. They might sulk and talk back when being disciplined. Or in more extreme cases, they might leave home, use illegal drugs, commit crimes, and spend time in jail.

How Some Celebrities React to Parental Divorce

Because of their celebrity status, many entertainers are interviewed about their personal lives. In some cases, reporters include questions about a star's reaction to his or her parents' divorce. For example, award-winning singer and actor Justin Timberlake's parents divorced when he was three years old, and during an interview as a young adult he said, "I'm humbly and honestly finding out that I have a lot of issues with that. . . . I'm finding more and more that . . . I'm going to break the chain because that's what you want to do, break the chain of your parents." He hopes he won't make the same mistake as his parents in regard to relationships.[3]

Nicole Richie said her life came crashing down when she was about eight years old and her parents, famous musician Lionel Richie and his wife, Brenda Richie, divorced. In a 2004 interview with Oprah, Nicole recalled, "When my dad divorced my mom it was kind of like him leaving me also. . . . I just really didn't understand why he wasn't returning my phone calls, or why I couldn't see him whenever I wanted to. That was the most hurtful thing to me."[4]

Not all celebrities are upset when their parents divorce. Actor and film director Johnny Depp remembered hearing his "parents argue and thinking: 'Come on, this is torture. Just split!' They stuck it out until I was 15, but I'd seen it coming for years. When they finally did divorce, I thought: 'OK, this is the right thing.'"[5]

Brooke Hogan, daughter of wrestler-dad Hulk Hogan (his real name is Terry Bollea) and his wife, Linda, was thankful when her parents divorced in 2009. As she put it in an interview, "I was relieved to hear that the divorce was finally signed, sealed and delivered. . . . They weren't good together. . . . So it's like OK, everything's over, everything's done, you guys don't have to hate each other anymore."[6]

Noncustodial Moms

"There are an estimated 2.4 million noncustodial mothers in the United States," according to an *ABC News 20/20* report aired in June 2013. During the *20/20* show about noncustodial moms, hosts Alyssa Pry and Gail Deutsch questioned how the public and children react when moms opt out of marriage and leave their children with their ex-husbands. The public often blames women who make that choice, frequently branding them as "evil" or "inhuman" or worse. Some women even get death threats. However, the *20/20* hosts said these mothers are likely acting in the best interests of their children.

There are many reasons why mothers forgo custody. In some cases, after a divorce fathers are better able to financially care for children than mothers are. Sometimes men hire lawyers who manipulate divorce proceedings in order to obtain custody of their children. Judges on occasion make decisions that force mothers to release their offspring to the fathers.

In a 2009 major feature "What Kind of Mother Leaves Her Kids?" in *Marie Claire* magazine, three women told their stories to Lea Goldman. All three moms left after a divorce to pursue careers. They described the emotional difficulties, the defensiveness, agonizing, and longing after parting with their children. But their lives and their children's lives apparently have been productive.

The hosts of the *20/20* show interviewed noncustodial mom Talyaa Liera, who left her family and lives in Seattle. Her daughter, Serena, and her brothers live in Pennsylvania with their father. The children, now teenagers, did not carry on a blame game and have a good relationship with both parents. As Serena put it, "When [mom] first left, it was really difficult. I would cry all the time. It was really hard," Serena said. "But now, I'm not that way. I'm more me, I think, than I was before, because I figured out who I am without my mom. . . . When I realized that she really is happier, I can be happy without her being here all the time. . . . I really love my mom a lot."[7]

Who's to Blame?

Despite the fact that every state has some form of no-fault divorce law, some couples still want to place blame on their spouse for their marital breakup, as do some children of divorce. An article by Sam Margulies in *Psychology Today* provides some explanations. Margulies wrote, "When misfortune strikes most of us want to know why. Illness, hurricanes and other natural disasters are obviously no-one's fault and simply have to be endured without whatever satisfaction comes from having someone to blame. But the failures of human relationships are much more complex. Divorce is about the failure of a relationship in which at least one partner but usually both are disappointed in the behavior of the other." He added, "Most divorces are the product of a hundred small wounds, sins of omission and commission and failure to care for and feed the relationship. Marriages don't end suddenly; they erode over time. Nevertheless, it is common for people to seize on one or two actions or character flaws of their mates in explaining the divorce." This happens because "few people are prepared to accept responsibility for their own contributions to the failure of the marriage." The "more comfortable" route is to blame a spouse rather than oneself; "It is generally easier to garner sympathy from friends and family that way."[8]

A similar opinion came from an author and teacher Lisa Arends, who writes a blog on *HuffingtonPost.com*. In 2013, she stated,

> The blame frequently starts within the dissolving union. One partner often holds the other responsible for the destruction of the marriage. They can be quick to list the faults and transgressions of their ex, pointing fingers at another as a way of avoiding having to look at themselves. This is frequently performed behind a shield of righteousness, painting the blaming spouse into a victim role where they have no responsibility for their own actions and their own happiness.[9]

Placing blame also makes most people feel better. If problems or failures (whether in marriage or in other relationships) are someone else's fault, the sense of guilt, worry, and grief may disappear. By blaming others, individuals do not have to be responsible for their mistakes or actions. In other words, they become victims, which in some way provides a feeling of security. Victims are not at fault so that must mean they are in the "right" or okay.

Blaming Themselves

Young children's common reaction to parental divorce is to blame themselves for the family breakup. At a young age, children are self-absorbed—the world revolves around them. Their parents have told them what to do, how to behave, where they can go, what they can wear, and so forth. Perhaps they have heard their parents argue about how a child should be disciplined for not doing household chores, for poor grades at school, for an argument or fight with peers, or for using inappropriate language. They then might conclude that something they have done or have not done has caused their parents' marriage to fail. But that is not the case, recording artist Justin Bieber told *Twist* magazine in 2010. He said, "I think a lot of kids have had their parents split up, and they should know that it wasn't because of something they did."[10]

Teens also blame themselves for their parents' divorce, even though they may understand very well that they are not responsible. It may help to ease the pain of parental divorce just to find fault with oneself. By blaming themselves, teens may be trying to hide their feelings of helplessness. Or perhaps teenagers have guilt feelings because they have not tried to convince their parents to seek counseling or other help to save their marriage. But that is not any child's responsibility. In 2013, nineteen-year-old Hailee Smith of Indiana, whose parents divorced when she was a youngster, put it plainly: "Kids of divorce are not to blame. It's not their fault. Just because parents can't work out the problems with each other, that doesn't mean they are blaming the kids."[11] In short, divorcing or divorced parents are the ones accountable.

More Finger Pointing

In some cases parents blame their teenagers for causing conflicts, separations, or divorce. A teenager who calls herself CrackyGirl complained on ExperienceProject.com that her parents "always have to fight every month. And it's always me who witnesses them. I have a 14 year old sister, but she goes away and stays in the room until dinner. I cannot stand them always fighting. Fine, I'm a 17 year old but I cannot interfere, because they constantly blame me for the reason" they are fighting.[12]

Should daughters be blamed for fights and divorces? Some experts seem to infer that. For example, Notre Dame psychologist Anita E. Kelly wrote an article in 2010 for *Psychology Today* in which she noted, "In generation after generation across many countries, parents of girls divorce more than do parents of boys." As she explained in her article,

Economists Gordon Dahl (at the University of Rochester) and Enrico Moretti (at UCLA) discovered the following facts in 2003: In the United States, the parents of a girl are nearly 5 percent more likely to divorce than

Some couples play the "blame game"—he blames her, she blames him for marital problems that lead to divorce.

the parents of a boy. The parents of three girls are close to 10 percent more likely to divorce than the parents of three boys. . . . [O]ne conclusion we might draw is that wives with daughters are less likely to stay with their husbands because they know that with a girl, they'll never be lonely or without help. Thus, they may be less willing to tolerate any bad behaviors from their husbands (and less willing to stay married) because they don't need their husbands as much.[13]

Nevertheless, Kelly and the economists did not reach a final conclusion. They left it up to readers to speculate on why more parents of girls divorce than parents of boys.

Whatever the statistics about divorces among parents with girls, females are not the only ones targeted for blame. Along with blaming their spouses, some couples with marital problems may accuse in-laws of causing conflicts. Or they contend that interfering friends, vindictive co-workers, or spiteful neighbors stir up marital troubles. The truth is that unless a partner is abusive, is unfaithful, has married for fraudulent reasons, has committed a crime, or is mentally ill, both spouses probably share some of the blame for a miserable marriage.

Can Minor Children Divorce Their Parents?

Rather than blame their parents for divorcing, some teenagers and preteens threaten to divorce their parents. Can that happen? It is unusual, but the answer is yes. It is called emancipation. The word itself means being free from others' control. When a person turns eighteen, she or he is legally an adult and is automatically emancipated. A minor who receives parental consent to join the military also becomes emancipated from his or her parents.

Minor emancipation laws differ by state, and not all states have such statutes. In order to divorce their parents, minors must petition the court or other legal entity. Usually they have to be at least fourteen years old and provide reasons for their emancipation. Abuse and neglect are legitimate reasons for emancipation. But minors must also show that they have a consistent source of income and can manage money responsibly—that is pay for food, housing, and all of their bills, including medical, dental, and insurance. Minors also have to attend school, usually until the age of sixteen.

Teenagers under the age of eighteen who are working and can support themselves make up the majority of emancipated minors. In most cases, they are usually film celebrities, musicians, or other well-paid entertainers. They are not likely to be employed in minimum-wage jobs.

It Happened to Miley Cyrus

Miley Cyrus was born in 1992 and was named Destiny Hope because her parents, country singer Billy Ray and Leticia (Tish) Cyrus, believed their daughter would accomplish great things with her life. "But she has always been called Miley, a modification of 'Smiley,' because she had such a happy disposition," wrote David Hiltbrand of Knight Ridder News Service in 2006. That was the year Miley got braces and prepared for her role in Disney channel's *Hannah Montana* show, a teen comedy-drama.[a]

Miley played the part of a young teen who was an average school girl by day but at night was a famous pop singer named Hannah Montana. Her father Billy Ray played the role of Hannah's dad in the show. The series debuted in 2006 and ended in 2010, when Miley was eighteen years old. That year her father filed for divorce from her mother—not an unusual event except that Miley blamed herself for the breakup. In her view, her parents were so involved in their efforts to make her a celebrity that they neglected time for each other. In fact, Miley went on with her career and became a pop star with millions of followers. Her father noted that Miley's fame had affected the family and that was the reason he filed for divorce in 2010.

In 2011, Miley's parents reconciled and the family was back together. But in 2013, the couple divorced, citing "irreconcilable differences." Meanwhile, Miley, who has had up-and-down relationships with her parents, has kept working on new albums and booking appearances. Apparently she has changed her Disney image to become a sexy performer. But critics around the globe denounced her twerking performance at the 2013 MTV Video Music Awards. To twerk is "to dance to popular music in a sexually provocative manner involving thrusting hip movements and a low, squatting stance," according to the *Oxford Dictionary Online*. Some critics called her dance moves "bawdy," "raunchy," "embarrassing," and "a nightmare." On the other hand, Cyrus was pleased that she received thousands of tweets about her performance, publicity that so far has enhanced her career.

For example, Ariel Winter, a teen actress in the TV series *Modern Family* (which debuted in 2009), began seeking emancipation in 2012 when she was fourteen years old. Ariel's mother Chrisoula (Crystal) and father Glen Workman are divorced and have been in court over custody of Ariel. In a highly publicized family feud, Ariel accused her mother of emotional abuse, which Chrisoula adamantly denied. Chrisoula argued that her daughter wanted to be emancipated so she could have sexual relations with her eighteen-year-old boyfriend. Ariel's mother told reporters and the court that she caught her daughter and boyfriend (now an ex-boyfriend) in bed. Since late 2012, Ariel began living with her older sister Shanelle Gray's family. The court granted Shanelle Gray legal guardianship of Ariel. For her part, Ariel reported in 2013 that life with her sister's family is "definitely more normal—and that'll help me grow up like I'm supposed to."[14]

Drew Barrymore is another child actress who filed to divorce her parents. A member of a celebrated stage and screen acting family, Drew herself was famous at a young age, becoming a star with her role as Gertie in *E. T. the Extra-Terrestrial* (1982). A few years later she began abusing drugs. Her mother would take her to night clubs and buy her drinks and her mom's friends gave her marijuana. By the time she was a teenager, Drew was addicted to drugs and practically ruined. But she got treatment and was rehabilitated. While in the treatment center Drew's father would call frequently to ask her for money. In 1990, at the age of fifteen, she petitioned for emancipation, telling the court that her mother and father were bad influences. The court agreed and granted her emancipation in 1991.

Another young celebrity who divorced his parents is Macaulay Culkin, the star in the movie *Home Alone* (1990) and *Home Alone 2: Lost in New York* (1992). Macaulay accused his parents of mismanaging the millions of dollars he earned and was granted emancipation from his parents at the age of fourteen. Unfortunately, divorcing his parents did not trigger further success. Macaulay has been accused of drug abuse and has played few roles since the 1990s.

At the age of fifteen Michelle Williams did not particularly want to divorce her parents. Instead, she wanted emancipation so she would not be governed by child labor laws that set rules for wages, hours worked, and safety requirements for individuals under age eighteen. As an independent singer, songwriter, and actress, she was able to advance her career and gain success.

Former child stars of the past have also divorced their parents. One is Melissa Francis, who played Cassandra Cooper Ingalls on the TV show *Little House on the Prairie* from 1981 to 1982. Melissa tells of her mother's physical and mental abuse in her memoir *Diary of a Stage Mother's Daughter* (2012). Her mother, who had great mood swings and was manipulative, wanted Melissa emancipated as a fifteen-year-old so her daughter could work longer hours. Melissa told Hollie McKay on *FoxNews.com*, "I didn't have a driver's license, how would I get to school? I wasn't organized enough at 15 to pay the rent, manage my schedule, go on auditions, work and take care of my basic needs. It didn't seem possible to break free," she said. "But I realized if I was going to seize the reins from my controlling stage mother, I had to be able to take charge of my life."[15] And she did, going on to get a bachelor of arts degree in economics at Harvard and eventually becoming a TV business anchor.

Taking Sides

It is not unusual for offspring to be torn between parents following a divorce. Unfortunately, that is part of the blame game. Sometimes even adult celebrities such as Ashlee and Jessica Simpson publicly take sides when their parents split up. Apparently the parents, Tina and Joe Simpson, parted in 2012 and divorced in 2013 because of Joe's reported homosexuality. Joe is a former minister and manager of Jessica's fashion line. Jessica told reporters that her mom was dealt a terrible blow after years of marriage so she supports Tina. But Ashley, who blames her mom for not giving Joe enough attention during their marriage, has been on Joe's side.

Of course, not all children of divorce tell the world that they support one parent or the other after a family breakup. But taking sides is a common consequence for offspring of divorced parents, say lawyers, psychologists, clergy, and other counselors. When young children and teenagers hear a parent discuss how the marriage went wrong, they begin to resent the parent they think is at fault, which can damage the relationship for a lifetime.

Most teens and young adults try not to think about their parents' separation or divorce. The young man from the Philippines whose parents broke up when he was eighteen noted, "I was thinking to myself that I never really cared about divorce . . . as long as my [younger] sister was okay." He recalled, "I didn't see my sister cry but I cried when they first told me."[16]

Children of divorce tell themselves it is not a big deal so they won't hurt so much. Still they want some kind of explanation regarding the situation. But if they talk about it with either mom or dad, they fear they will be persuaded to take sides when all they really want is to have a relationship with both parents without one of them being jealous, angry, or vindictive.

Sometimes "parental alienation" occurs. The term used by legal experts and family counselors simply means that one parent tries to alienate a child from his or her other parent. "[A] twelve-year study commissioned by the Family Law Section of the American Bar Association of over 1,000 divorces found that 'parental alienation,' the programming of a child against the other parent, occurs regularly, sixty percent (60%) of the time, and sporadically another twenty percent."[17] The study found that "[o]ne of the 'basic techniques' alienating parents use is to send the message, either overtly or subtly, that the target parent is insignificant or irrelevant to the child." For example, a custodial parent may refuse to speak about the nonresidential parent, sending the message that he or she hardly exists. Another method is to destroy photographs of the target parent or not let a child keep photos of that parent. An "insidious but powerful method of excluding the target is for the alienating parent to refuse to acknowledge any positive experiences the children have [with the target parent]."[18]

Another way to describe alienation is to think of it as a form of brainwashing. For example, a father might ask his teenager to look at his mom as she "really is," or a mother might find every opportunity to contemptuously detail a dad's faults—he did this or that wrong. Another ploy to get children of divorce to take sides is telling them in a reproachful manner: "You act just like your mother," or "You talk just like your father." Such comments are likely to make progeny wonder which part of themselves they should find objectionable since they are products of both parents.

Twenty-one-year old Natie was familiar with parental alienation. In 2013, she wrote on ExperienceProject.com,

> From an early age, my mother has told me what a horrible person my father is. Positive things about him rarely crossed her lips. And when I was finally old enough to think 'Hey, why do I still have to see this man if he's such a bastard?' I began acting out towards him. In my mind, everything my mother told me was fact, and this man who shared my DNA was no longer deserving of my respect. I began to hate him. . . . I am 21 years old now and trying hard to have a relationship with both my parents, but how does it help when my mother keeps reminding me that my father hurt her? I am trying to let go of my pain concerning both of them, but her stories about him don't help.[19]

A sixteen-year-old boy seeking advice in 2011 on the Internet site Annie's Mailbox, lived with his biological mother and stepfather and was concerned because his mom blamed him "for most things and nearly always takes my stepdad's side when we have a disagreement. For example, on one of my report cards, I had two 97s and two 94s. Those are pretty solid grades, but Mom yelled at me for not doing better. She also gets mad when she thinks I'm giving her 'attitude,' even when I'm not." He explained that his biological father had been out of work and was behind on child support so the teenager had to listen to his mother and stepfather complain about his dad. He wrote, "I love my dad. I also love my mother and stepfather, but I don't know how to talk to them anymore because I know they will judge me."[20]

Children, whether youngsters or teenagers, want to see their parents—biological or stepparents—as reliable and capable authority figures. "Trying to

The Children's Bill of Rights in Divorce

Many organizations have developed "Children's Bill of Rights in Divorce" and have posted these on the Internet. The New Jersey Chapter of the Association of Family and Conciliation Courts adapted and expanded the American Bar Association's version, which says that children of divorce have the following rights:

1. The right to be treated as important human beings, with unique feelings, ideas, and desires and not as a source of argument between parents.
2. The right to a continuing relationship with both parents and the freedom to receive love from and express love for both.
3. The right to express love and affection for each parent without having to stifle that love because they fear disapproval from the other parent.
4. The right to know that their parents' decision to divorce is not their responsibility and that they will live with one parent and will visit the other parent.
5. The right to continuing care and guidance from both parents.
6. The right to honest answers to questions about the changing family relationships.
7. The right to know and appreciate what is good in each parent without one parent degrading the other.
8. The right to have a relaxed, secure relationship with both parents without being placed in a position to manipulate one parent against the other.
9. The right to have the custodial parent not undermine visitation by suggesting tempting alternatives or by threatening to withhold visitation as a punishment for the children's wrongdoings.
10. The right to experience regular and consistent visitation and the right to know the reason for a cancelled visit.[b]

Off the Bookshelf

From its title, *The Divorce Girl: A Novel of Art and Soul* (2012), the book appears to be only for girls, but it should appeal to youth and adults of both genders. Written by Kansas poet laureate Caryn Mirriam-Goldberg, the story is humorous as well as sad as it follows Deborah Shapiro, a teenage photographer in a Jewish family of the 1970s. Her parents, Harold and Bev, divorce, and Deborah takes sides, turning against her mom, who suffers from depression because of the death of one of her children and withdraws from everyday life. In the divorce settlement Deborah opts to stay with her father, who keeps the family home in New Jersey and demands that his daughter do the housekeeping and cooking. Her mother moves to an apartment and is granted alimony and custody of the couple's other two children, eleven-year-old Roger and young Missy.

The arrangement is full of conflict as self-centered Harold Shapiro constantly criticizes Deborah. When she does not meet his expectations, he threatens to send her to live with her mother. It's a refrain that appears in almost every chapter. Deborah's life becomes even more chaotic when she discovers that her father has a lover, Fatima, who owns a Greek diner. Harold owns a taxi company in New York City, and he and Fatima decide to operate a joint business, a stall at a large flea market. Deborah works there every weekend and sometimes works as a dispatcher at the taxi company. At both places she gets acquainted with eccentric characters who represent a variety of ethnic backgrounds.

Eventually, Deborah develops a relationship with Fatima, who tries to "mother" the teenager. But Harold cheats on Fatima and begins an affair with another woman. After that affair ends, Harold finds another partner and marries her. All of these varied situations plus her observations of her home life and natural settings serve as subjects for Deborah's photography, which is her passion. Her camera is like an appendage and with it she chronicles her life. She is mentored by a crass, outspoken woman named Liz, who sells jeans but holds a photography class at the back of her shop once each week. Liz helps Deborah learn the art of photography and encourages Deborah to set up a darkroom in her family home to develop her film.

As the story develops, Deborah faces one crisis after another in somewhat soap-opera style. She becomes so disillusioned with her life that she thinks about ending it. She actually writes a suicide note but falls asleep before she does anything. When found, she admits she doesn't know how to kill herself. She also is faced with an unbalanced father who attempts suicide but fails. Both Deborah and her father are counseled by a rabbi, who calls himself a radical. The rabbi holds weekly youth sessions that Deborah attends in a suburban temple.

The crises that follow include Deborah's knock-down fight with her father, her first love and discovery that the boyfriend is homosexual, and her realization that her father's "second wife" does not support her. Somehow she manages to pick herself up after every defeat. She even gets a scholarship to attend a fine arts college and is able to reconnect with her mother. It is exactly the kind of ending that most children of divorce would like—except this is fiction.

Reality TV and Divorce

Real fighting couples. Real families falling apart. Real TV shows that allow viewers to take sides as couples air their grievances. One reality show of this type is *Divorce Court*, where couples argue in front of a real judge, who is municipal court judge Lynn Toler of Cleveland Heights, Ohio. The show has become the oldest of courtroom dramas, first running from 1957 to 1969, then from 1985 to 1992, and once again since 1999. In 2011 the show began to feature couples who are cohabiting or "shacking up," as the judge puts it. Toler told Michael Logan of *TV Guide Magazine*, "The marriage rate is dropping significantly and unwed couples who live together have the same problems as those headed toward divorce. Who's getting out of the apartment lease? Who gets the car? Who gets Fluffy? By the way, I'm kicking and screaming about this change. Hate it, hate it, hate it!" She explained, "I'm old-school. I don't believe in shacking up and hooking up and having two or three baby daddies. Society has evolved, and we need to address this so that our show keeps providing a service people can use. But I say, 'Get married or don't do it at all!'"[c]

Most couples on *Divorce Court* and similar reality shows about divorce are not famous, but Pennsylvanians Jon and Kate Gosselin gained celebrity after their highly publicized family breakup. The couple and their eight children (fraternal twin girls and sextuplets—three girls and three boys) were featured on TV specials *Surviving Sextuplets and Twins* and *Sextuplets and Twins: One Year Later.* Those specials on the Discovery Health Channel were the basis for a series of reality TV shows called *Jon & Kate Plus 8.*

The series was about the daily lives of the Gosselin family, first airing in 2007. But after Jon's highly publicized affair in 2008 and the couple's divorce in 2009, Jon left the show and it was retitled *Kate Plus 8.* It focused on the challenges of a divorced mother raising the children and the bickering between Jon and Kate, such as disagreements about finances and how to parent. On TV news programs, commentators reported on the couple's he-said-she-said accusations—in other words, the public hassle continued as he blamed her, she blamed him.

Kate Plus 8 was cancelled in 2011 after airing 150 episodes. Nevertheless, the family still has been featured in news stories. In 2011, Kate also launched a website, Kate Plus My 8, on which she shares her hopes for another TV show plus information about the family (in 2013 the twins were teenagers and the sextuplets were nine years old).

destroy the child's belief in the other parent deprives that child of one of the essential elements of his or her well being. Seeing a parent degraded and humiliated is deeply disturbing to a child. It inflicts long-lasting damage in ways that a child—even an older one—does not fully understand," wrote legal experts in a pamphlet distributed by the Virginia State Bar.[21]

BEING IN THE MIDDLE

"I hated being in the middle. They still say things to me . . . seven years after the divorce, about the other parent, and they expect me to laugh at a bad joke about them or to say something bad about them."—nineteen-year-old Nicole in Voices of Children of Divorce by David Royko[1]

Being in the middle of parental divorce is the subject of an entire chapter in Royko's book of interviews with young people. The interviewees identified only with fictitious first names have reactions similar to Nicole's. For example, Riza, eighteen, said, "Like my mom would say something about my dad. . . . Or my dad would say something about the way my mom handles things." Or Loretta, twenty-one, declared, "I always felt like I had to defend Dad because Mom was always so angry, and . . . accusing him of this and that." Or Barb, eighteen, complained, "My mother would say, 'Go tell your dad that you need money for clothes. . . . And tell him that your brother needs some more medication.'"[2]

Another way that divorced or divorcing parents put children in the middle is to ask, Who do you want to live with—your mom or dad? "During my childhood, it was a question that was often put to me," wrote Tanith Carey, an adult child of divorce. "And it caused me a lifetime of pain."[3]

Sandi Greene of Arizona was eighteen years old when her parents separated and twenty-one when they divorced. She noted on FocusontheFamily.com that she

> often felt caught between my parents. In the midst of their pain, my parents would slip phrases in such as "Your mother did this," or "Your father is at fault." While I understood they were only releasing frustration and hurt, I felt caught in the middle by their negative comments about one another. Asking me to relay information to the other parent, or getting upset because I decided to spend Christmas with one of them and not the other, only contributed to my feelings of resentment and frustration.[4]

On the website ExperienceProject.com, a young adult female who uses the name LonexWolf wrote in 2011 about her parents' divorce:

> For years, my mother had a "Me against Him" attitude towards my dad, in the sense that everything he did, she took it as a further declaration of war, instead of peacefully, casually talking to him about it. There are divorces in which both sides call a sort of truce. Some of my friends, their parents live this way, even giving a friendly smile and a hug when they see their ex spouse, for divorce is not something final and severing. Divorce just means the marriage didn't work out, which is no reason to raise the pirate's flag and attack.[5]

On the same website, a twenty-one-year-old who calls himself batteredsoul wrote in 2012 that his parents divorced when he was three years old, but they made it his "responsibility to be the messenger between them. . . . I have grown up having to deal with the emotional beat downs from them that really only makes me realize that I am the common denominator between them and without me they would no longer have to think hear or talk to one another ever again. It's a really stressful burden to carry."[6]

Hear No Evil, Speak No Evil, See No Evil

That maxim often is found on figurines of three animals—sometimes rabbits but generally so-called wise monkeys. One is covering its ears, the second is covering its mouth, and the third is covering its eyes. Some say the proverb originated on a Japanese Shinto shrine. Others say it is of ancient Buddhist origin.

Regardless, today the saying also represents advice that children of divorce receive from counselors and others: Don't listen to or carry hateful messages back and forth between parents who are divorced, such as a father saying, "Tell your mom not to pick you up early. This is my time, not hers." Or "Tell your dad this is the last time he'll see you until I get the child support payment." In other words, children get caught in the middle of divorced parents' arguments and bad-mouthing. Some websites on divorce even use photos of individuals imitating the actions of "hear no evil, speak no evil, see no evil."[a]

These girls are imitating the slogan hear no evil, see no evil, and speak no evil.

In their guidebook for individuals seeking divorce, Alan J. Hawkins and Tamara A. Fackrell wrote, "One teenage girl we know confided that her parents had put her in the middle of their divorce. Her mother inappropriately confided in this young girl many of her relationship problems. This stripped her of the carefree innocence she once had. The girl began to fail in school and felt burdened by her parents' expectations that she take messages back and forth and smooth conflicts between her divorced parents."[7]

Children of divorce also feel torn during special occasions. They want both parents to attend concerts, plays, sporting events, or graduation ceremonies, for example. Sometimes, they have to find ways to share time with parents who do not want to sit near each other at such events. Or when it comes to holidays or birthdays, they may have to choose where to spend it. However, as Hailee Smith reported, she was very young when her parents divorced so the idea of celebrating "two holidays and two birthdays" with double the gifts seemed like a great benefit. That changed as she got older and realized her "biological father was not really there" to be a role model for her.[8]

Off the Bookshelf

The fictional character Drew Marsh, a teenager, has no doubt about whose side he is on after his parents, George and Linda Marsh, divorce. He supports his mom. Drew and his mom share points of view every other chapter in the novel *Replacing Dad* (1993) by Shelley Fraser Mickle. The novel is set in the small Gulf town of Key Palm, Florida, where Drew; his younger sister, Mandy; and preschooler George the Second live with their parents. George the First, as Linda calls her ex-husband, is principal of a K–12 school with about a hundred students. George has left the family for a fifth-grade teacher at the school.

Drew does not display anger toward his dad. In fact, he and his siblings visit with him on weekends. But as the eldest child, Drew understands the many obstacles his mother has to face as a single parent. With few job skills (she planned to be an artist), she works at the only job she can find—a clerk in the office of the town dump. Before going to work, Linda must drop off George the Second at day care and take Mandy to school and then pick them up in the evening. Drew is eager to get his driver's license so that he can help out with the transportation.

On the day Drew receives his learner's permit, he has an accident—with his mother and siblings in the car. At a traffic signal, he backs into the car behind him, a vintage Mercedes owned by the new doctor in town, Mark Haley. Not much damage is done to Haley's car, and he doesn't raise a fuss. Linda's insurance company pays for repairs to her car with its smashed-in trunk, but she decides to use the money to buy a station wagon that she calls the Granny Apple.

The family attempts to settle into a routine of sorts and go along with Linda's positive spirit, but their lives are hardly without turmoil. The roof in the house leaks. A pet dog dies. Mandy is afraid of poltergeists. And Drew's date with his first girlfriend doesn't go well.

Drew also has to supervise George the Second, who insists on wearing an old bunny suit everywhere he goes. One day while Linda is at work, George puts a rock (more likely a good-sized stone) up his nose, and Drew has to find someone with a car to take his brother to see Dr. Haley. However, in the medical office, George manages to sneeze and eject the rock. While the family is in his office, Dr. Haley is impressed with Linda's medical knowledge, albeit limited, and he offers Linda a job as an assistant. She agrees, even though she has no academic background for the position.

Over the weeks, Linda and Mark begin to develop a close friendship and Drew hopes the two will marry. But one day he sees Dr. Haley and a young woman walking on the beach and he mistakenly believes that the doctor has betrayed his mother. He does not realize that Haley is a widower and the young woman is his daughter. Drew decides he has to fix things and confront Haley—even do him bodily harm, if necessary. But without knowing Drew's intentions, Dr. Haley surprises the teenager, asking him if it is okay to marry his mom. The response? Yeah.

Custody Issues

Custody issues in a divorce can be divisive and they sometimes can place offspring in the middle. Where will they live—with mom or dad? Which parent will they visit and when? What if one parent moves to another state? Who will make the decisions regarding their basic needs, health care, and education?

Parents can make custody and visitation arrangements in a private agreement, and usually the mother becomes the custodial parent. Children then see their father on preplanned visits, such as weekends or summer vacations. But sometimes parents cannot agree, and a court has to decide such issues, putting children in the middle.

When children appear in family court while their custody is being determined, the young people can become highly stressed. Some U.S. family courts are using therapy dogs to help relieve that stress. Therapy dogs are especially trained and certified to appear in court, and they are being utilized nationally in varied cases. For instance, in December 2013, Pasco County, Florida, circuit judge Lynn Tepper allowed two therapy dogs in her court during a hearing in which a girl was extremely anxious as attorneys debated over who should have custody of her and her younger sister. Hugging the dogs helped calm the girl. A similar change occurred in another case, Judge Tepper told a *Tampa Bay Times* reporter, "A teenager was "getting more and more agitated," but after stroking one of the dogs "[y]ou could see her calming down," the judge explained.[9]

According to the legal website Nolo, "Almost all courts use a standard that gives the 'best interests of the child' the highest priority" and these depend on many factors, including

- the child's age, sex, and mental and physical health;
- the parent's mental and physical health;
- the parent's lifestyle and other social factors, including whether the child is exposed to secondhand smoke and whether there is any history of child abuse;
- the emotional bond between parent and child, as well as the parent's ability to give the child guidance;
- the parent's ability to provide the child with food, shelter, clothing, and medical care;
- the child's established living pattern (school, home, community, religious institution);
- the quality of the child's education in the current situation;
- the impact on the child of changing the status quo; and

- the child's preference, if the child is above a certain age (usually about 12).[10]

Sometimes custody agreements may need to change, especially when children of divorce are teenagers and have needs that differ from those of younger children. Teens often have very busy schedules. Not only are they in school, but they also may be involved in team sports, band, or other extracurricular activities, and/or may have part-time jobs. Also they may want to spend more time with friends. Thus, they may prefer to live with their noncustodial parents in order to have home bases closer to all their commitments.

Ruth Bettleheim, a marriage and family therapist, pointed out in a 2012 *New York Times* opinion piece that "a custody agreement that meets the needs of a toddler is unlikely to be right for a teenager." She contended,

> [A]ll parenting plans should be subjected to mandatory binding review every two years. The review should include a forum for children to speak privately with a mediation-trained lawyer. The conversation should be recorded to ensure that the child was not pressured or asked leading questions. Children should not be forced to state preferences but invited to speak if they choose. Many children will decline, as they are deeply reluctant to hurt a parent. But occasionally, the need to advocate for themselves outweighs these fears. When they do speak up, their wishes should be honored as stated, not as interpreted by an expert or lawyer.[11]

Special-needs children, however, may have little choice in custody arrangements following a divorce. Custody usually is granted to the parent who has the most time to devote to the care of a special-needs child or to a parent who lives near a medical facility where the child is receiving care. The added stress for the custodial parent was described by Lisa Helfend Meyer, whose daughter was diagnosed with autism. She wrote in 2011 on *HuffingtonPost.com*,

> According to the most recent Centers for Disease Control and Prevention (CDC) statistics, the number of children diagnosed with autism spectrum disorders has grown to 1 in 110 children today, while another CDC study indicates that 1 in 10 children aged 4–17 has been diagnosed with Attention-deficit/hyperactivity disorder (ADHD). Combine these sobering statistics with the ever-rising divorce rates and you have a perfect storm of people navigating the very rocky waters of divorce with the added pressure of needing to effectively co-parent a child with special needs long after their marriage is over.[12]

Parents Caught in the Middle: Same-Sex Couples

When same-sex couples with children divorce, the partners sometimes resort to legal battles over custody of the children. On *NBCNews.com* Judith Messina reported in 2013 on problems encountered by Mercedes Counihan and Molly Bishop, who married in Connecticut in 2009. Bishop became pregnant in 2010 by means of a sperm donor "who shared Counihan's biracial heritage [and] Bishop gave birth to a son. Two years later, the two women are battling for custody. Counihan's name is on the child's birth certificate, but she did not legally adopt him, a move that lawyers say would have protected her rights as a parent. Counihan said she has now spent $100,000 arguing for those rights."[13]

Another more complex case was settled by the Florida Supreme Court in 2013. The state's high court issued a ruling on a custody battle between two lesbian women in Florida; their names were not released for a news report in the *Tampa Bay Times*. One of the women donated an egg that was anonymously fertilized and implanted in the other woman. Both women contributed funds to pay for the implant and agreed to raise a child together. The child was born in 2004, but in 2006, the women split up and one of them left the United States, taking the child with her. She and the child were found in Australia. The Australian woman denied her former partner rights to the child, citing a Florida law that says "anonymous egg and sperm donors who sign away their parental rights at the time of donation cannot later claim they have a parental right to the child." Her former partner in the United States sued for her parental rights. The case eventually was decided by the Florida Supreme Court, which ruled that if the case involved a heterosexual couple in the same situation as the lesbian couple, there would be no argument—both of the partners would have equal rights. The Florida court, in a four-to-three opinion, determined that it was in the best interests of the child for both women to have parental rights.[14]

Child custody cases are not the only legal muddle that can occur when married couples of the same gender want to divorce; they can only do so in states where same-sex marriages are legal. By late spring 2014, seventeen states and Washington, D.C., have legalized gay marriage.[15] Divorce is not possible in states that ban or do not recognize marriages of two women or two men—no marriage, no divorce. Thus if a marriage has taken place in a state that allows couples of the same gender to marry, the couple may have to move to that state in order to obtain a divorce or dissolution order. As a result, their children may be more confused, uncertain, and anxious than ever before. Such a situation will probably continue to be true for the near future, although state laws have been changing since the U.S. Supreme Court struck down the Defense of Marriage Act in June 2013 and ruled that same-sex marriage is legal in California, allowing other states to follow suit.

> ⚠ **Did You Know**
>
> ◎ A *Guardian ad Litem* is a person who acts on behalf of those unable to speak for themselves in legal actions. Although a Guardian ad Litem may be appointed by a court for a variety of situations (such as for someone mentally incompetent), in custody cases a guardian may be an advocate for a child, determining his or her best interests when deciding which parent should be the primary custodian. A guardian has access to all information regarding the child and can speak to all persons involved with the child. Some of the decisions made by the judges and even the caseworkers follow only the rules and legal maneuverings and what might be best for the child is ignored. A guardian speaks up in court if there are issues that go against the well-being of the child, and tries to make sure the child's side is heard and that the court is aware of all pertinent matters.

Extended Family Matters

Children of divorce or of unmarried couples who separate may be caught in the middle when close relatives such as grandparents want more access—that is, visitation rights—to grandkids. That became a major issue in a case—*Troxel v. Granville* (2000)—that ended up in the U.S. Supreme Court. The case began in Washington State when an unmarried couple, Tommie Granville and Brad Troxel, ended their relationship in 1991. Two years later, Troxel committed suicide. The couple had two daughters, and when Granville remarried, her husband adopted the girls.

Because Troxel had often taken the girls to visit his parents, Jenifer and Gary Troxel, the elder Troxels wanted to continue seeing their grandchildren, but their mother, Tommie, limited the visits to one per month. So Jenifer and Gary Troxel filed a lawsuit for the right to increased visitation. Washington State law allows a court to order visitation if it is in the best interest of the child, in spite of a parent's objections. The case was heard by the State Supreme Court, which ruled that the state statute was unconstitutional. When the case reached the U.S. Supreme Court, the majority of justices ruled that unless there are allegations that a child's parents are unfit, the wishes of the parents should be given priority in resolving visitation disputes.

"Recognition of grandparents' rights by state legislatures is a fairly recent trend, and most of the statutes have been in effect for less than 35 years," according to the *Encyclopedia of Everyday Law.* "Every statute requires courts to consider the best interests of the child before awarding custody or visitation to grandparents." Most state laws include the conditions for grandparent visitation if parents divorce. If children of divorce are adopted, the rights of grandparents may be terminated, although there are exceptions.

For example, in Arizona, "[a]doption cuts off the visitation rights of the grandparents unless the adoption is granted to a stepparent." But in California, "[a]doption does not automatically cut off the visitation rights of grandparents." In Georgia, if a child is adopted by a stepparent or a biological relative, grandparents have visitation rights. In Virginia, grandparent visitation is determined at the time a parental divorce is granted. Whatever the various laws, courts have ruled that some statutes violate either the state or federal constitution because they infringe upon the fundamental right of competent parents to raise their child in the manner they see fit, including the right to decide with whom the child will associate.[16]

What if grandparents, aunts, uncles, or other relatives want legal custody of children following parental divorce? Like many other custody issues, circumstances help determine the answer to that question. A court might allow a close relative to have custody if parents have abandoned, neglected, or abused their children. In some cases if children of divorce have lived with grandparents who have acted in loco parentis—in place of the parents—for an extended period (perhaps a year or more), judges may grant the grandparents legal custody. Usually other close relatives cannot have legal custody of children of divorce unless they, like grandparents just described, have served as parents for a long time.

Religious Conflicts

In some divorce cases, one parent may want his or her children to attend religious services that the other parent finds objectionable. For example, a Catholic father and Jewish mother may argue over what religion is appropriate for their children after a divorce. Or a Mormon father and a Catholic mother who divorce differ on whose religion is the "best" for their children. Or a mom who is a member of an evangelical church and a father who is a strict Methodist divorce and cannot agree on which church their children should attend. So the children are caught in the middle. Where do they worship? What should they believe? Whose religious views are "right"?

Because of the numerous interfaith marriages in the United States, courts across the country often have to intervene when there are religious conflicts after a divorce, even though judges do not want to choose one religion over another. If a child is considered mature enough (generally, children over twelve years of age), a judge is likely to allow the child to decide his or her own faith. In other words a child can exercise his or her right to freedom of religion as guaranteed by the First Amendment to the U.S. Constitution ("Congress shall make no law respecting an establishment of religion"). But young children seldom have a choice. When divorced parents cannot reach an agreement, state courts make the decisions. However, there is no uniform standard that courts follow when determining what religion children of divorce should follow.

A Massachusetts Supreme Court case *Kendall v. Kendall* (1997) was widely publicized and called attention to religious conflicts after divorce. It involved Jeffrey Kendall, who belongs to a fundamentalist Christian church, and Barbara Zeitler Kendall, an Orthodox Jew. When the couple divorced, the father told the court that he "believes in Jesus Christ and that those who do not accept the Boston Church of Christ faith are 'damned to go to hell' where there will be 'weeping and gnashing of teeth.'" He said he would never stop trying to save his three children. He also cut his son Ariel's hair (the curls customarily worn by Orthodox Jewish males), which violates orthodox practices. The court ruled that the father

> shall not take the children to his church (whether to church services or Sunday School or church educational programs); nor engage them in prayer or bible study if it promotes rejection rather than acceptance, of their mother or their own Jewish self-identity. The [father] shall not share his religious beliefs with the children if those beliefs cause the children significant emotional distress or worry about their mother or about themselves. Thus, for example, [Jeffrey Kendall] may have pictures of Jesus Christ hanging on the walls of his residence, and that will not serve as any basis for restricting his visitation with his children. But, [he] may not take the children to religious services where they receive the message that adults or children who do not accept Jesus Christ as their lord and savior are destined to burn in hell.

The judge further forbid the father to cut Ariel's hair, but allowed him to have "the children with him at events involving family traditions at Christmas and Easter." The couple's joint custody was retained.[17]

In another case in Illinois, a Roman Catholic man married a Jewish woman and converted to Judaism. He agreed to raise their children as Jewish. However they divorced in 2010, and by then he was the father of a young daughter, whom he thought should be baptized in the Catholic church. His ex-wife knew nothing about the baptism until she received a photograph of the event from her ex-husband. He had to appear in court and was faced with prison time if he took the child to church again.

These cases just happen to represent interfaith Christian and Jewish couples who divorce, but could include a Jehovah's Witness and an atheist or a Muslim and a Christian or a Presbyterian and a Greek Orthodox or a Bahá'i and a Baptist. The point is, "[w]hen courts are asked to answer the question of what religion a child should follow after a separation or divorce, they often balance two competing interests, the best interests of the child, and the rights of the parents," according to FindLaw.com. The legal post added,

> On one side, courts routinely answer questions about what is in the best interests of a child and have become quite proficient with these types of issues. On the other hand, the First Amendment of the United States Constitution protects the parents' freedom of religion as well as their right to raise their child under the religion of their choosing. Often, in a case where a court must make a decision about the child's religious upbringing, one parent will argue that raising the child under the other parent's religion will put the child's welfare in danger. When faced with this question, the court must weigh the benefits and costs of one parent's First Amendment rights versus the best interests of the child.[18]

In 2010, Naomi Schaefer Riley reported in the *New York Times* that she "commissioned the polling firm YouGov to conduct a nationally representative survey of 2,450 Americans, adjusted to produce an oversampling of couples in interfaith marriages. It found such unions were becoming more common, without regard to geography, income or education level. Jews were the most likely, and Mormons the least likely, to marry outside the faith. Muslims fell somewhere in the middle." She also found that "[c]ertain faith pairings seem more likely to result in divorce. While roughly a third of all evangelicals' marriages end in divorce, that figure climbs to nearly half for marriages between evangelicals and non-evangelicals. It is especially high (61 percent) for evangelicals married to someone with no religion."[19] So if there are children, what happens to them when their parents divorce? That question was not answered in Riley's survey. In fact she learned that before marriage many interfaith couples do not discuss the religion of their future children and the possibility of conflicts.

Ann Kass, a district judge in the state of New Mexico, wrote on AllLaw.com that a number of children of divorce in her court have experienced problems with religious conflicts. An example: A child's parents "had not practiced any religion during the marriage" but "after the divorce, each parent had selected a different religion, and each was critical of the other's choice." Other children's parents had a common religion while married but changed religions after divorcing. Judge Kass explained how the courts in New Mexico determine religious issues for children of divorce:

First, the "status-quo" is determined. What religion did the parents choose for the children when they were married and making joint decisions? That religion is the children's "status-quo-religion," and neither parent may change it unless both parents agree or the court allows it.

If, during the marriage, the parents chose no specific religion for the children, then the "status-quo-religion" for the children is "no specific religion," and neither parent may then enroll the children in any specific denomination without the other parent's agreement.[20]

Nevertheless, "status-quo-religion" may have little meaning in some cases, such as one in Arizona. Richard Franco, a young Mormon man, married Sandra Fromm, a young Catholic woman, in a civil ceremony. A church wedding was not allowed because Fromm was pregnant. They had no discussion previously about what faith their child should follow. So there was "no specific religion" in the household. However, the couple argued about religion constantly and eventually divorced. They had joint custody, but Sandra accused Richard of domestic violence, saying he had slapped their daughter. He denied that happened, and his daughter did not say she was abused. The case went back to court, and in 2009 a judge decreed that Franco could not take his children (a fourteen-year-old son and ten-year-old daughter at the time) to services of the Latter-day Saints. The judge also ruled that the mother, who had sole custody, would determine the religious upbringing of the children.[21] In this case, did the judge, not the parents, decide what religion the children should follow? It is debatable.

Adult Children of Divorce in the Middle

When a long-time marriage ends in divorce, the effects on adult children of that union can be as devastating as it is for teenagers. A 2012 study conducted by Susan Brown and I-Fen Lin of Bowling Green State University in Bowling Green, Ohio, documented how the divorce rate among long-time married adults has changed between 1990 and 2009. The researchers found that "The divorce rate among adults ages 50 and older doubled between 1990 and 2009. Roughly 1 in 4 divorces in 2009 occurred to persons ages 50 and older." They noted that the "rise in divorce among middle-aged and older adults is not only likely to shape the health and well-being of those who experience it directly, but also to have ramifications for the well-being of family members (e.g., children and grandchildren)."[22]

Chuck Barney of the *Contra Costa Times* reported in the *Seattle Times* that "older [divorced] parents often expect, or demand, their adult offspring to take sides. And they tend to want to confide in them—sometimes to an uncomfortable

Youth Survey on Parental Divorce

In 2009, the Wilmington Institute Network, which helps families "fulfill their potential," published the Gordon Poll Youth Survey of 1,000 teenagers from age fourteen to eighteen. The poll asked, "In a divorce, what do teens want parents to know about their feelings?" Responses were posted online and, like other youth, many in the survey expressed their pain, frustration, anger, and confusion about parental divorce. They also wanted to be assured that they were not at fault. Some comments were about being caught in the middle. For example, teens didn't "want to feel like their parents are competing for them (trying to either fight for custody or just who gives the best presents)." Or "They feel helpless and feel stuck in the middle. Mom tries to convince you that Dad is a bad person, and Dad tries to convince you that Mom is the one in the wrong." Or they "hate when you fight and drag us into it." Or "kids want parents to know that they are put under a tremendous amount of stress from going back and forth to houses. Sometimes they have to even move to another state and start a new life, school and make new friends." Or they "want their parents to know that [they] are not something to push and pull here and there. The constant tug-of-war is enough to stress out even the most carefree child."[b] The numerous responses are available online. And young people are encouraged "to view the results to better understand their peers."[c]

extent." One example he cited is a woman who did not want to be named and believed that

> in some ways it's worse for someone my age to go through this than a young child. . . . Little kids are resilient. They adapt as they grow up. I've had 34 years of Mom and Dad being together. I thought I had this perfect family, and it's all been shattered." She added, "On the night my dad left, my mom told me some things about him I'd never heard before—things that made me even more mad. . . . It's awkward. My mom had always been a private person. Now, it's like she wants to act like a friend and tell me everything. It's a lot to handle.[23]

Barney further reported that a twenty-six-year-old woman's parents divorced after thirty-two years of marriage, and "both her mother and father filled her in on the graphic details of their sex lives, arguments and other issues." She said, "If I had been 15 or younger, they wouldn't have told me a lot of that stuff. . . . At one point, I got them both on the phone and set some ground rules. I drew a line in the sand. It was a weird kind of role reversal."[24]

It Happened to President Reagan's Family

The split in Ronald Reagan's family happened years ago—in 1949 when Reagan was a well-known Hollywood actor, and his wife was equally well-known actress Jane Wyman. They appeared to have a "perfect," harmonious family: daughter Maureen and an adopted son, Michael. When Reagan and Wyman divorced, the two children stayed with their mother since joint custody was not a common practice at the time.

Ronald Reagan was remarried to another actress, Nancy Davis, and they had two children: Patricia Ann (Patti) and Ronald (Ron) Prescott. Over the years Reagan left an acting career for politics, serving as governor of California from 1967 to 1975 and as U.S. president for two terms (1981–1989). From time to time, the four Reagan children—Maureen, Michael, Patti, and Ron—have been in the middle of public controversy regarding their parents.

Patti Davis (using her mother's maiden name) was controversial in the 1970s when she became a member of a rock band and activist against nuclear power, publicly distancing herself from her parents. She wrote *A House of Secrets* (1986), which accused Nancy Reagan of being obsessed with appearances and propriety. For many years, she was estranged from her parents, but eventually apologized for her actions.

The other three Reagan children also put themselves in the middle of parental differences. Maureen Reagan campaigned for a U.S. Senate seat in California in the early 1980s, but President Reagan did not support her. Some in his inner circle called Maureen unqualified. However, Maureen campaigned for her father's reelection in 1984. She died of skin cancer in 2001.

Michael Reagan wrote *On the Outside Looking In* (1988), which described a strained relationship with his father and his long ordeal with the emotional effects of sexual molestation at a summer camp when he was eight years old. He has since written and talked about his mental turmoil, his conservative politics, and his long-running disagreement with his liberal half-brother Ron Reagan, a talk-show political pundit.

Although many offspring of divorce—children or adults—find themselves stuck in the middle of parental disagreements through no actions of their own, the Reagan family was in the center of conflict partly because they are the offspring of a widely loved former president. However, they also chose to publicly express their views, putting them in the middle of parental divorce issues.

WORRYING ABOUT MONEY

"After my father was officially moved out of our house, he filed the divorce proposal, and thus the three-year court battle began. As the weeks played out, I saw my mom go to court over the things that she needed to take care of us, but that my father was trying to deny her. . . . My mom wasn't fighting for everything my dad owned or anything absurd, she was simply fighting for what she needed to pay for health insurance, doctors and orthodontist appointments, and other basic needs."
—Morgan Thomas writing for *YourTeenMag.com*[1]

Few people can escape the continual barrage of information about money woes and inadequate or loss of income. Recession, falling stock prices, bank closings, unemployment, job losses, home foreclosures, homeless shelters, food giveaways—on and on the drumbeat goes. For children of divorce it is common for money to be a major issue. Most children of divorce live in single-parent households, usually those headed by their mom, and they visit a nonresidential parent, usually their dad. They may worry that Mom is no longer going to have enough money to live on and perhaps will lose her house so the family will not have a home.

The young man who calls himself batteredsoul attested that after his parents divorced, he was expected to carry messages back and forth between parents. "The messages relayed were mostly due to money situations which brought a rise to a completely new set of arguments and frustrations."[2]

A female college student vented about finances in 2010 on a website for adult children of divorce:

I'm almost 21 years old and my parents have been divorced for a little over one year. I attend college four hours away from home and am financially dependent on my parents. Sometimes I feel as if money is the only reason I continue to try to work on my relationships with my parents. I am constantly put in the middle of their arguments. They agreed they would both pay half of the finances of my sister and I. This may be hard to follow but I'll try my best . . . my mother will need money for one of us girls, but my dad will refuse to pay it because [by his reasoning] if she has the money to come visit us, or go do leisurely things then she does not need his money. However, her boyfriend is who pays for her leisurely activities. My sister and I are the ones affected by this bitterness.[3]

Teenage Mallie reported in a 2012 online post to "Judge Tom" that following her parents' divorce, "[my father] is taking the house and my mother is taking one of the cars and some of the furniture. She makes much, much less money than him and she had already confirmed that he's not paying for child support. I don't understand how child support works. I'm very concerned about this because she'll need to buy/rent another house in the area and my two siblings and I will live with her for the majority of the time." In response to this post the judge could only advise Mallie "to express an opinion through a lawyer appointed for you or through a guardian. Courts differ regarding speaking with teenagers in divorce cases. If you get the chance, let your feelings be known to all involved."[4]

The website DivorceInfo.com contains a section on "Adolescents and Divorce." In an undated advice on money, the website states,

Adolescents are more likely to have financial worries than are younger children. This is due in part, of course, to the intense focus on self that comes to full flower during adolescence. Teenagers have things they want to buy, places they want to travel, and experiences they want to savor, and they are understandably focused on making sure their parents can afford them. In addition, however, adolescents are more aware than younger children about the limitations imposed by money. They suspect the divorce may have direct financial ramifications for them, and they're usually right.[5]

An academic study published in 2011 in the *Journal of Adolescent Research* noted the common worries of adolescents whose parents are divorced: "(a) being poor/struggling for the necessities of life, (b) attaining/maintaining a high quality of life, (c) job-related matters, (d) (in)ability to care for future family or parents, (e) educational expenses, (f) negative interpersonal consequences, and (g) managing money."[6]

Managing Money

According to one news report, 87 percent of teens say they know little about managing money.[7] One reason money issues are important is that divorce often

Part of money management is paying bills on time.

occurs because of disagreements about bank balances and debt. "A 2013 survey by the American Institute of Certified Public Accountants and Harris Interactive found that money causes more arguments among men and women than other typical domestic disputes. A full 27 percent of respondents said their spats started over money, more than problems with kids (16 percent) or chores (13 percent)," according to a *Daily Mail* report about U.S. money problems.[8] And if parents divorce, teens themselves could be embroiled in money disputes as well as being clueless about everyday finances.

Some U.S. teenagers are beginning to learn about money issues. For example, in 2011, eighteen-year-old Megan Wurm became a national ambassador for the

"Top 10 Money Myths Held by Teens"

In 2009, the Consumer Federation of America and FoolProofMe.com, which teaches young people about money and financial responsibility, surveyed teens to determine what kind of misinformation they have about money. Here are the top ten myths posted on the Internet:

1. I don't have to worry about credit at my age.
2. Bad credit can't keep me from getting a job.
3. All loan companies have the same rates.
4. All credit cards are alike.
5. The job of financial advertising is to tell the truth.
6. It's OK to bounce a few checks.
7. It's OK to make minimum payments on a credit card.
8. Paying late occasionally can't hurt my credit.
9. Fine print isn't important.
10. Young people don't have credit scores.[a]

The truth is that all of these myths are baseless. Good credit is important for job seekers, renters, insurance companies, and people seeking loans (a car or student loan, for example). Employers, landlords, insurers, banks, and businesses frequently check credit information to see if the people they are dealing with are responsible. So bouncing a check and making late payments on a credit card negatively affect a person's reliability. As for contracts or other legal forms, the fine print should be read and understood before signing the documents.

Money Matters program sponsored by the Boys & Girls Clubs of America and the Charles Schwab Foundation. She began the program when she was in seventh and eighth grade and said she learned that "the basic personal finance lessons were the most important—learning how to budget, save, and run my own life financially. Now that I've gotten to the point where I am trying to figure out how to pay for college, the scholarship information from the program is coming into play." Being ambassador allowed her "to share the knowledge I've gained with teens across the nation." When asked why she thought that important she said,

> The earlier you learn about the importance of money and how to use it responsibly, the easier your adult life will be, and the less likely you'll be to go into debt. . . . I know how easy it is when I get my paycheck to go on a mini shopping spree—I think to myself, "Well, I have all this money, so one or two little things won't hurt." Soon I'm $30 shorter on cash than I was a few hours ago, with nothing but empty food wrappers and music download bills to show for it. When I get to that point, I'm a little annoyed with myself at first for letting my impulses get the best of me, and next time I get my paycheck I'm a lot less likely to go out and spend it on trivial purchases.[9]

In Ohio, the Department of Education instructed high schools in 2010 to begin teaching financial literacy. According to the *Cleveland Plain Dealer*, "students often tell area business teachers that their parents don't understand or use banks, can't grasp their credit card statements and don't have any money saved." Because parents are not teaching their children about finances, Cleveland's North Ridge High School students "are required to take one of three financial literacy classes." These are "personal finance, introduction to business and surviving on your own." When completed, students are expected to know such financial matters as "how to decipher a car lease contract, invest in a retirement account and prepare their own tax return."[10]

Other state education departments require schools to teach personal finances, but not all of the programs make the grade in terms of financial literacy. So said the Center for Financial Literacy at Champlain College in Vermont, which used national data to grade "all 50 states on their efforts to produce financially literate high school graduates." The center published its report in 2013, noting "40 percent of states were given grades A or B. Sixty percent of states have grades of C or less." Only seven states received an A grade: Georgia, Idaho, Louisiana, Missouri, Tennessee, Utah, and Virginia. Eleven states received Fs: Alabama, Alaska, Arkansas, California, Connecticut, Delaware, Hawaii, Massachusetts, Nebraska, Rhode Island, and Washington. In its introduction to its report, the center declared that

> negative financial outcomes and low levels of consumer knowledge and confidence have made it crystal clear that financial literacy in America should be a national priority. Moreover, studies have shown that financial literacy is linked to positive outcomes like wealth accumulation, stock market participation, retirement planning, and avoiding high-cost alternative

> ! **Alimony**
>
> Although court-ordered, alimony—sometimes called spousal support—is not the same as child support. In divorce proceedings, a court may order one of the parties to pay the other a certain amount of money based on need or circumstances. For example, one of the spouses may not work outside the home, so the court may order the other spouse who earns an income to pay for maintenance of the stay-at-home spouse. Traditionally, a husband paid alimony to his former wife, but currently a former husband may be entitled to alimony from his former wife, depending on who is the chief wage earner. The alimony could be temporary, granted for a specified time, or permanent (that is, until the payer or recipient dies or the recipient remarries). State laws differ on the extent of time of the alimony and in the amount granted.

financial services like payday lending and auto title loans. To avoid another financial crisis in the future and to improve personal finance outcomes for American citizens, our nation must be educated in personal finance. A great place to start is with our K–12 students.[11]

Child Support Issues

Lack of child support adds to money problems after parental divorce. Usually child support is arranged when a couple divorces, separates, or annuls a marriage. Courts typically require a noncustodial divorced parent—whether the mom or dad—to support his or her minor child or children. If there is joint custody, the parent with the highest income might be (but is not always) required to pay the other parent to help with expenses.

If support payments to the custodial parent are inadequate or nonexistent, a court may have to step in. The U.S. Department of Health and Human Services (HHS) has an office of child support enforcement. If parents are unable or unwilling to pay child support, they may be directed to state programs to improve job skills or find employment. In addition, many states try to ensure that parents responsible for support do not accrue so much debt that they are forced to abstain from seeing their children—until they pay.

The child support enforcement handbook explains that

[t]he child support program is a federal/state/local/tribal partnership to collect child support: We want to send the strongest possible message that parents cannot walk away from their children. Our goals are to ensure that children have the financial support of both their parents, to foster responsible behavior toward children, and to emphasize that children benefit when both parents are involved in their lives.[12]

What if a parent simply refuses to pay and moves out of the state where the divorce was granted? The handbook states, "In addition to actions that can be taken through law enforcement and judicial proceedings (such as citations for contempt of court and filing of state and federal criminal charges), over the years, Congress has provided the child support program with strong enforcement tools including: wage withholding, offsetting federal and state income tax refunds, and the ability to secure liens on property."[13]

Statistics show that after a divorce most nonresidential fathers *do* pay child support, but in split families, money problems persist when there is inadequate financial support. In her book *The Love They Lost* (2000), Stephanie Stahl included interviews from 120 adult children of divorce, many of whom report moms having to make "constant pleas for money." She explained, "Some fathers had remarried and were more concerned with supporting their new families. Many remember waiting for a check that never came, or came too late, or was for the wrong amount. Several told of lying about a father's salary on financial aid forms for college when he refused to pay for tuition, because they wouldn't qualify otherwise." Some of the interviewees constantly worried about money while they were growing up and as adults still feared not having enough money to survive.[14]

In a more positive view, associate professor of social work Edward Kruk wrote,

More often than not, fathers are involuntarily relegated by family courts to the role of "accessory parents," valued for their role as financial providers rather than as active caregivers. This view persists despite the fact that fathers in two-parent families, before divorce, typically share, with mothers, responsibility for the care of their children. This is both because fathers have taken up the slack while mothers work longer hours outside the home, and because fathers are no longer content to play a secondary role as parents. Most fathers today are keen to experience both the joys and challenges of parenthood, derive satisfaction from their parental role, and consider active and involved fatherhood to be the core component of their self-identity.

It Happened to Abigail Dalton

Abigail Dalton of LearnVest, a financial planning program, revealed on a website post how her parents' divorce turned out to be a lesson in money matters. She explained,

> I come from a relatively wealthy background—I grew up in a safe, affluent suburb of New York City, where I was raised by two parents with advanced degrees, and went to excellent schools with kids in similar situations. For much of my life, I didn't have to really worry about shopping for school supplies or getting the clothes I wanted or having money to go to the movies or other incidentals. It was all given to me, just like it was given to my friends.

But then her parents divorced when she was fifteen years old. Her mother discovered that her father was a "big spender" and "had also been buying regular tickets to visit his girlfriend in Greece. The money went fast." Since the family income was depleted, Abigail suddenly "had to learn relatively quickly what it meant to have a handle on your money—and your life." She noted that her "mother was adamant that we stay in our house and school district. Her desire to make sure we weren't totally uprooted from our lives, regardless of finances, meant that I soon had to rely on myself for all of those financial incidentals I had always received from my parents."

Abigail described three lessons that have stayed with her. First, "It is *essential* as a woman (and for anyone in a relationship, although women are particularly vulnerable) to know where your money is and . . . never rely on someone else to manage" it. Secondly, she learned how to budget:

> From gas for my old Honda (a hand-me-down from my grandmother), to movie tickets for nights out with friends, I learned how much money I would need and what I could go without. I picked up more babysitting shifts than I ever had before, took summer jobs at the local Barnes & Noble and as a tutor, and managed (and saved) my own money.

Finally, because her college fund was nonexistent, she learned how to get finan-cial aid and supplement it with part-time jobs.

In conclusion, she wrote. "[D]ivorce can seem like the worst thing to happen to a family, [but] what we went through turned me into a more responsible adult than I might otherwise have been, and for that I'm incredibly grateful."[b]

Yet, as Dr. Kruk noted, "divorced fathers in particular are devalued, disparaged, and forcefully disengaged from their children's lives."[15]

Living in Poverty

More than 46 million people or 15 percent of the U.S. population were living in poverty in the United States in 2011. Poverty is measured in various ways, de-pending on the agency or organization, according to data from the U.S. Census Bureau. The Census Bureau sets a threshold, or a bottom line, for the amount of income indicating a family is impoverished. In 2011, the poverty threshold for a

Did You Know?

Families headed by single mothers often struggle with money problems. According to a 2007 data brief by Mark Mather of the Population Reference Bureau,

Most single-mother families have limited financial resources available to cover children's education, child care, and health care costs. Seven in 10 children living with a single mother are poor or low income, compared to less than a third (32 percent) of children living in other types of families. While part of the problem is fewer potential earners in female-headed families, many of these families are also at a disadvantage because of problems collecting child support payments from absent fathers. In 2007, only 31 percent of female-headed families with children reported receiving child support payments during the previous year. It is especially difficult for young, never-married mothers to collect child support because many of the fathers in this situation have very low wages.[c]

household of four was $23,050. People with half that amount of income were considered in deep poverty.[16] The nation's official poverty rate in 2012 was 15 percent, which represents 46.5 million people living at or below the poverty line. This marked the second consecutive year that neither the official poverty rate nor the number of people in poverty was statistically different from the previous year's estimates. The 2012 poverty rate was 2.5 percentage points higher than in 2007, the year before the economic downturn, according to a 2013 Census Bureau report.[17]

As has been stated frequently, some divorced parents and their children are living at the poverty level and they along with other poor families have to find ways to survive. In order to put food on the table, some families receive help from food banks that supply staples or food kitchens that give away free meals. Some are able to get help from the U.S. government food program called Supplemental Nutrition Assistance Program (SNAP) or state food assistance programs. SNAP recipients use government-issued cards (similar to credit or debit cards) to buy food. The dollar amounts on the cards vary by state and depend on the size of a family and its annual income. Other food assistance programs include federally funded school meals and the Women, Infants, and Children program; the latter provides money to states to help feed pregnant women, mothers, and children.

For income assistance, poor families, if qualified, may get help from federal and state government programs. The first federal assistance program began in the 1930s during the Great Depression, but it was reformed in the 1990s when Congress passed a law signed by President Bill Clinton that gave the control of the welfare system to the states. "The type and amount of aid available to individuals and dependent children varies from state to state. Most states offer basic aid such as health care, food stamps, child care assistance, unemployment, cash aid, and housing assistance," according to WelfareInfo.org.

The federal government offers grants to states through a program called Temporary Assistance for Needy Families (TANF), which helps each state operate its own welfare program. "The TANF grant requires that all recipients of welfare aid must find work within two years of receiving aid, including single parents who are required to work at least 30 hours per week" and two-parent families must work 35 to 55 hours per week. If aid recipients do not comply with work requirements, they could lose benefits.[18]

Easing Money Troubles

Some youth who have experienced divorce and struggle with finances try to ease their money problems by working at part-time jobs to help with income, but in a poor economy it is not easy to find employment. An example is high school senior Melissa of Lokeford, California (near Lodi), who searched more than a year to find a job so she could help her family. Her mom is supporting herself and four children on an annual income of $22,000 as a teacher's assistant. In 2012, Tony Lopez reported Melissa's family story on CBS and explained that "[f]or teenagers in our state, the unemployment rate is at a staggering 35 percent. It's the highest in the nation behind only Washington, D.C." After Melissa found a part-time job at a thrift shop, she was able to use her paycheck to help pay family bills. She said it felt "good because I can help my mom now."[19]

When jobs are available for teenagers, they often are in fast-food restaurants, grocery stores (as baggers), agriculture and construction, and yard maintenance. Such jobs usually pay minimum wage, which in 2013 was $7.25 an hour, set by the federal government. In December 2013, fast-food workers in numerous cities engaged in one-day strikes to demand higher wages. Many strikers and media commentators pointed out that fast-food companies earn millions in profits each year but do not share their good fortune with employees. However, some states and local governments across the country have raised their minimum wage higher than the federal level. Washington State's minimum wage was set at $9.19 per hour as of 2013 and Oregon, California, Nevada, and Illinois were paying hourly minimums of $8.00 or slightly above.[20]

A Fast-Food Budget

In July 2013, the fast-food giant McDonald's decided to help its employees live on the minimum wages they receive for their work. The corporation posted ideas for budgeting along with a sample form to complete. Perhaps a teenager without a family would find the budget useful, but many people across the United States, including finance experts, were highly critical of McDonald's suggestions. Its budget form shows earnings from two jobs for a monthly net income of $2,060. That assumes earnings of about $12.80 an hour for a forty-hour week, which is way beyond what a fast-food worker receives.

The McDonald's sample budget claimed that an employee needs at least $24,000 a year to survive, but in itemizing expenses there was no provision for basics like clothing and food, unless those needs were assumed to be part of the allotment of $100 in the "other" category. Although health-care insurance was budgeted at $20 per month, that is far less than most insurance premiums.

Laura Shin, a *Forbes* magazine contributor, interviewed Carman Iverson, a twenty-eight-year-old single mother in Missouri who has four children and receives some child support payments. She tries to live on the minimum wage she earns at McDonald's. "I'm a cashier, I clean the lobby, I do order take-in, I hand out food to customers, I do the cashier at the back window where I take the money. I've been on the grill, I've worked at the table where they make the food and wrap it up—I've done everything that they got in there," she said. She would like to work a forty-hour week but has only been scheduled for twenty to twenty-seven hours, depending on what the manager has decided. Her take-home pay has been between $400 and $600 per month.

Iverson takes public transportation to work, has no phone, and pays about $100 per month for electricity. Her rent is $650 per month, which she cannot pay, but she said, "I have a landlord that works with us." In other words, she has accumulated rental debt. She uses food stamps to feed her family, but usually runs out before the end of the month and had to ask her sister for help. If she continues to work at McDonald's, she said, "I want to make more than $10 an hour. Because I'm the best worker they got there in the morning time. People who've been there longer than me come and ask me, and I've only been there a year. So I know I'm the strongest they have during the morning time." Iverson said her long-term goal "is to earn my GED, and become a pharmacy technician so I know I have enough money to take care of me and mine."[d]

If and when teenagers are employed, their employers are required to follow U.S. Department of Labor (DoL) rules. For example, a teen under the age of fourteen is only allowed to do certain jobs such as delivering newspapers and babysitting. Fourteen- and fifteen-year-olds are allowed by DoL rules to work up to three hours on a school day, up to eighteen hours in a school week, up to eight hours on a nonschool day, and up to forty hours in a nonschool week. Youth age sixteen to seventeen may work in a variety of jobs including those located in offices, grocery stores, retail stores, restaurants, movie theaters, amusement parks, baseball parks, or gasoline service stations. However, they are prohibited from working in jobs declared hazardous by the secretary of labor. Hazardous jobs include mining, meat packing or processing, using power-driven bakery machines or paper-product machines, roofing, and excavation operations, plus others. When young people reach eighteen years of age, they are no longer subject to the federal youth employment laws.[21]

There are special DoL rules for minors employed as farm workers. If under the age of sixteen, minors cannot operate machinery like corn and cotton pickers, trenchers, fork lifts, or power post hole diggers. Rules also forbid working in pens with large breeding animals like bulls and boars or in grain and fruit storage bins. The prohibitions do not apply to youths employed on farms owned or operated by their parents or to fourteen- and fifteen-year-old students enrolled in vocational agricultural programs.

Beside federal labor laws for minors, many states have legal standards for youth employment in agriculture. "When both state and federal youth employment laws apply, the law setting the most stringent standard must be observed," the DoL has declared.[22]

Even when jobs are scarce, youth can help ease money problems by

- bicycling instead of using the family car,
- collecting and selling recyclables (aluminum cans, for example),
- organizing a yard sale,
- reducing use of utilities (electric, water, phone) and personal cell phones,
- walking dogs for a fee,
- finding free leisure activities (such as skating or going to a park),
- buying necessities on sale,
- organizing a swap to exchange items with friends or neighbors,
- collecting coupons to save on groceries and other items,
- selling used items on Craigslist or similar website,
- detailing cars, and
- doing yard work.

Workforce Readiness

Teenagers who have experienced parental divorce often have another worry connected with family money problems. Statistically, studies say, teens of divorced parents may become school dropouts. High school dropouts, whether from intact or broken families, are 72 percent more likely to be unemployed as compared to high school graduates.

The Alliance for Excellent Education, which is based in Washington, D.C., says on its website that the organization "works to improve national and federal policy so that all students can achieve at high academic levels and graduate from high school ready for success in college, work, and citizenship in the twenty-first century. The Alliance focuses on America's six million most at-risk secondary school students—those in the lowest achievement quartile—who are most likely to leave school without a diploma or to graduate unprepared for a productive future." In a 2011 report the Alliance noted,

> Every school day, nearly 7,000 students become dropouts. Annually, that adds up to about 1.2 million students who will not graduate from high school with their peers as scheduled. Lacking a high school diploma, these individuals will be far more likely than graduates to spend their lives periodically unemployed, on government assistance, or cycling in and out of the prison system.[23]

Most high school dropouts see the result of their decision to leave school very clearly in the slimness of their wallets. The average annual income for a high school dropout in 2009 was $19,540, compared to $27,380 for a high school graduate, a difference of $7,840. The impact on the country's economy is less visible, but cumulatively its effect is staggering.[24]

The alliance is just one of numerous institutions and programs that try to help teenagers prepare for the workforce. Junior Achievement, for example, helps students understand the connection between classroom subjects and the skills they need for real-world jobs. SkillsUSA is a national organization serving "teachers and high school and college students who are preparing for careers in

Off the Bookshelf

Lack of adequate income in a single-mom household, a biological father who seldom appears, and a pesky twelve-year-old sister, Sweet Caroline, are just a few of the problems that Sanskrit Zuckerman, a child of divorce, faces in this novel, *Since You Left Me*. The story by Allen Zadoff is set in the modern-day Los Angeles, California, area and is told from the viewpoint of witty, irreverent, and sometimes snarky sixteen-year-old Sanskrit. As he repeatedly tells people, his mother named him after an ancient Indian language. He also has a Hebrew middle name, Aaron, but he doesn't want to be called that because he claims to be a nonbeliever even though he is a student at a prestigious Jewish Academy (paid for with funds from his late grandfather). He also regularly attended the local synagogue before his parents divorced.

Throughout the novel, Sanskrit's professed lack of faith is challenged by classmates and teachers (called professors) and other school staff. He also struggles with the idiosyncrasies of his divorced parents. To earn a meager income, his mom is a yoga teacher and is seldom at home, expecting Sanskrit to take charge. His mother falls in love with a Hindu guru and plans to move to India with him.

Sanskrit's father is an absent-minded inventor of sorts who wanted to establish his own business but could not get the financial help he needed from his father, Abe Zuckerman, called Zadie by the family. When Zadie died, he left a large trust for Sanskrit, on the condition that his grandson get a good Jewish education and become a faithful Jew. Otherwise the money would be given to a charity for researching Tay-Sachs disease, a rare genetic disorder that destroys nerve cells.

"Without Zadie Zuckerman's money I'd be a public school kid, and Mom would be panicked about paying for college," Sanskrit muses. "If Zadie hadn't bought this house when my parents got married, we'd be living in an apartment in some crappy suburb. . . . And if Zadie hadn't survived the Holocaust, none of us would be here in the first place. Not quite true. Mom would be here, but not the rest of us."[e]

As teenagers are wont to do, Sanskrit rebels. His rebellion begins with a fabrication that sets off repercussions throughout the entire time span of the book. His mom does not show up at a school parent conference as she is expected to do, and Sanskrit is so frustrated that he eventually tells the school personnel that his mother has had a terrible accident. The lie leads to other lies and reactions within the Jewish school and community that involve Sanskrit in one predicament after another—some humorous, some distressing, some bitter. All the while he is trying to get his family back together and without admitting it is taking a spiritual journey; he's attempting to find his way to *HaShem* (God).

---

trade, technical and skilled service occupations, including health occupations. It was formerly known as VICA (Vocational Industrial Clubs of America)."[25] Students who attend technical career classes may learn automotive, construction, and health technologies; childcare; accounting; retail sales and marketing; cosmetology; culinary arts; and entrepreneurship.

Volunteering is another way teenagers can get a proverbial "foot in the door" for a possible paying job. Many schools have service learning programs: Students in elementary and secondary schools and colleges participate in organized service that is conducted in and meets the needs of a community, thus providing firsthand knowledge and skills for a future job. Boys & Girls Clubs of America offer a Job

Ready program; members, ages sixteen to eighteen, learn the skills and knowledge necessary to enter and compete in the workforce. The YMCA sponsors a Teen Corp Job Readiness program in which teen volunteers aged fifteen to nineteen learn work skills in real-job settings and receive job-readiness training. Cities also offer volunteer opportunities for teens in parks, nature trails, museums, animal shelters, and other public facilities to gain job readiness skills.

COPING WITH ADDICTION, DEPRESSION, AND JAILED PARENTS

....

"You know, kids like to think that they're rebelling against society. But if they drink and drug, they're going along with the crowd. I say if you want to be a rebel, rebel against drugs and alcohol. I'm clean and sober, and I'm proud of it."
—*eighteen-year-old Emmy Hall, a child of divorce and recovering drug addict[1]*

Emmy Hall was only twelve years old when her parents divorced, and she was hurt and lonely. To make herself feel better she had her first drink, following the suggestion of a classmate. From then on through her teen years, she turned to alcohol to calm her distress and she soon became addicted not only to alcohol but also to drugs such as heroin, cocaine, and methamphetamine (meth). She was kicked out of school and became an official runaway.

At the time she told her story, Hall was eighteen years old, and she said,

At one point, I weighed 86 pounds. One day when I had no place to stay, no money and no food, I sent up a little prayer for those three things. I'm not sure what made me do it, but I went and turned myself in to the Los Angeles police as a runaway. I got what I had asked for—an 8 by 8 cell for shelter, food, and transportation back home to a detention center in Oregon. I stayed there for two weeks, thinking I'd get out and go back to my old ways. That was when my probation officer told me I was going to rehab. The facility was way out in the middle of nowhere, and at first I just sulked. There was no escape, so I just told them what I knew they wanted to hear. I had a negative attitude, though. My heart wasn't in it, and the only thing I could find to abuse was a pen. I managed to mutilate my arm with it.[2]

Fortunately, after several months, Hall's attitude changed and she said, "I began to join group activities and talk and work on my problem. Two months later, I graduated from the program and went to live with my dad. I stayed with him for a year and a half. Then I went to live with my mom." She also continued her studies and graduated from high school. But she did not think she was cured. "I have to be really careful to stay away from stuff. I am an addict. It's in my genes," she said. She received help from a program called On Track.[3]

Like Emmy, other young adults sometimes use illegal drugs and alcohol to ease their emotional turmoil due to their parents' divorce. On the website FamilyinDivorce.com, Everett wrote about his reaction to his parents' divorce:

Early in high school I started drinking, skipping school, bad grades, getting in trouble at school, joining a "gang," smoking pot, lying to my mom, etc. Without going into much detail, I am sure you get the picture of where things were heading. I was even dropped off at school one day in a police car after they had picked me up and questioned me about a burglary in the neighborhood. Though I was just skipping school and had nothing to do with the break-in, all my friends thought I was sooo cool for being dropped off at school in a police car. Mom didn't think it was cool.

The real heart breaker that opened my eyes was when I had somehow stumbled my way home in a drunken stupor one night. It was the summer between my Freshman and Sophomore year in high school. My mom came to my room with a glass of water and looked me in the eyes and said, "Everett, don't hurt me again." And then she walked away.[4]

"Adolescents are capable of expressing their distress about the divorce in alarming new ways," wrote Daniel Pikar in an article for *Sonoma County Medicine Magazine: Parenting*. He confirmed that "[t]eenagers can use or abuse illicit drugs or alcohol, precociously engage in sexual activities, physically hurt themselves, run away, or get in trouble with the law."[5]

In 2011, the National Center on Addiction and Substance Abuse at Columbia University (known as CASA) conducted online surveys about alcohol and drug use, questioning 1,000 high school students, plus 1,000 parents of high school students and 500 school personnel. CASA's report noted, "All teens are influenced by messages from today's culture to smoke, drink or use other drugs and three-quarters have done so," adding that some teens "have personal characteristics or life circumstances that place them at even greater risk of using addictive substances or more prone to becoming addicted to them. Some have a "genetic predisposition toward developing an addictive disorder" or a "family history of substance misuse or addiction." A teen who has been abused or bullied, has mental health problems, or has experienced parental divorce or lives in a single-parent family is also at risk for addiction.[6]

According to the CASA report, "The stress of a divorce on the family can reduce the bond between children and parents, making children more vulnerable to negative peer influences. Nevertheless, "research finds that youth substance use is affected more by family attachment and relationships than by family structure. That is, children may better be able to avoid substance use when growing up in a nurturing single-parent home than in a less nurturing two-parent home."[7]

Whatever the family structure, many young people are influenced by popular music and song lyrics that refer to the use and abuse of illicit drugs. The message

Some teens abuse alcohol and other drugs when parents divorce

could be, "If it's okay for entertainers, then it's okay for me." Online chats, blogs, social media like Facebook, and other electronic communication are other ways that teens learn about and then experiment with alcohol and addictive substances. In fact, some youth have proudly posted online photographs of themselves drunk or using drugs.

The U.S. National Institute on Drug Use (NIDU) issued its annual survey "Monitoring the Future" in December 2012, which showed that over five years there have been significant increases in marijuana use among tenth and twelfth graders. The survey also showed that from 2007 to 2012 teens reported their drug use within the month before the survey. The increases ranged from 14.2 percent to 17 percent among tenth graders and from 18.8 percent to 22.9 percent among twelfth graders. Among high school seniors it was at its highest point since the late 1990s. These increases parallel softening attitudes for the last several years about the perceived risk of harm associated with marijuana use. In addition, many of the drugs used by twelfth graders are prescription or over-the-counter medications. The survey showed, as it has in the past, that most teens obtain prescription drugs like amphetamines, tranquilizers, or narcotics other than heroin, for free from friends and family; roughly 68 percent of twelfth graders, for example, report getting prescription pain relievers this way.[8]

Nevertheless, there was good news in the NIDU survey: cigarette smoking, alcohol use, and the use of inhalants have decreased among high schoolers. In addition, a CASA survey of high school students found that a majority—95.3 percent—saw driving while drunk as "very dangerous." Other behaviors students regarded as "very dangerous" were listed along with the percentages of those responding:

Behaviors	*Percentage Students Saying Behavior "Very Dangerous"*
Using illicit drugs other than marijuana	91.5
Mixing alcohol and prescription drugs	90.0
Driving while high on prescription drugs	88.1
Using inhalants	82.0
Misusing pain medications (opioids)	80.0
Misusing tranquilizers	79.8
Driving while high on marijuana	79.7
Binge drinking	77.6
Mixing alcohol and energy drinks	64.7
Getting drunk	59.3
Smoking cigarettes	56.4
Using marijuana	52.1[9]

It Happened to Kurt Cobain

Singer and song writer Kurt Cobain was just nineteen years old in 1988 when he formed Nirvana, the "grunge" band that earned worldwide recognition, followers, and praise. But as he was growing up in the logging town of Aberdeen, Washington, his childhood was full of disruptions and the uproar of his parents' ever-present fighting. When he was nine years old, Cobain's parents divorced and he became withdrawn. He sometimes found refuge inside his bedroom closet. In several biographical accounts, he said that after the divorce he never felt loved or secure again.

Both of Cobain's parents remarried, but the families were dysfunctional due to alcoholism. Cobain lived with his father and friend Jenny and her two children for a time. At first he had a good relationship with Jenny; "she provided him the female attention he was lacking." But that changed after his father married Jenny, because of Cobain's "internal conflict: If he cared for her, he would be betraying his love for his mother and his 'real' family," writes biographer Charles R. Cross. "Kurt had held on to a hope that [his parents'] divorce was a temporary setback, a dream that would pass."[a]

In 1982, Cobain left his father's place and went to live with his mother. About this time, his uncle gave him an old guitar, which Cobain learned to play. Music relieved some of his misery with his parents. But music also inspired an interest in punk rock and the lifestyle of rock and roll bands.

He began experimenting with drugs and alcohol in high school, increasingly "drinking and drugging. Cobain also got into fights with his mother who was also drinking a lot, and he could not stand his stepfather. Cobain spent much of 1984 and 1985 living in various places. He spent time living with friends when he could and sleeping in apartment building hallways and a hospital waiting room when he did not have any other place to crash."[b]

Cobain's life was never what anyone would call "ordinary." Like his parents and other members of his extended family, he struggled with drug and alcohol addiction, depression, and the tendency to be suicidal. He was diagnosed early in his life with attention deficit disorder and later with bipolar disorder. Although he had much success in the entertainment world, his mental health deteriorated and in March 1994 he attempted suicide by taking an overdose of prescription drugs. When that failed, he tried again. In April 1994, he killed himself with a shotgun. He was twenty-seven years old.

> ! **Did You Know?**
>
> On NIDA for Teens, a website run by the National Institute on Drug Abuse, teenagers have posed numerous questions about substance abuse. One question was about overdosing, which brought this response:
>
> An overdose is when someone takes too much of a drug or medication, causing serious, harmful symptoms or even death. If someone takes too much of something on purpose to commit suicide, for example, it is called an intentional or deliberate overdose. If the overdose happens by mistake, it is called an accidental overdose. For example, a teenager might try to get high by taking a parent's prescription opioid painkiller and end up in the emergency room—or worse. More overdose deaths are caused by people abusing prescription opioids than by any other drug, including heroin or cocaine.[c]

Symptoms of Depression

Frequently, studies, reports, personal stories, and other accounts tell of children and teens suffering depression when their parents divorce. Unfortunately, drugs and alcohol may be used (and abused) in order to overcome depression. The staff at the renowned Mayo Clinic defines teen depression as

> a serious medical problem that causes a persistent feeling of sadness and loss of interest in activities. It affects how [a] teen thinks, feels and behaves, and it can cause emotional, functional and physical problems. . . . Teen depression isn't a weakness or something that can be overcome with willpower—it can have serious consequences and requires long-term treatment. For most teens, depression symptoms ease with treatment such as medication and psychological counseling.[10]

Even when parents are happily married, teenagers are inclined to have mood swings and feel gloomy or sullen every now and then. But a broken family can turn teens' world upside-down. Their physical and emotional lives are changing. They have other stresses as well. They are experiencing hormonal changes and have fears about how they are going to manage when their parents split up. All of this turmoil can trigger depression, particularly during the two-year period just after parental divorce—that is the time when teenagers are at the highest risk for depression. If there is constant conflict and financial problems, those factors add to the possibility teens will sink into a mental condition that needs to be addressed either by a licensed counselor, medical doctor, psychologist, or psychiatrist.

- Some of the symptoms of depression include
- being irritable and crying often,
- losing interest in once-enjoyable activities,
- complaining frequently about stomachaches or headaches,
- withdrawing from friends and social events,
- sleeping more or suffering insomnia,
- being excessively critical of self,
- behaving inappropriately at school or at home,
- doing poorly in studies at school, and
- making threats about committing suicide.

It is important to remember that teenagers can exhibit some of these symptoms (such as often being irritable) *without* being depressed or experiencing parental divorce. But if symptoms occur—especially threats of suicide—over a two-week period, teenagers should tell a school counselor or parent about how they feel. A trusted adult may be able to help them get therapy. If untreated, depression can lead to substance or alcohol abuse, eating disorders, or even suicide.

Youth Suicide

While some young people whose parents divorce threaten to commit suicide, they seldom carry out that threat. Several factors, however, can put a young person at risk for suicide, such as drug addiction, family violence, death of a family member, problems with peer relationships, being bullied, and having access to weapons. The U.S. Centers for Disease Control and Prevention (CDC) maintains statistics on suicide and states that for youth "between the ages of 10 and 24, suicide is the third leading cause of death. It results in approximately 4600 lives lost each year. The top three methods used in suicides of young people include firearm (45%), suffocation (40%), and poisoning (8%)." However, the CDC reports,

More young people survive suicide attempts than actually die. . . . Each year, approximately 157,000 youth between the ages of 10 and 24 receive medical care for self-inflicted injuries at Emergency Departments across the United States.

Suicide affects all youth, but some groups are at higher risk than others. Boys are more likely than girls to die from suicide. Of the reported suicides in the 10 to 24 age group, 81% of the deaths were males and 19% were females. Girls, however, are more likely to report attempting suicide than boys. Cultural variations in suicide rates also exist, with Native American/Alaskan Native youth having the highest rates of suicide-related fatalities. A nationwide survey of youth in grades 9–12 in public and private schools in the U.S. found Hispanic youth were more likely to report attempting suicide than their black and white, non-Hispanic peers.[d]

The American Foundation for Suicide Prevention (AFSP) supports projects and programs that provide suicide information and ways to prevent it. AFSP formed in 1987 because many of its original founders were concerned about the dramatic rise in suicide among teenagers as well as the elderly.

When Parents Are Addicted

The stories of Kurt Cobain and Chase Block tell not only of having to deal with divorced parents but also point to the statistics about parents who are addicted to drugs and are in jail. A report in 2010 from the Pew Charitable Trusts included these statistics on U.S. parents in prison:

- 2.7 million children have a parent behind bars—1 in every 28 children (3.6 percent) has a parent incarcerated, up from 1 in 125 just 25 years ago. Two-thirds of these children's parents were incarcerated for non-violent offenses.
- One in 9 African American children (11.4 percent), 1 in 28 Hispanic children (3.5 percent) and 1 in 57 white children (1.8 percent) have an incarcerated parent.[11]

Even if parents go to rehabilitation centers or attend recovery sessions like Alcoholic Anonymous, they may relapse, disappoint their families, and create emotional turmoil and confusion in the family.

Off the Bookshelf

Chasing Happiness: One Boy's Guide to Helping Other Kids Cope with Divorce, Parental Addictions and Death (2010) is by teenager Chase Block of Jacksonville, Florida. In an online post Chase said he wrote the book when he was fourteen years old because he wanted "to help other kids whose parents were divorcing." But before he began working on the book, his mother, who suffered from depression and was addicted to sleeping pills and alcohol, committed suicide. Chase wrote "about the shock of my mom's suicide, my grief and guilt, and my own suicidal thoughts."[e]

Chase explained, "As hard as it was to get through those waves of sorrow after my mom died, I knew I had to just make myself keep going. I always knew that with all that I'd been through, I could really help other kids. We usually listen more to each other than parents or teachers."[f]

In the book, Chase wrote, "Sometimes just knowing you're not the only one with a certain kind of problem really helps."[g] The last chapter, "Encouraging Words," includes ideas for keeping a good sense of humor, relying on friends, and persevering.

According to the Substance Abuse and Mental Health Services Administration, reporting in 2012,

> 7.5 million children under age 18 (10.5 percent of this population) lived with a parent who has experienced an alcohol use disorder in the past year. . . . 6.1 million of these children live with two parents—with either one or both parents experiencing an alcohol use disorder in the past year. The remaining 1.4 million of these children live in a single-parent house with a parent who has experienced an alcohol use disorder in the past year. Of these children 1.1 million lived in a single mother household and 0.3 million lived in a single father household.[12]

When divorced, separated, or unmarried single parents are addicted to alcohol or drugs, life in their households can be frenzied and unpredictable. Children usually are confused about what to expect since the rules change regularly and parents can be demanding at times and apathetic at others. Children also are likely to have negative feelings about themselves. Some believe it is their responsibility to stop their parents from alcohol or other drug abuse, and they blame themselves for their dysfunctional parents. If they are required to do most of the cooking and cleaning plus other household chores, they often feel resentful.

Many children whose parents are addicted will not invite friends to their home. Usually, they are forbidden to talk to anyone about their family problems. Some children are left alone for long periods and thus feel isolated, abandoned, or useless—or all three. Or they may live with constant fear that authorities will force them into foster care if their parents' addiction is discovered. (If a divorced parent excessively abuses drugs, he or she could lose visitation or custody rights or even parental rights.)

The Child Welfare Information Gateway (CWIG) of the U.S. Department of Health and Human Services compiles statistics and reports on adoption, foster care, child abuse and neglect, child and family well-being, and parental substance abuse. In 2012, CWIG reported,

> Approximately 47 States, the District of Columbia, Guam, and the U.S. Virgin Islands have laws within their child protection statutes that address the issue of substance abuse by parents. . . . For example, in 20 States the manufacture or possession of methamphetamine in the presence of a child is a felony, while in 9 States, the manufacture or possession of any controlled substance in the presence of a child is considered a felony. Nine States have enacted enhanced penalties for any conviction for the manufacture of methamphetamine when a child was on the premises where the crime occurred. Exposing children to the manufacture, possession, or distribution of illegal drugs is considered child endangerment in 11 States.[13]

Parental addiction and divorce seem to forecast insurmountable obstacles for children. But the obstacles can be overcome. Consider Erin Brady of Connecticut, who won the Miss USA contest in 2013. Erin's parents, Judith and Francis Brady, divorced when Erin was very young; in addition her father has struggled with alcoholism, although he has been recovering. Her father's addiction "taught me to stay grounded, focused," she told a reporter for the TheDay.com. "You can't choose your parents, but you can learn from their mistakes."[14]

After graduating from Portland (Connecticut) High School, Erin left home when she was eighteen years old. She went on to college, paying her way by working as a waitress, and earned a degree in finance and a minor in criminal justice from Central Connecticut State University. She became a financial accountant and also a role model for her two younger sisters. When she won the Miss USA contest, she noted that one of her goals is to use her celebrity to help children who live with parents who are addicted. "I think it's so important to talk about it. . . .

I think I can be a great example to showcase that you don't have to fall into that path."[15]

Another inspiring story is that of Dana Lynn Hee, winner of a gold medal in Taekwondo at the 24th Olympic Games in Seoul, Korea, in 1988. According to her online biography, she was a "child of divorced, alcoholic parents, [and] endured abuse, abandonment, and despair." She "passed back and forth between an orphanage, suicidal family members, halfway houses, a commune, government shelter, and finally a foster home." As a result, she had "little self-esteem or self-confidence, and a huge fear of failure. To her, nothing seemed possible . . . and she struggled to escape a lifelong habit of running from her fears." She seriously considered suicide. However, in her twenties she changed her life and began training in martial arts to prepare for the Olympic Games. After winning the gold medal in 1988, she became a motivational speaker, then in 1993 began a modeling and acting career, appearing as a stuntwoman in dozens of films and TV series. In the film industry, she has been a top stuntwoman and has survived countless injuries. As she says on her personal blog, "I feel very fortunate to have been able to accomplish so much . . . and change my entire life from victim to victorious." She wants to give back and "help elevate the human spirit."[16]

A Taboo Subject: A Divorced Parent in Jail

News stories frequently tell of drug abusers being sentenced to prison, and many of them are divorced parents with minor children. A 2010 report from CASA said, "In 2006, American prisons and jails held an estimated 1.0 million" parents who abused drugs. These incarcerated parents had "more than 2.2 million minor children. . . . Almost four-fifths of incarcerated mothers (77 percent in state prison and 83 percent in federal prison) reported being the primary daily caregiver for their children prior to their imprisonment compared with 26 percent of fathers incarcerated in state prisons and 31 percent incarcerated in federal prisons."[17]

In spite of the statistics, the impact on children of incarcerated parents is seldom the focus of discussions about divorced moms or dads. For that reason the producers of *Sesame Street* decided in 2013 to introduce a new blue-haired muppet named Alex who is sad because his father is not around. When friends ask him why, he says, "My dad's in jail. . . . I don't like to talk about it. Most people don't understand." Alex misses his father so much that he says, "Sometimes I just feel like I want to pound on a pillow and scream as loud as I can." The video story about Alex is not shown on the regular children's show, but is part of an online teaching kit for adults called *Little Children, Big Challenges*. However, producers say the video "can be a useful tool for kids" to help them understand difficult and sensitive topics.[18]

Watch This Documentary!

It's titled *Undroppable* and is the name of a social media campaign as well as a documentary released in 2013. Well-known filmmaker Jason Pollock is creator and producer of the documentary along with Adam McKay, Sharon Chang, and Scooter Braun (Justin Bieber's manager). The team has a partnership with the Get Schooled Foundation, a nonprofit established in 2010 to use the media to help improve high school graduation rates. The purpose of *Undroppable* is to call attention to the high dropout rate in American high schools and to do something about it. An estimated 1 million students failed to graduate in 2013. But some young people have been able to complete high school in spite of extremely difficult odds—parental addiction, imprisoned parents, domestic violence, and neighborhood shootings. "It's like a war zone" going to school and home every day said a Chicago teen Shawndtrana Campbell. Why does she and others keep trying to get an education? "It's to prove to yourself, I can do this," said Jaurees Gaines who comes from a single-parent family. He graduated as the valedictorian of his Chicago school and is going on to college.

Videos from the documentary can be seen at Undroppable.com and they feature students like Cynthia Gallardo, who attended East High School in Des Moines, Iowa. Gallardo explains on the video how difficult it was to stay in school. "My mom wouldn't have money to pay the rent, or she wouldn't have money to pay bills, and we would have to move all the time. . . . I remember there was about two months where we actually moved five or six times." Gallardo also tells about domestic violence in her home and how upset she became when her mother was hurt. In addition, she became pregnant and had a baby when she was a junior in high school. Yet, she graduated and went on to community college.

Pollock also filmed other students and teachers at East High School in Des Moines and in Collins Academy High School west of downtown Chicago; New Bedford High School and Whaling City Junior/Senior Alternative School in New Bedford, Massachusetts; Academy at Palumbo Liberal Arts High School in Philadelphia, Pennsylvania; Joplin High School in Joplin, Missouri; and La Causa in Los Angeles, California. Students in these schools tell their stories on Undroppable.com and YouTube videos.[h]

It is indeed a difficult if not an off-limits subject, says the Council on Crime and Justice (CCJ), a nonprofit agency in Minnesota. In a 2006 study that included thirty-four children, ranging in age from seven to eighteen, CCJ included a report on a nine-year-old who said it was hard to talk about his dad in prison "because you know how kids are? They like, oh where's your dad? We don't hardly see him as often. It's always mom picking you up. And then it starts . . . then I tell them well, he's in prison. And then they start being smarty pants, and then it turns into a whole conversation, and for like, it takes me awhile to get the darn thing out of my head."[19]

What about older children and teenagers? How do they cope? Some teens in the CCJ reported on how strong their mothers became after their fathers were imprisoned. One anonymous seventeen-year-old boy admired his mother because of

her ability to keep going. I mean, she has to take care of two kids that are trying to be really active. I do football, then shot-put and disc and a lot of times she has to give me rides during track season and my sister was doing theater so, she had to try and work both of us in there. And then she had to deal with all the money situations and trying to keep our house up and everything. . . . [I wish that] Mom could get a good job. Because we are always kind of behind on our payments. We have to find ways each month to get extra money so, maybe if she could get a good job that could at least pay the bills pretty well.[20]

Writing in a blog for the *Prevention Researcher* (which ceased publication in September 2013), editor Colette Kimball noted that incarceration of a parent "can be a severe and traumatic disruption" for all children's lives, including many teenagers. She told of Mary, a teen whose father is in jail. Mary said,

After my father went to jail, my mother started looking for a job. Now she works from 1 a.m. until 7 a.m. at a factory. Friday mornings she comes home at 8 a.m., and then at 10, she has to go to work at a hair salon so she just sleeps two hours. . . . My mother is a great person and strong too. But now that she's the one who's in charge of this family, sometimes the situation is too much stress for her, and she screams a lot and fights with us.

Yet, Mary continued her schooling and said that she tries "to concentrate on what the teacher is saying and . . . show a happy face. It's hard."[21]

LEARNING TO COPE WITH DIVORCE

"I do not exactly know why physically acting out was my way to deal with [parental divorce]. Today, I make conscious choices revolving around bettering my emotions, helping others, and most important, constantly working at removing anger and turning it into positive action."
—*comment from Amy, a fictitious name for an adult child of divorce[1]*

Creigh, who maintains the website DivorceandTeens.weebly.com, has experienced family divorce as a teenager, and has survived negative aspects as well as found some "silver linings." Creigh wrote, "Having a divorced family teaches you a lot of different skills that you probably wouldn't have learned otherwise," adding,

> When you finally leave home, you come out more independent than other kids your age, and a lot more mature. You learn to manage money, negotiate, and stand up for your own rights. Essentially, you learn to take charge of your own destiny. To this day, I'm an incredibly independent person. . . . I value my independence far more than most people do, and that's caused me to be far more financially and emotionally stable. I'm not trying to say divorce is a good thing—it's not. It's a horribly painful experience. But I would be a liar if I said that I hadn't gained important skills and matured as a person after my parents divorced. That, to me, is the most positive thing that can come out of a bad situation.[2]

"Divorce does not always have to be a bad thing," agreed teenager Annie Carter, writing in *YourTeenMag.com* in 2012. She explained,

> While it can be very upsetting and challenging, attitude can make a big difference. When I was in seventh grade, my parents separated, and my

mom moved out shortly afterwards. At first it was hard to bear, but then I grew used to my living situation, and now I cannot imagine living any other way. . . . Overall, I have come out with a relatively positive outlook on my experience. While the changes that came with my parents' divorce were hard to become accustomed to, I have found that things can always turn out all right. I have been lucky enough to maintain good relationships with both parents, and them maintaining a good relationship with each other made some of the transition easier on my siblings and me. In the end, I have learned that in situations such as this, I could dwell on how life could be or accept how it is and make the best of the situation.[3]

Not every child who experiences parental divorce makes such a constructive adjustment, according to Richard Niolon, professor of clinical psychology. He explained in a 2010 article that

[d]ivorce does not appear to have consistent effects across all children and across all ages. Older children may be more sensitive to family conflict and feel more pressure to intervene, which could increase their risk for problems, but they also have more emotional resources to help them cope, which could decrease their risk. Younger children may have less ability to sense and intervene to stop arguments, possibly leading to less risk, but they also have fewer cognitive resources to make sense of events and emotions, possibly leading to higher risks. Thus, determining how any *specific child* will deal with a divorce entails understanding that child's strengths and the demands of the specific situation.[4]

Dealing with the Aftermath of Parental Divorce

Perhaps one of the most difficult problems a child of divorce faces is the loss of one parent. To repeat an oft-stated truth: children often have emotional challenges as they try to adapt to changes in their family structures. If young people have been sheltered from economic worries, they are likely to have a hard time liv-

Did You Know?

Some experts say that children find divorce more difficult to accept than death. Years after parental divorce, some offspring hang on to the belief that their parents will reconcile and they will have an intact family again.

ing with a custodial parent who has few financial resources. Abigail Dalton, whose affluent parents divorced, explained that soon afterward, "I had to rely on myself for all of those financial incidentals I had always received from my parents."[5]

Some single parents become depressed because of financial strains, and as a result, children have even more problems adapting to their family circumstances. Children might have to face other changes, such as moving to a different home, changing schools, and going back and forth from one parent's household to the other's. They might also have to adjust or try to adjust to a divorced parent dating and getting married again.

When pressures become so great that a child of divorce or a divorced parent cannot cope in a healthy manner, he or she could be at risk for developing an eating disorder. In other words, if young people or adults experiencing divorce also have issues regarding their body image, they may want to make themselves feel socially "acceptable" or more appealing by being thin and having "ideal" bodies. In that pursuit they could be tempted to engage in unhealthy eating, which can become a psychological disorder with damaging physical results. These disorders include anorexia nervosa, bulimia nervosa, and binge eating. Anorexics starve themselves to stay thin, bulimics consume food and vomit or use laxatives to keep from gaining weight, and binge eaters consume excessive amounts of food that often leads to weight gain, guilt, and a cycle of on-again, off-again compulsive eating .

However, there are multiple causes of eating disorders. Stress is certainly a factor, but as WebMD points out, "Eating disorders are complex, and experts don't really know what causes them. But they may be due to a mix of family history, social factors, and personality traits." People may be at risk if they are facing "stressful life events, such as divorce . . . or losing a loved one."[6]

Although females seem more prone to eating disorders than males, a variety of studies have shown that after a divorce, boys have more adjustment problems than do girls. "However, problems related to sex differences tend to be reported only when children live with [single] mothers. When children live with their custodial father or a remarried family, girls exhibit poorer adjustment, whereas boys fare better than those in mother-custody homes," a fact sheet from Ohio State University Extension notes. The university's fact sheet also states,

> Gender differences in adjustment are likely to depend on multiple factors such as sex of custodial parent, parenting style, marital status, parent-child relationships, and amount of contact with non-custodial parent. Most children's adjustment problems occur within the first two years following their parent's divorce or remarriage. Still, some children, who appear to be adjusting well early-on, will experience a reemergence of problems during adolescence. Research indicates that while behavior problems are common at the time of divorce, they typically diminish as time passes.

Most children will eventually adapt successfully to this life transition and have no long-term ill effects.[7]

Like Creigh and Annie, many teenagers have discovered that their parents' divorce results in some unexpected positives. Michelle New, a clinical child psychologist, reviewed a 2010 article on KidsHealth.org that described successful ways teens cope with their parents' divorce:

Many teens find their parents are actually happier after the divorce or they may develop new and better ways of relating to both parents when they have separate time with each one.

Some teens learn compassion and caring skills when a younger brother or sister needs their support and care. Siblings who are closer in age may form tighter bonds, learning to count on each other more because they're facing the challenges of their parents' divorce together.

It Happened to Amy

She does not want her real name used, so she will be known here as Amy. She told her story about the effects of her parents' divorce. As an adult, the memories are still with her even though events happened while she was growing up in California. But she learned to adjust. Amy wrote,

I am looking back and remembering what it was like to be a child, a pre-teen, a teenager, with divorcing/divorced parents . . . and an only child to boot. My first memory is that of the last altercation between my mother and father. It took place in the house they owned together. I was about four. They were yelling at each other. I just remember hearing and seeing it and it stuck.

Soon after that, I discovered that my father had been in some sort of accident with his car and that my mother and I needed to go pick him up. We did. I was scared.

Fast forward some time, not sure if it was weeks or months but I was introduced to the server at the restaurant my father and I frequented. She soon became my stepmother. As a child without siblings, there is not a single person to talk to about the sadness of your parents' divorce. I could not go to kindergarten or daycare and discuss the trials and tribulations of divorce. All I could do was stuff it, and so I did for probably nine years.

My parents did not go to court and put me through that type of turmoil as they decided to handle their custody and like issues on their own. Here is how the visitation went: one parent would have me for the majority of the school year and I would visit other parent every other weekend. The every-other-weekend parent would be the parent to keep me that summer . . . or I would go visit my grandparents for weeks or months in the summertime. I do not think I minded the visitation arrangement because I knew of no other way. I liked having two houses, two bedrooms, etc. What I did not like was the transition from one house to the other. It was almost as if my personality, thoughts, feelings, emotions, and psyche had to change in transitioning from Mom's house to Dad's and step-mom's house.

Some Fridays my dad would "forget" to pick me up at a school bus stop. I would wait and wait. Sometimes it was an hour or more—as a 6th grader, one's perception of time is not all that impressive so it may have been longer or shorter but it felt like an eternity. When it became obvious that he was not coming, I would make other arrangements, or walk to my mom's because it was clear he wasn't going to pick me up. At least not then and there. This single act has stayed with me until now, and when I see the school, unfortunately that is one of the memories that stand out. I wish it were not.

When you are an only child of divorced parents, you are the go-between. The one that hears negativity from both sides. You are the one who is caught in the middle, and the one who feels there is no place to turn. With that comes anger. Since I had no idea how to categorize or place my anger, I took it out physically. On my mother and on myself. To this day, the guilt (unfortunately) still haunts me. Mom has forgiven me, I have forgiven her, but I still have terrible feelings associated with my bouts with physical violence.

As Amy explained in the opening quote, she constantly works "at removing anger and turning it into positive action. I exercise every single day of the week. Without this, I believe I would still be stuck. I help others achieve their fitness goals, control their eating, and listen to their problems. My studies in psychology help me process emotions and find answers to why we act the way we do. Emotional well-being is connected with physical well-being and I strive to achieve this always."[a]

A sympathetic friend can help a teenager adjust to her parents' divorce.

Coping well with divorce also can bring out strength and maturity. Some become more responsible, better problem solvers, better listeners, or better friends. Looking back on the experience, lots of people say that they learned coping skills they never knew they had and feel stronger and more resilient as a result of what they went through.[8]

Learning to Adjust

When teens and adults try to adjust after their parents divorce, what do they do? The answer depends, as it often does, on the individual and the circumstances. In some cases, it takes years to figure out healthy ways to deal with a family breakup. Usually, the most difficult time is during the first year after a divorce. But once again that depends on the individual and whether there are negative factors like addiction or high conflict in the household. There is no situation or time frame that applies to everyone. Nevertheless, there are strategies that work for many young people. Some examples include

- writing in a journal to express feelings,
- listening to soothing music,

- playing an instrument,
- dancing,
- exercising,
- getting involved in team sports,
- meditating,
- watching a movie,
- reading a good book or story,
- volunteering at a charity or religious center,
- talking to a counselor or member of the clergy,
- confiding in a friend, and
- starting a new hobby.

Many individuals such as family therapists, psychologists, divorce attorneys, teachers, school counselors, and medical practitioners can help people cope with parental divorce. Support groups are also helpful resources. Some groups are connected with local churches, synagogues, or temples or are community groups established by social workers and divorce counselors. Others are organizations such as Banana Splits (as described on page 128) and online support groups such as I Am a Child of Divorce (www.iamachildofdivorce.com), which launched its pilot program for teenagers in 2013. Online group chats, videos, and instructions for helpful activities are part of the program.

Another source is DailyStrength.org, where users discuss their life challenges and support each other through online communities. One of the communities is children of divorce and focuses on adults and youth as well as parents concerned about the effects of divorce on their children.

The support website ExperienceProject.com and its "I Have Divorced Parents" section include stories from teenagers and young adults whose parents divorced. Some of its members have shared their hurt and memories of discord. But they also have provided examples of positive outcomes that can occur following a divorce.

How Adult Children Deal with Divorce

Jann Gumbiner, a licensed psychologist and clinical professor at the University of California, Irvine, College of Medicine, is "the daughter of a divorce." She noted in a 2011 article for *Psychology Today*,

> During the 70s, when the psychological literature first discussed the effects of divorce on children, the general view was that divorce doesn't have to harm children. But, it does. Children, even intelligent ones or older ones,

What Are Banana Splits?

No, they are not always ice cream sundaes. Across the United States, support groups in schools are called Banana Splits, named for families that have split apart. These groups are made up of students helping other students. For example, teens who have already dealt with their own parents' divorce offer their advice and support as they mentor younger children dealing with the same difficult problems. Banana Splits allow young children to safely express their feelings without fearing a negative backlash. Children of divorce also learn to develop coping skills and to increase their self-esteem.

Social worker Lila Margulies has guided Banana Splits in an independent school in New York City since 2004 and in a website article she included the views of some participants. One youth had this to say about Banana splits: "I think I have allowed myself to open up to more people and to take everyone else's advice. Now when things are screwed up between my parents I can actually say something and not only help myself cope but help with the actual problem." Another young person said, "Banana Splits enables people to make friends and find connections with people they otherwise might not have." One more student explained,

> I like sharing personal problems with other kids my age who might feel the same way as I do about my parents' separation issues. I am able to express myself at a more open level and I am comfortable sharing with my peers because of Banana Splits. Banana Splits has allowed me to hear what kids my age have to say about their personal lives and has given me a chance to reach out to them if they need my help with those problems or vice versa.[b]

Information about Banana Splits is available online at http://www.banana splitsresourcecenter.org/.

often think it is their fault. There is a lot of self blame. Grades suffer. I lost my motivation in school. My grades went down. Not studying was a form of rebellion, anger and apathy. . . . Without a father around, I was very promiscuous. I sought affection from adolescent boys. I was unsupervised and got into trouble. There was no one to set limits, no one to ask where I was going.

Her concluding remark: "My parents' divorce has had lifelong effects on me and I am still feeling them."[9]

Many adults whose parents divorced while they were children have carried their pain into their twenties, thirties, forties, and sometimes longer. Consider laurenashley of Colorado, who was twenty-five when she wrote in a 2011 blog that she was a "product of a 'broken home'" in the 1990s. She explained, "[I] was one of those kids that was supposed to end up all kinds of weird because I didn't have a dad around. In elementary school, I was the only one out of my group of friends that didn't have 2 parents." She added,

I constantly felt like a pariah. Not only were my parents in the process of a nasty divorce, as soon as the divorce was all said and done with, my dad disappeared out of my (and my brother's) life. For several years . . . half of who made me "me" was gone. And I was crushed.

I never felt anger towards him. Just a longing to have him back. My Daddy-o. The longing helped to foster a deep insecurity. That I wasn't good enough for anyone or anything.[10]

Her father reappeared again when she was a sophomore in high school. But then "he vanished again a few years later. . . . Almost instantly I felt that deep crushing pain. A lost little soul. I didn't know who I was. My relationships suffered. I felt so alone. I lost my job. And I felt like I deserved to be hurting like I was." Yet, over the years, she managed to reassess her life and concluded that she was not the one "missing out" because of her father's absence. Instead it was "his loss."[11]

There is a common perception that adults who are no longer dependent on their parents are able to "get over" the distress of parental divorce, forget about it, and go on with their lives. Adult children of divorce frequently say they seldom get support from family and friends who might help them cope. As adults they are expected to be stable and mature enough to deal with parents who divorce after twenty or thirty plus years of marriage. But the effects of divorce sometimes can last for decades, as Kim King noted in response to an online forum. "My parents divorced when I was about 9; I am now 49. It is an experience you never recover from," she wrote. "There was so much anger with my father and guilt on my part that it took years (until I was 25) to come to terms with the fact that it wasn't my fault, that he had caused the situation. My mother never talked bad about him in front of me and always tried to work things out with him. His behavior was selfish and revolved around relationships with other women. That is very difficult . . . to come to terms with."[12]

An adult on Reddit.com explained,

I'm in my 30's now. My parents divorced when I was 7. I've dealt with depression and low self-esteem ever since. I'm doing a lot better now. I started seeing a counselor . . . and it has helped tremendously. I have also talked about the divorce extensively with both my mom and dad. That was probably the biggest help. For the longest time I felt abandoned by my father. I finally had a heart to heart talk with him and learned his side of the story. Hearing his side of the story gave me insight into why he handled the situation the way that he did.[13]

Donna Ferber, a psychotherapist in Connecticut, wrote on her blog,

With younger children, parents often go out of their way to, as much as possible, protect their kids from conflict. With adult children, it may be just the opposite. Parents experiencing divorce often seek out their adult children for counsel and support. . . . Frequently older children are made privy to information they really shouldn't/don't want to have—dad's affair with his secretary or mom's refusal to have sex. Parents . . . tend to see their adult children as "friends" and confide in and rely on them for support, friendship, allegiance. They often minimize their children's need [for] comfort and support as they face their parents' divorce.[14]

In 2013, Kasey Edwards, author of several books on thirty-somethings, wrote on *HuffingtonPost.com* that her parents divorced after thirty-two years of marriage, but Edwards noted that she "didn't feel entitled to grieve publicly. . . . Unlike when children are young, people don't concern themselves with the emotional, physical and financial toll of divorce on adult offspring. I felt silly being so upset, because it wasn't about me." She added,

Watching the family home and assets being packed up and fought over shatters your world, no matter how old you are. It was as if my safety net in life had gone. There was no safe refuge, physically or emotionally, that I could run to if I needed it. My parents we so engrossed in their own pain and anger they no longer had any concern for me, other than as a pawn in their own drama.[15]

Dr. Sylvia Mikucki-Enyart of the University of Wisconsin–Stevens Point has been conducting a study of people who were eighteen years of age or older when their parents divorced and were living independently at the time. According to graduate student Christopher Brundidge, who has been part of the interview team, the study is "important because being an adult adds completely new dimensions to relationships between children and parents. Having less dependence on a parent can create a variety of different perceptions, expectations and raise many different questions then [sic] a dependent youth might have." The initial stage of data collection for the study began in 2013 on the UW–Stevens Point campus, and graduate student Brundidge noted that he and other team members "have been surprised by the amount of emotion that individuals still possess despite already being an adult in addition to the separation from their parents. The level of complexity that exists when one is an adult dealing with their parents getting divorced is extremely insightful, and I myself personally did not imagine some of the scenarios."[16]

M. Gary Neuman, a psychotherapist, rabbi, and best-selling author, conducted a study of 379 adults whose parents divorced when they were children. His findings are the subject of his book *The Long Way Home for Adults Who Were Children of Divorce* (2013). Eighty-nine percent of the adults studied said their parents' divorce "had a negative impact on their life" with 80 percent reporting "severe sadness or depression." In addition, "[t]he majority feel their parents' divorce has undermined their self-confidence and ability to trust," and more than half "lack self-confidence in their love relationships," Neuman noted. Money fears, difficulties dealing with conflicts, and temper problems were other effects that plague participants in the study.[17]

Some Positives for Children of Divorce

Two psychology professors, Lisa Laumann-Billings and Robert E. Emery, at the University of Virginia, Charlottesville, wrote in 2000, "Researchers find that most children from divorced families function normally, but some clinicians assert that young people are disturbed even many years after a divorce." They pointed out that differences are probably because "research typically focuses on notably problematic behavior (disorder), whereas case studies emphasize more subtle inner turmoil (distress)." In one study "college students reported painful feelings, beliefs, and memories about their parents divorce on a reliable new measure, but they also reported accepting the divorce and having few psychological symptoms. Distress about family life was greater among students from divorced than from married families." Another study "replicated these findings in a community sample of young people from low-income divorced families. In both studies, greater distress was associated with children's residence, frequency of contact with fathers, interparental conflict, and psychological symptoms."[18]

In a 2013 article for *Scientific American*, Hal Arkowitz and Scott O. Lilienfeld reported that "only a relatively small percentage of children experience serious problems in the wake of divorce or, later, as adults," adding that "many children experience short-term negative effects from divorce, especially anxiety, anger, shock and disbelief. These reactions typically diminish or disappear by the end of the second year. Only a minority of kids suffer longer."[19]

The two authors cited one 2001 review of the literature on divorce by sociologist Paul R. Amato, then at Pennsylvania State University. Amato

> examined the possible effects on children several years after a divorce. The studies compared children of married parents with those who experienced divorce at different ages. The investigators followed these kids into later childhood, adolescence or the teenage years, assessing their academic achievement, emotional and behavior problems, delinquency, self-concept and social relationships. On average, the studies found only very small differences on all these measures between children of divorced parents and those from intact families, suggesting that the vast majority of children endure divorce well.[20]

Psychologist E. Mavis Hetherington of the University of Virginia conducted a twenty-five-year study that included "an in-depth examination of 1,400 families and over 2,500 children, many followed for more than three decades."[21] Details of her findings were included in her book *For Better or For Worse: Divorce Reconsidered* (2002), written with journalist and co-author John Kelly. This academic work provides a basis for a somewhat optimistic outlook on the effects of divorce as opposed to the many studies predicting gloom and doom after marital breakups.

The late Judith Wallerstein (1921–2012), divorce psychologist and lead author of a widely read and quoted *The Unexpected Legacy of Divorce: The 25 Year Landmark Study* (2000), noted in 2011 that when children experience divorce, many of them

> learn to get along, to meet changing conditions, to acquire socially adaptive skills that stand them in very good stead when they grow up—skills of tact and diplomacy that work well in the business world, in law offices, and in marketing. As one young man told me, "Some call this resilience." Others regard this as learned behavior. No matter its roots, children of divorce have social skills of which they are justly proud.[22]

What are those social skills? In general young people may learn how to

- get along with diverse individuals,
- negotiate when there are conflicts,
- be a mentor for others going through divorce,
- communicate with adults as well as peers,
- stand up for their own interests,
- become independent, and
- be discriminating when considering future relationships.

Although she certainly does not claim to be an expert, Leslie Sheline noted, "Divorce has taught me a lot of what not to do but, even now over halfway through my twenties, I still am not too sure what is right to do. However, I know that between my husband and me, divorce is not a word that dwells in our thoughts. Relationships have their ups and their downs. The key is to help each other up every now and then."[23]

Parenting and Family Stabilization Courses

Beginning in the 1970s and 1980s, judges, family law attorneys, and legislators began considering programs to reduce parental conflict after a divorce. Officials noted that arguments between ex-husbands and ex-wives had long-lasting negative effects on couples' children, and research shows that if children have good relationships with their parents, negative effects are reduced. Currently, most states have established parent education classes or family stabilization courses for divorcing couples with minor children. These courses help divorced parents focus on ways to assure that their children are able to adjust constructively to their changing family status.

In most states, local courts require couples with minor children to take these courses, and the courses are mandatory statewide in about twenty states. The Extension Services of West Virginia conducted a national survey between 2009 and 2010 and found that Arizona, Connecticut, Florida, Illinois, Iowa, Minnesota, and Utah are among the states that have a statewide mandate for divorce education classes. That is, couples will not be granted a divorce unless they participate in these courses, which are usually about four hours in length.

In Florida, for example, the law states, "The court may hold any parent who fails to attend a required parenting course in contempt, or that parent may be denied shared parental responsibility or time-sharing or otherwise sanctioned as the court deems appropriate." The Florida Department of Children and Family

Off the Bookshelf

Divorce Is Not the End of the World: Zoe and Evan's Coping Guide for Kids (2008) was written by the Stern family team—Zoe and Evan (sister and brother) with their mother, Ellen Sue Stern, author of numerous books. This paperback is an updated and revised edition of a book written when Zoe and Evan were teenagers in 1998. Ten years later they include upbeat advice from their perspectives as young adults who have experienced divorce. Twenty short chapters discuss topics ranging from "Why Did This [Divorce] Have to Happen?" to "Rewards, or The Good Things Nobody Tells You about Divorce."

The book includes children's and teenagers' questions sent to Zoe along with her responses. "Evan's Quick Tips" in each chapter are helpful suggestions for readers. These tips are followed by "Ten Years Later" written by either Zoe or Evan. They tell concisely what each has learned over the years. Mom also has her say in each chapter.

Services provides each judicial circuit with a list of approved course providers and sites at which the parent education and family stabilization course may be completed. A certificate of completion must be filed with the local Clerk of Court office before a divorce is granted.

Required courses include topics such as anger management, strategies to resolve conflicts, child custody arrangements, co-parenting plans, children's rights, dating, and blending families. In some states, parents can take classes online, but a court must be willing to accept an Internet certificate of completion. That is usually determined by a judge in a jurisdiction where the divorce process takes place.

Susan L. Pollet, an attorney and director of the New York State Parent Education and Awareness Program, and Melissa Lombreglia, a student at Hofstra University School of Law, conducted a nationwide survey on mandatory parent education for divorcing and separating parents. Published in 2008 in the *Family Court Review*, the authors concluded that the education programs are "an effective tool to improve the lives of parents and children throughout this country. It opens the door to accessing resources to continue the process of reorganization of families in a way that is most beneficial to all concerned. The sheer numbers of families who need this education is [*sic*] staggering—the goal now should be to get as many of them to attend as possible."[24]

10

LIVING IN A STEPFAMILY

··

"I didn't accept what she [stepmom] had to say at first. . . . I was rebellious.
I ran away once and I started fights all the time just because I wanted to see what
she would do, how she would react, try to push her buttons. . . . And now we have a love
for Donna and just accept what she has to say because she has a lot of wisdom."
—Andy, a teenage participant on a PBS show, In the Mix[1]

Many children of divorce, especially teenagers, say they have conflicting emotions when their divorced parents begin dating and then remarry. Some have expressed embarrassment or disgust—they think it is inappropriate. Others resent another person who might try to replace his or her biological parent. Some young people who have experienced their parents' divorce are wary about remarriage. They are not enthusiastic about living in a stepfamily.

Still others are pleased with the idea that their parents have found someone with whom they can share their lives. Nineteen-year-old Hailee Smith, a child of divorce, wrote, "When your parents start dating again and finally are ready to get re-married it's not always a bad thing. My step-dad is the best father I could ask for. Yes, I said father because sometimes it takes a step parent to fulfill where a biological parent lacks."[2]

In some cases, when divorced parents plan to remarry, teens lose all hope they once had that their biological parents would reunite. In a PBS show *In the Mix* on divorce and stepfamilies, Chris put it this way: "In my brain, it was like, there's no other way, my parents are together, they're together, they're not gonna see anybody else. Then all of a sudden, they're divorced and they're seeing other people, it just—it doesn't fit in." Another participant said, "Having to be shared between two parents and two different households for a couple of days a week, taking two completely different bus routes, it's hard to get adjusted to." And Chris added this about traveling between families:

The schedule is so confusing. I can't even keep it straight sometimes. It's like; I have Monday nights with my mom, and every other Tuesday night I have with my dad. And then Wednesday night I have with my dad, Thursday night I have with my mom, Friday night I have with my dad. And Saturday all day I'm with my dad and at night I sleep at my mom's house, and Sunday I'm with my mom and Sunday night I'm with my mom. And then it goes back to Monday night when I'm with my mom.[3]

In California, teenagers involved in the San Jose Urban Journalism Workshop write for the *Mosaic*, a publication by high school students. One *Mosaic* article described the effects of shuttling back and forth between split families. "People don't realize how lucky they are to live in one home," Shani Chabansky, a sixteen-year-old at Gunn High School in Palo Alto told student reporter Sabrina Mercado. "I feel like I don't have a home to call my own. . . . I have to move stuff all over the place. It's not as easy as people think." According to Mercado, "Shani admits living with one parent would be less hassle, but she doesn't want to choose between them" because that would upset or offend one of the parents.[4]

Teenager Chase Block, who wrote the book *Chasing Happiness*, has had definite opinions about his father's divorce, dating, and remarriage, and his experiences with a stepfamily. His father, in his fifties, dated Tara, a twenty-eight-year-old model, for only three months before he proposed. Chase wrote, "My brother and I agreed Tara was beautiful, and she seemed nice, but we told Dad a few months was WAY [Chase's emphasis] too soon to make a decision about something as important as marriage. I strongly recommended to Dad that he wait longer, and get to know Tara better. They hadn't even had an argument yet, and you can tell a lot about a person's true nature by the way he or she fights—or refuses to speak—when angry."[5]

Unfortunately, Tara called off the wedding "just ten days before the ceremony." Chase wrote that his father was "completely devastated." His dad "hadn't seen it coming, even though my brother and I warned him. Kids are much smarter than you think."[6]

Then six months later, Tara came back and the two married. However, the marriage did not last, and Chase noted, "Even though I saw the divorce coming, it was still a rough time for everyone. My brother and I had worked hard to create a kind of family life with our new stepmother, and it was tough to watch it all fall apart."[7]

The Holiday Dilemma

Holidays are some of the most difficult times of the year for children whose biological parents have split up and have established two different households.

In stepfamilies, the dilemma at holiday time may be trying to find a middle road between a tradition customary in the nuclear household and a different tradition in a blended family. How do children of split families determine where and with whom to spend, for example, Passover, Easter, Thanksgiving, Hanukkah, Christmas, Kwanza, New Year's Eve, and Holy Days of varied religions? It is not an easy question to answer when a stepfamily does not share the same religion or cultural rituals as the biological family.

"The holiday season brings families together from all over the globe to participate in the happy festivities surrounding Christmas," wrote Tayce Taylor, a California high school senior in 2012 and contributing blogger for *HuffingtonPost.com*. "But for me, my Christmas makes it even more apparent how divided my family is." Although she got to see each parent for a week during the holiday break, she noted, "It is hard to see all of my friends whose parents are together, and I have to remind myself that I am not like them and it is not my fault. All I see during the holidays is big families celebrating Christmas together, while my family will never be like that again."[8]

Some stepfamilies that include different religions and faiths start their own tradition. For example, stepfamilies with Jewish and Christian members combine some customs from Hanukkah and Christmas customs (like decorating a tree) and calling it a Hanamas celebration. Another way some blended families combine celebrations is to create holiday meals that include favorite foods from each of the diverse families. Or as is more common, members of stepfamilies may move between their biological parents' households and their blended family households.

For teenager Taylor Stone, "the hardest thing about her parents' break up is finding a way to spend equal time with both parents," according to a reporter for Lingnaore High School's the *Lance* in Frederick, Maryland. "In the past, my family always had a huge Halloween party," Taylor told reporter Kate Mannarino.

It's a Fact

Stepfamily Day is on September 16 and was first celebrated in 1997 to show appreciation for stepparents and extended families. The first celebration originated with Christy Borgeld of Michigan. In 2000, U.S. Representative Debbie Stabenow of Michigan recognized Stepfamily Day as a way to celebrate the importance of stepfamilies throughout the United States. The U.S. Congress has yet to designate an official national holiday, but celebratory events occur across the nation. They include family potlucks, campouts, making family scrapbooks, and dozens of other activities.

"But this year [2013], we did not have one. I had to have a party on my own," Taylor explained. Another student, Seth Brooks, declared, "We always used to have family night all the time, especially on Sunday nights. Now it's just trying to do your own thing. We try to make something happen, but it never really works. I usually go to Nebraska the day of or the day after Christmas to see my dad," he reported. "I spend the rest of the holidays with my mom."[9]

Stepfamilies

Family therapists and others who work with or are part of stepfamilies want to take the "step" out of stepfamily, wrote Carol Morello of the *Washington Post* in 2011. She noted that families want to become known by alternative names such as "blended families, bonus families or para-kin," the latter meaning to support or to be on the side of, rather like paralegal. In addition, Morello explained that even Hallmark "has stopped publishing greeting cards using the word 'step.' A spokeswoman said there are too many varieties of nontraditional families to justify it, though 'step' is an option for personalized cards on the company's Web site."[10]

Stepfamily, however, is still a well-used term. In fact, author Patricia L. Papernow titled her 2013 book for therapists and other professional helpers *Surviving and Thriving in Stepfamily Relationships: What Works and What Doesn't* (Routledge). Nearly all sections of the book refer to stepfamilies and tell how to meet their challenges.

Creating a new stepfamily frequently requires numerous changes. When families are combined, some child or children in a stepfamily may lose some privacy and have to share a bedroom. Meal times, food customs, family income, and rituals may be altered. If the custodial parent moves to a new neighborhood, children's friends, school, sports fields, and hangouts may change drastically.

When a stepfamily forms, here is how teenager Nick described it on the PBS show *In the Mix*: "[You] just jump in with two new siblings, and you don't know how it's going to be you know. So, I was sort of like wasn't sure what it was going to be like." At the beginning, Nick said, "[m]e and Andy, and Alex and Ashley actually didn't get along very well. . . . Like we would argue a lot. He [Alex] would make fun of me. Stuff like that. And I get annoyed very easily." As for Ashley, she refused to sit next to her two stepbrothers.[11]

On the program, Alex explained what happened:

We would be like . . . we would team up on each other. . . . I was very used to it just being myself or me and my brother. I wasn't used to having two other people. You know, I wasn't used to having . . . or sharing, you know, even the food—bigger portions of food. I would kinda always try to keep my distance, but I would always be short tempered with them. They would take . . . Like, we'd have these big fights over little things. Like we'd fight over a whiffle ball bat or something. You know if they took my whiffle ball bat I would yell at them.[12]

An adult child of divorce living in California had a somewhat different view about parental divorce and her new stepfamily. She believed that she became "more grounded" and has experienced more diversity than she would have if her parents had stayed married. "Children from split homes have to grow up faster and become more self-sufficient, for this, I feel lucky," she declared during a 2010 interview. She also believed that having to plan her own visitations with either parent helped to make her realize that is not what she wants for her children. Bottom line: She said she has been blessed with her two half-sisters that she helped to raise. "I can't imagine my life without them."[13]

Terry Gaspard and Tracy Clifford, a mother and daughter team who are both children of divorce, maintain a website that offers advice for people in stepfamilies. For example, sixteen-year-old Maggie has had trouble relating to her stepdad and wrote,

From the start, my stepdad tried to treat me like his own daughter but whenever he came close, I'd push him away or say something mean. I never really developed a father-daughter relationship with my stepdad. To this day, I still have a closer bond with my real dad, even though I don't see him very much since he married Karen and they have a new baby.

The problem is that I've always felt torn between my two dads and living in their different worlds. I've always felt as if I had to choose between them. My family was split apart after the divorce. I lived with my mom and felt like I had to take sides.[14]

Gaspard, who is a licensed therapist, explained that while growing up she had a similar problem. She "had to adjust to both a stepdad and a stepmom. My two sisters, who were teenagers when our parents divorced, never accepted my stepmother or stepbrother. In my case, I was younger and bonded with my stepmom and stepbrother, but considered my stepdad to be a rival. . . . I felt that if I was close to my stepdad, I was being disloyal to my real dad." Gaspard added that "stepfamily life is by far the most challenging for adolescent girls. Based on my research, girls have more difficulty coping with life in a stepfamily during adolescence than when they are younger. In most cases, living in a stepfamily means taking one day at a time."[15]

Another team that offers help for stepfamilies is Bonus Families, an international nonprofit organization founded in 1999 that substitutes the term *bonus family* for *stepfamily*. Melanie Ford and Anee Mew have been editors of the Kids and Teens Department of the organization, and they have answered questions from children of divorce living in a bonus family. For example, Stacy P. wrote that her friends complain about their stepparents, but she feels differently. "I like my stepmother. She's always been a great friend to me. It makes me feel kind of weird, like I'm the one who has a problem."[16]

Melanie responded that she, too, likes her stepmother. "She came into our family as a friend, not as my mom. She was an authority figure, I have to admit, but I never felt like she was trying to take my mom's place, so I listened to her. I'm not saying things were always perfect. She knew I had a mother that I adored, and the only way I wouldn't resent her was for her to not try to replace my mom."[17]

Alex, a teenager writing for BonusFamilies.com, described his initial reaction when his divorced father remarried a woman named Gill:

> When people called Gill my mom, I would become so enraged and I would snap back: 'She's my STEPMOM!' This rage did not last long. . . . [A] friend told me how he felt about his relationship with his stepmother and how he didn't want to show her any love because he thought he would be betraying his mom. The first thing I thought was "that's stupid"—just because you love your step parent, that doesn't mean you're betraying your biological parent. . . . [N]ow when people ask, 'Is that your mom?' It's easy for me to say 'No, that's my Bonus Mom.' Because she is. But, it has taken time—it didn't happen overnight. I guess we all had a lot of growing up to do.[18]

After her parents divorced, Avaz wrote in 2013, "[I] was always in solitude and never wanted to associate with anybody from school. I had major trust issues and didn't really understand the meaning of a friend." On ExperienceProject .com she explained that her parents remarried and that her mother

> used to always call me and complain that my dad's new wife will be evil like that of cinderella. . . . I can laugh about it now though. This "new wife" was actually the exact opposite. . . . In fact she was probably one the nicest people I have ever encountered . . . because of this simple reason, I was very angry about it. . . . [I]t actually took me a while to figure out why I couldn't bring myself to like her, but eventually it hit me. I just wasn't used to affection. . . . I did appreciate the fact that she wanted to help me and have a better life like the other kids did. . . . She just overdid it and eventually the kindness just reached my limit. I was literally throwing things all around my room and I had a lot of negative thoughts running through my mind putting all my hate on her . . . when she did nothing except try to help me.

Off the Bookshelf

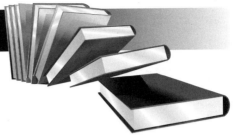

Lord of the Deep by Graham Salisbury, published in 2001, has won numerous awards. The story focuses on teenager Mikey Donovan and his stepdad, Bill Monks, who is skipper of a charter boat in Hawaii, taking customers out to deep-sea fish off the Kona coast. Before Mikey was born, his father disappeared. Mikey believes his father ran away and deserted him and his mom. Mikey and his single mom are happy together, but he does not like all the boyfriends that come calling. Still, he understands why. His mother is beautiful—"a dark-skinned Filipino-French Polynesian."[a]

Mikey is pleased that his mom has chosen Bill, and that they have a son, three-year-old Billy-Jay, who was born blind. Mikey loves his half-brother and the way both his mom and Bill care for Billy-Jay. In Mikey's view, he has a "real" family, and he clearly idolizes Bill, whom he calls "Lord of the Deep." He wants to be exactly like him. He convinces Bill that he should be a deckhand on his fishing boat, the *Crystal-C*. Bill takes him on when he loses a deckhand, and two rather obnoxious brothers, Cal and Ernie, charter the fishing boat for several days. On the second day Cal brings his teenage daughter, Alison, who is aloof and does not want to be there. But as the day wears on, Alison and Mikey begin a friendship.

Because they caught nothing on the first day, Cal and Ernie hassle Bill, urging him to find some action. From this point on, the story is full of nonstop adventure and a lot of information about snagging mahimahi, marlin (swordfish), and other fish along with techniques for handling a deep-sea fishing boat. Before the end of the three-day charter, Mikey discovers that his stepdad, Bill, has human weaknesses that he did not expect. He wrestles with that knowledge, but as the story concludes Mikey still wants Bill to be part of his family.

Avaz ended her story on a hopeful note, writing that she is learning to trust and trying to achieve happiness.[19]

Same-Sex Stepfamilies

The American Association for Marriage and Family Therapy (AAMFT) reported that studies estimate "between 1 and 9 million children in the United States have at least one parent who is lesbian or gay." In addition, AAMFT noted that "There are approximately 594,000 same-sex partner households . . . and there are children living in approximately 27 percent of those households." Same-sex households are not the same as same-sex marriages. But the households could be same-sex stepfamilies. "There is not a 'usual' gay family," AAMFT noted. "Some same-sex couples may decide to have a child within their relationship, while others may bring children from previous heterosexual or same-sex unions. The rise in same-sex parenting is partially due to the increase in options available for same-sex couples to become parents. Although most children of same-sex couples are biological children of one of the parents, a growing number are the result of donor insemination, surrogacy, foster care and adoption."[20]

There is no exact data nationwide on same-sex families primarily because the U.S. Census Bureau and other national agencies do not have a common definition for what a stepfamily is. In addition, some couples do not reveal their sexual orientation in order to avoid harassment or discrimination. They could lose a job or child custody or face violence.

Seldom are same-sex couples and their children even considered stepfamilies. Rather, the stepfamily is thought to be and often portrayed as a structure of heterosexual couples, such as a biological mom, stepdad, and her children or a biological dad, stepmom, and his children.

Yet, many family researchers as well as same-sex stepfamilies themselves would like more information to help them understand their families' challenges. These are often heightened by social attitudes toward homosexual relationships. For example, consider two lesbian women (call them Jane and Susan) who marry, and Susan has a daughter from a previous heterosexual relationship. They form a stepfamily, but the women do not publicly reveal that they are a same-sex couple because of numerous protests against homosexuality in the town where they live. Susan's daughter is being bullied at school because she once befriended a gay student. Both Jane and Susan would like to talk to the school personnel about the problem, but they fear if they do so they would be exposing Susan's daughter to even more harassment.

Some other problems same-sex stepfamilies may confront include how to deal with ex-husbands or wives who strongly disapprove of gay and lesbian relation-

When stepfamilies form, they can include children in varied age groups.

ships; or how to handle the lack of support from extended family. They may also be faced with religious issues—intolerant faith organizations that want to "reform" homosexuals. Thus knowing where to get help with any kind of conflict is a concern for many same-sex stepfamilies.

Stepfamily Myths and Facts

Anyone who has read or heard fairy tales like *Cinderella, Hansel and Gretel,* and *Snow White and the Seven Dwarfs* will recall the portrayals of controlling, selfish, and evil stepmothers. The stepmother in *Cinderella* forces her stepdaughter to do all the menial work and wait on the woman's biological daughters who live like princesses. In *Hansel and Gretel,* the stepmother orders her husband to take her stepchildren into the forest and abandon them. Snow White's stepmother orders a servant to kill her stepdaughter. In such stories, the stepmother is not only filled with malice but also is jealous of her stepchildren. Usually in these tales, the victims of the stepmother's venom are young girls, but some have been boys—princes in line for a throne, for example—who run away to escape a stepmother's death plot.

Other stepfamily stereotypes are also prevalent. A stepfather may be portrayed as a molester or a demanding tyrant. Stepchildren may be shown as brats

It Happened to Max Sindell

Max Sindell, a child of multiple divorces, is the author of *The Bright Side: Surviving Your Parents' Divorce* (2007). He wrote,

My parents got divorced when I was six, and this was my dad's second divorce. (I had three half brothers from his first marriage who lived with us too.) My parents' divorce was far from amicable and they fought over my custody. Eventually, my father moved to Colorado while my mother stayed in California. I was lucky enough to get to fly back and forth by myself from the time when I was eight years old, and got to see my dad each summer. Later, when they both lived in the San Francisco Bay Area, I took the opportunity to take control of my own schedule and experimented with various ways of living in two houses at once. During all this time I also got to learn about parental dating and step-parents as both of my parents variously dated, remarried, and even divorced and married again.[b]

Sindell decided to write a book about his experiences when he was a teenager and attending the Interlochen Arts academy, a fine-arts high school, but it took several years before the book was actually published. After graduating, he enrolled in Johns Hopkins University and earned a BA degree in writing in 2007. That same year his book was published.

About his parents' multiple divorces, he said that even though they were confusing, "I was lucky enough to have my parents, brothers, and step-parents all help me with good advice. They helped me see the bright side of all these new experiences, and they helped me keep a level head and a positive perspective." In his book, he wrote, "Rather than focus on all the negatives, I realized that there are a lot of positive experiences and new opportunities that can come to us through divorce, and I wanted to share that with every other kid out there who's going through what I went through."[c]

intent on making life wretched for the family. Stereotypes of wicked stepparents and miserable stepfamilies have been part of myths from ancient times to the present. Perhaps they persist in the United States because of films and modern print renditions of folktales. Also, in spite of the many diverse family structures, the stepfamily does not meet the unrealistic expectation for the "ideal" nuclear family of mom, dad, and the biological kids. So by default the stepfamily is supposed to be deficient—less than "perfect."

However, *The Brady Bunch*, a sitcom that played from 1969 to 1974, tried to dispel the myth about dysfunctional stepfamilies by portraying a "perfect" blended family. The show itself dramatized a myth. It was about a suburban California mother, Carol, whose marriage was over; she had three daughters and remarried Mike Brady, a widower with three sons. No character on the TV show explained why Carol's previous marriage ended. Writers of the show had planned to present Carol as a divorcée. But producers declared that was unacceptable, no doubt because divorce would not fit in with the ideal family concept. So viewers either assumed Carol had divorced or that she was a widow. The show in current times is as unrealistic as the negative stereotypes of stepfamilies.

In real life, stepfamilies thrive and "are one of the predominate [*sic*] forms of family in America today," according to the Stepfamily Foundation.[21] A *Psychology Today* article written in the 1990s but reviewed in 2012 included some positive findings about stepfamilies, for example:

- Contrary to myth, stepfamilies have a high rate of success in raising healthy children. Eighty percent of the kids come out fine.
- These step kids are resilient, and a movement to study their resilience— not just their problems—promises to help more kids succeed in any kind of family, traditional or otherwise.
- The biggest source of problems for kids in stepfamilies is parental conflict leftover from the first marriage.
- Expectations about women's roles and responsibilities are at the root of many problems that develop in stepfamilies.
- Stepfamilies experience most of their troubles in the first two years.

❗ Did You Know?

People who divorce are likely to marry again, numerous reports have shown. A 2010 report from the National Center for Family & Marriage Research noted, "In 2010, the overall marriage rate was approximately 37 per 1,000." That is, "37 marriages occurred per 1,000 men and women aged 18 and older."[d] Many of these remarriages created stepfamilies, although there are no exact data. The Pew Research Center surveyed 2,691 adults in October 2010, and 42 percent said "they have at least one step relative. Three-in-ten have a step or half sibling, 18% have a living stepparent, and 13% have at least one stepchild."[e]

- After five years, stepfamilies are more stable than first-marriage families, because second marriages are happier than first marriages.
- Stepfamilies are not just make-do households limping along after loss. All members experience real gains, notably the opportunity to thrive under a happier relationship. [22]

Watch This Video!

The film *Stepmom* (1998) is a comedy-drama starring Julia Roberts (playing the stepmom, Isabel) and Susan Sarandon as the biological mother, Jackie. Others in the cast are Ed Harris, in the role of Jackie's ex-husband, Luke; Jena Malone, playing twelve-year-old Anna; and Liam Aiken as seven-year-old Ben. Although it is an older film, it is available on DVD and likely can be borrowed from local libraries.

In the story, the parents, Jackie and Luke, are divorced and Luke is dating Isabel, a young and ambitious fashion photographer. Jackie and Luke have joint custody of their two children, who not only must deal with their parents' divorce, but also with the fact that Isabel, who lives with Luke, appears to be trying to replace their mother.

As the drama unfolds, one scene after another reveals conflict. Jackie, a full-time mom, is highly critical of Isabel, who continues with her career while trying to endear herself to Anna and Ben. In one instance, Isabel takes Anna and Ben to Central Park, where she is doing a photo shoot. She is so intent on her work that she loses Ben, who has wandered away. Police find him, but Jackie is livid and vows to prevent Isabel from ever having anything to do with her children. She does whatever she can to brainwash the children against Isabel to the point where Ben offers, "Mommy, if you want me to hate her I will."

Isabel, however, does not give up and over time is able to gain the trust and goodwill of the children. That becomes crucial when Isabel learns that Jackie has been diagnosed with terminal cancer. Jackie does not tell her family about her disease, but Isabel learns the truth and helps inform the children and their dad. Slowly the two women reconcile as it is clear that Isabel is going to actually replace Jackie in her role as stepmom.

A Biblical "Stepmother"

The biblical story of Hannah is primarily a sad tale, but ends on a triumphant note. Hannah was one of Elkanah's wives and was childless; his other wife was Peninnah, who had borne numerous children. Ancient Israelites felt blessed if they had large families, so when a woman was barren she was an embarrassment. In fact, she was hardly considered worthwhile until she had children. Nevertheless, Hannah cared for Elkanah and Peninnah's children and was like a stepmother to them.

At least once a year, Elkanah took both wives and his children to the temple in Shiloh on a feast day to worship and make sacrifices. According to the New International Version of the Bible,

> Whenever the day came for Elkanah to sacrifice, he would give portions of the meat to his wife Peninnah and to all her sons and daughters. But to Hannah he gave a double portion because he loved her, and the LORD had closed her womb. Because the LORD had closed Hannah's womb, her rival kept provoking her in order to irritate her. This went on year after year. Whenever Hannah went up to the house of the LORD, her rival provoked her till she wept and would not eat. Her husband Elkanah would say to her, "Hannah, why are you weeping? Why don't you eat? Why are you downhearted? Don't I mean more to you than ten sons?"[f]

Along with Peninnah's harassment, Hannah had to endure contempt from Eli the priest, who thought she was drunk. Actually Hannah was praying intently but silently only moving her lips. She was pleading for a child. Hannah told Eli she was "deeply troubled" and was "praying here out of my great anguish and grief." Eli gave his blessings, and Hannah and the family went back home. Not long afterward, Hannah became pregnant and delivered a son named Samuel who became a priest and one of the great prophets of biblical times.

The American Psychological Association (APA) notes:

The most difficult aspect of stepfamily life is parenting. Forming a step-family with young children may be easier than forming one with adolescent children due to the differing developmental stages. . . . [R]esearch suggests that younger adolescents (age 10–14) may have the most difficult time adjusting to a stepfamily. Older adolescents (age 15 and older) need less parenting and may have less investment in stepfamily life, while younger children (under age 10) are usually more accepting of a new adult in the family, particularly when the adult is a positive influence.[23]

On its help center, APA advised stepparents to "establish a relationship with the children that is more akin to a friend or 'camp counselor,' rather than a disciplinarian. Couples can also agree that the custodial parent remain primarily responsible for control and discipline of the children until the stepparent and children develop a solid bond." Additionally, "Families might want to develop a list of household rules. These may include, for example, 'We agree to respect each family member' or 'Every family member agrees to clean up after him or herself.'"[24]

STAYING CONNECTED AND COMMUNICATING AFTER DIVORCE

"Sometimes . . . I feel I'm just loved by only my mother and that my father doesn't want to have anything to do with me."—teenager Allycia-Ashely, a child of divorce, writing in a winning essay[1]

When parents divorce, children frequently have problems communicating or staying in touch with one of the parents. In a response to an article on parental divorce on the website FamilyLobby.com, a teenage girl wrote,

> My parents are currently getting a divorce, and my dad is trying everything to keep me and my two siblings out of the loop. He thinks his three teenage children shouldn't know anything about what is going on in the divorce. He refuses to respect us enough when we beg him to let us know his side of the story. He has basically abandoned us emotionally to our mom. He's a coward in my mind now, and won't even answer my phone calls. . . . My father claims it's not our problem and we shouldn't have to worry about it, but it is our problem because it is our life that it is affecting as well. I have lost all respect for my father, and now the best male influence in my life is my younger brother who is twice the man now as my father will ever be.[2]

When a daughter's relationship with her father is damaged, the result may include emotional problems such as low self-esteem, lack of trust, and even depression. "The father-daughter relationship is by far one of the most understudied, yet there is evidence that the father's impact on his daughter's psychological well-being and identity is far-reaching," wrote clinical social worker and author

Terry Gaspard in a May 2013 blog. She added, "A daughter's sense of self, for instance, is often connected to how her father views her. While this isn't universal, a girl stands a better chance of becoming a self-confident woman if she has a close bond with her father."[3]

Gaspard also wrote about the mother-daughter connection after divorce. She pointed out that even though mothers usually have custody of children, few studies have focused on how mothers and daughters connect. "Most of what we know about this topic comes from psychologist E. Mavis Hetherington's landmark study of 1,400 divorced families over a period of thirty years," Gaspard noted. Hetherington, with co-author John Kelly, wrote *For Better or for Worse: Divorce Reconsidered* (2002). According to Gaspard, the study found that after divorce "preadolescent girls develop close supportive relationships with their mothers but that this shifts during adolescence when there is more upheaval in their lives." The study showed "there is a notable increase in conflict between adolescents and their mothers post-divorce. Given this information, it makes sense that fathers can be a good buffer between mothers and daughters if they maintain an active role in their lives."[4]

Lack of Connections

The lack of connection with both of their divorced parents is a common issue for young people who express their feelings about parental relationships after divorce. In 2003 the Children's Rights Council (CRC) sponsored a teen essay contest based on the theme, "What does 'The Best Parent Is Both Parents' mean to you?" The U.S. Congress honored three winners. One was sixteen-year-old Charles B., who wrote,

> [I]t has been particularly hard growing up from a boy to a young man. I was never one of those children who had a "camping trip with dad" or was "painting with dad." These were all things that I had to do on my own. This lack of experience still has its effects today.
>
> It still seems that even today I am the one in the household who must complete the so-called "man" tasks of the house. In doing this, it has always hurt me that I had to teach myself how to complete these jobs and I had no male figure there to guide me. The only way I ever learned was by teaching myself. Often in my self-taught lessons I have become frustrated and depressed on the whole situation. Another situation that is particularly hard for me is seeing fathers with their children all over the place. Seeing this is a very depressing sight for me, making me feel as if I have missed a part of my childhood.[5]

Another winner, fifteen-year-old Yolanda, explained in her essay that after her parents' divorce she lived with her single mom and younger brother:

[My mother] worked two jobs trying to support her family, alone. I know that my mother only wanted the best for my brother and I, but it felt like I was the mother to her son because she was always gone. As I got older, I began looking for love in other places. Like boys, thinking they could replace the neglect, pain, and hurt that I felt from my father. After awhile I figured these boys couldn't replace the feelings that I felt, only my father can. So I took my frustrations out on my schoolwork. I was getting honors in middle school, but when I went to high school, it was a complete change.[6]

Allycia-Ashely, the third winner, also spent her teen years as a child of divorce, living with a single mother and her brother. "I'm sometimes angry of the fact that I can never get in contact with my father. I'm also angry because I know my mother personally, but not my father. Sometimes I think that most of the male population doesn't care about their children."[7]

A Penn State University study published in 2008 found that connections between fathers and teens (sons as well as daughters) are harmed the most in a divorce. The reasons are varied, but mothers are usually custodial parents and more involved with young children and teenagers. According to co-author of the study, sociology Professor Alan Booth, "As kids grow, they tend to grow 'away'—toward peers, school and the world. . . . The relationship with the father declines normally, just in the natural course of things. . . . Coupled with divorce, this distancing may result in further declines in father-child closeness." Usually dad moves out of the family home. As a result a father's time with his children is limited. "It's just hard for dads to keep up," Professor Booth noted.[8]

If divorced fathers and their daughters are estranged for long periods, they are likely to have difficulty communicating. But it is not always up to the dad to make the first attempt to reconnect. Linda Nielsen, a professor of adolescent and educational psychology at Wake Forest University in Winston-Salem, North Carolina, used the analogy of a father and daughter in a leaking boat. Dad knows nothing about repairs, but his daughter is an expert at such tasks. So it appears obvious who should take the initiative. Nielsen pointed out in her book *Between Fathers and Daughters: Enriching and Rebuilding Your Adult Relationship* (2008) that "dads are often less equipped or less confident than their daughters when it comes to fixing the leaks in a relationship—or steering it back on the right course."[9] As the title suggests, the book provides advice for improving father-daughter relationships.

Staying Connected over the Miles

Staying connected is even more difficult when one of the divorced parents moves a long distance away, from New York to Alaska, for example, or from the United States to Germany. Perhaps a parent takes a new job or wants to be near extended family or to get away from an ex-spouse. In such situations, the cell phone is one of the most convenient and accessible means for staying in touch. However, adolescents across the world are using social media such as Facebook to connect with their family members, including their divorced parents. Posting photos, status updates, and links to activities or fund-raisers that children and teens are participating in for school or sports are just some of the ways to connect. Using Instagram, which was purchased by Facebook in 2010, teens and their parents can simply post photos taken with a mobile phone using interesting filters to show events that have influenced their day-to-day lives.

When using sites such as Tumblr, people can blog about anything from health to aliens and everything in between. If parents can find their children's blog and "follow" them, they can have insight into their world. Tumblr can also be used to follow trends and other hipster events. In addition, Twitter is another popular social media site that offers additional methods of communicating via personal updates, hashtags, photos, and the like. Users can tweet their events of the moment, hour, day, and so on.

E-mail and Skype are also effective in communicating via long distance, although some families may not have access to computers or may not be computer literate. If electronic communication is not available, the U.S. Postal Service is an affordable alternative to send a letter, postcard, photograph, greeting card, video, book, or congratulatory certificate.

Travel can be a major problem when long distances separate family members of divorce. Jean McBride, a licensed marriage and family therapist in northern Colorado, wrote,

When one parent becomes a long distance parent, he/she tends to have less influence on how their child is raised. Children frequently lose contact with the long distance parent's extended family, which for children is yet another significant loss. Children typically have to travel to spend time with their long distance parent. They rack up hundreds of hours of travel time either on the road or in the air. This takes them away from their friends and daily routines. It also means that they may not be able to fully participate in sports or other extracurricular activities that occur on a weekly basis. And it makes seeing the other parent a BIG DEAL, instead of a regular part of the daily round.[10]

In his book for teens, *The Bright Side*, Max Sindell recalled the many times he traveled between parents after divorce—sometimes from one state to another—but he wrote,

> If my parents hadn't divorced, I would have never known about Aspen, Colorado. I would have never learned to ski. I would have never learned to travel by myself at eight years old. I would never have had the opportunity to explore Colorado with my father. I'd have never lived in an apartment in a major city. I probably would have never ended up going to boarding school. . . . All these experiences have greatly affected my life, and I wouldn't trade them for anything.[11]

Two Books off the Shelf

Two books—one nonfiction and the other a novel—include numerous ways that children of divorce try to communicate with their biological parents and stepparents. The first book is *Split in Two: Keeping It Together When Your Parents Live Apart* (2009) by Karen Buscemi, an easy-to-read paperback, written primarily for teenagers living in two different homes after a parental divorce. Among the eight chapters is one titled "The Family Bargaining Table," which offers advice on communicating with parents. Another is "The Daily Shuffle" (going back and forth between homes). Sixteen-year-old Dani expresses a common complaint of children in split families: "I feel like I have no one place to live. My home is always moving, so I never am really at one place."[a] On the other hand, seventeen-year-old Travers notes, "One bonus to having two houses is that I have two rooms and I get double the stuff."[b]

"Your Room—And Your Other Room" is a chapter on how to make each room feel like home. "I'm Supposed to Be Where When?" is about scheduling. "The Life of an Intrepid Traveler" describes ways to pack and haul stuff from one home to the other. "Cash Control" is about earning a little money. "Parent Patrol" tells how to keep the adults on track. The final chapter, "Now What?" describes what to expect in the future and provides some positive outcomes. Comic-strip illustrations, brief comments from the author and editor, and quotes from teenagers are included.

The second book *that Summer* (lowercase *t* in *that* intended) by Sarah Dessen is a novel that was selected as an American Library Association's "Best Books for Young Adults" for 1996. It tells the story of Haven, a teenager, who feels she is a misfit because of her five-foot-eleven size and the fact that she is still growing. But she also has problems communicating with her divorced parents—her mother, who attempts to be a "swinging single," and her father, a TV sports anchor who marries Lorna Queen, a meteorologist known as the "Weather Pet." Lorna is only a few years older than Haven's sister Ashley, an engaged young adult who is twenty-one. At their father's wedding, the sisters wear pink, fluffy dresses and Haven compares the two of them, describing her sister as "a short, curvy pink rose, and I was a tall, pink straw, like something you'd plunk down in a big fizzy drink."[c]

Told from Haven's point of view, this is also a tale of a teenager's attempt to connect with her earlier and happier life. Haven recalls *that Summer* when her family was intact and they spent a week at Virginia Beach along with Ashley's boyfriend, Sumner Lee, a fun-loving fellow. Sumner is often at the family's suburban home in Lakeview. However, Ashley suddenly breaks up with Sumner, and she soon is engaged to a conservative young man whom Haven considers boring and dislikes.

But meantime she also has difficulty dealing with her father's visitation time. Once a week he takes her to lunch, but they seldom really communicate. Her father is always distracted by one or another sports enthusiast who stops by their table. One day at lunch Haven encounters Ashley's former boyfriend, Sumner, who has left college and returned to Lakeview to work as a waiter. Haven attempts to get him interested in seeing Ashley again, hoping this will help re-create that carefree summer of the past. That does not happen.

To add to the muddled father-daughter relationship, the Weather Pet announces on TV that she and Haven's father are having a baby. As the chaotic story moves forward, Haven still manages some teenage wit and wisdom, eventually realizing that she cannot bring back the past and must look forward to the future.

Communicating

Teenager Griffin Mitchell of Cardinal Newman High School in California has been able to communicate with, stay connected to, and have supportive relationships with both of his biological parents following their divorce. He wrote in a 2011 blog for the Sonoma County *Press Democrat* about his mother's remarriage:

> It was awkward at first, seeing my mother with another man and, basically, having a second father, although I never looked at him in that sense. I just saw him as a third parent and not a second dad.
>
> My father, on the other hand, remained single and tried new combinations to find the right spouse and, naturally, I always had faith he would find the right woman. Before and during my mother and father's marriage, they were best friends, and that is the way they decided to keep it even after their divorce. I benefited in pretty much every way imaginable from my parents being close. Both of them would always attend my sporting events, and they would always communicate in a friendly manner regarding raising me. When it came to which parent I spent more time with, they divided the time up evenly.[12]

Communicating "in a friendly manner," as Griffin put it, is not always easy for divorced parents and their offspring to do. In fact, just talking to parents can be difficult for children and teens who want to communicate their feelings about divorce or to just gain the attention of their parents. One user on DailyStrength.com was a male teenager in Colorado who was having trouble communicating with his divorced mother, his custodial parent. He wanted to live with his father in Utah and wrote, "I love my mother, but she doesn't seem to make us (me and my siblings) her top priority. She is always talking to or texting her friends. In the car, at home, at work. It feels like a non-stop conversation between her and her friends. She most often texts, and when she does, if me or my siblings attempt to talk to her, she completely ignores us, doesn't respond, sometimes even yells at us for interrupting her conversation." He explained that he was miserable and felt "so much more loved and supported with my dad." Advice for him from others on the website ranged from giving his situation time to heal to talking to both his parents about how he feels.[13]

If young people are frustrated because parents are too distracted to pay attention to them or not interested in talking with them, then teens may have to take the initiative. If the talk cannot be face-to-face, some teenagers use their cell phones to have a talk with their parents, whether custodial or nonresidential.

Those calls are likely to be productive when young people (whether of divorced or intact families) ask their parents for advice or share good news, according to Robert S. Weisskirch, a professor of human development at California State University in Monterey Bay. Weisskirch surveyed 196 parent-teenager pairs in 2011 to determine the types of calls made. "When the parents call and have a lot of communication around 'what are you doing?' or 'who are you with?' or when they're angry at the child and upset or scared, the kids report more conflict in the family," he reported to Roni Caryn Rabin of the *New York Times*.[14]

Sometimes conversations with parents—however they occur—can be antagonistic if family members are impatient, angry, or hurting. It is common then to lash out. But one of the most important communication skills is to "cool it," experts say. That is, take time to think about how to say something in a tone of voice that is as neutral as possible. To have an effective conversation it is also helpful to know what the topic should be: About one's feelings? About an embarrassing problem? About the need for support? About a loss?

Listening is another important skill in effective communication. During conversations, discussions, and other speech communication, most people hear what others say, but they do not necessarily really listen. Like other communication skills, listening efficiently aids in understanding and in developing relationships, which certainly are an asset when families are struggling with divorce and when stepfamilies form.

Effective listening is hindered sometimes when in conversations people are not looking at each other—the listener, for example, is glancing around, looking at his or her cell phone, or jangling car keys or coins impatiently while the other person is talking. When listeners mentally judge a speaker and prepare to attack with counterpoints, they also are setting up barriers to effective listening.

Being able to catch nonverbal cues—getting messages sent with body language—is another skill that can aid in successful communication. In conversations, much of what people "say" is nonverbal. People who cross their arms while others are talking often send the message "I'm closed to your point of view" or "I'm not listening to what you have to say." Rolling the eyes and shrugging shoulders often give the impression that the listener is dismissing what the speaker is trying to communicate.

Experts on human behavior say people usually tense their bodies when they are listening with interest. That does not mean they are rigid. Rather, they are taking a position of "forwardness" or "openness" as they listen to what is being said.

Perhaps one of the most helpful communication messages in divorcing families and stepfamilies is a hug, handclasp, or pat on the back that signals "I care." Someone who offers a comforting touch can help ease another person's physical pain or hurt feelings. However, the way people use touch gestures usually depends on their personalities and what they learned during their growing-up years. Some people may have deep feelings of concern but are unable to reach out. Others easily express caring with sympathetic touches, which is a form of communication worth developing.

Write, Revise, Repeat

Of course having a conversation is not the only way divorced parents and their children can communicate. Anyone with e-mail access can send written or text messages, although those are not good substitutes for having a talk if possible. One divorced father, Ted Rubin, put it this way in a 2012 piece for *Your Teen Mag .com*:

> Nothing can replace face-to-face interactions with my teenage daughters. Although I do social media for a living, I never communicate with them through social media. I occasionally check Facebook to see what they are doing, but the last thing they want is their dad communicating with them in a visible format. When necessary, I send texts and phone calls. Although they rarely check email, I always send one before I fly to tell them I love them (just in case), so they will always know. Our most important moments are face-to-face, when I am truly paying attention and being involved in what they do.[15]

When corresponding by e-mail, it is always a good idea to be aware that miscommunication can occur. Using all capital letters, for example, usually implies that the writer is yelling or is saying "I'm angry" or "I'm disgusted" no matter what the words themselves indicate. E-mail messages also are long lasting. Using e-mail as a communication tool is effective if a sender chooses his or her words carefully and holds off on the Send button for a bit of reflection. That means writing, reading the message, thinking about how the receiver will interpret the words, then revising them and repeating the process if necessary.

Another effective communication tool is letter writing, which is nearly an obsolete activity. In fact, according to some parents and teachers, numerous teenagers lack the skills needed to write letters or to even address envelopes. Many teens simply depend on Internet access and electronic technology to communicate. So they struggle to write a letter to apply for a job, for example, or to send a thank-you note or an apology or condolence.

In some schools, teachers conduct letter-writing projects on specific topics, such as thanking parents, whether they are divorced, separated, or married. In one project, the teacher required teens to write at least five paragraphs, first selecting "the overall tone of the letter"—serious or humorous. "The overall message . . . is to say 'thank you' . . . writing a persuasive letter to inform their parents of their gratitude" for the years the teens have been alive.[16]

Letter writing goes both ways—from parents to teens, as well as from teens to parents. Numerous websites provide suggestions for how parents can write letters or postcards to their children. Jennifer Wolf on About.com offered advice for single parents (whether divorced or unmarried) and suggested making letter writing to children a traditional event such as for birthdays or holidays. In a letter a single parent can point out positive characteristics of a child, express hope for the future, and congratulations for an accomplishment. Of course that kind of communication can be spoken as well. But a letter can be read and reread and it "communicates love, pride, and commitment beyond the power of everyday spoken words," Wolf noted.[17]

This teenager uses basic tools for communicating: writing a letter, using a pen and a pad of paper.

! Divorce Poems by Teens

One way teenagers try to communicate their sorrow and hurt because of parental divorce is through poetry. On the website BestTeenPoems.com, one teenager told of his regret for not calling his divorced and drug-addicted mom and expressing his love for her before she died. Another poem titled "Daddy" described a teenager's feeling of abandonment by her father after her parents divorced. "What Happened to My Perfect Life," "Why Did You Leave Us," and "After Divorce, Fall In Between," are titles of other poems that can be read in full on the website. Also on the site are comments from teenagers who have read the poems. Many were touched and shed tears as they related to what the poets expressed.

The importance of written messages is underscored by a California adult whose parents divorced while she was a youngster. She wrote, "I still have cards from my Mom and Dad that I have saved for years and years. When I feel sad, sometimes I pull out these cards and/or photographs and re-read them to remind myself of my own value."[18]

What Is Conflict Resolution?

Conflict resolution is a concept and method for bringing about peaceful ends to disputes. Varied methods may be used in numerous situations where people oppose one another. Counselors, therapists, lawyers, and experts on families often focus on conflict resolution when there are major arguments during or following a divorce. Not all split families experience intense conflict. But divorce usually occurs because of disagreements, irreconcilable differences, or incompatibility. After divorce, conflict also may occur when stepfamilies form. Thus family members may seek ways to resolve discord.

In conflict resolution, communication is a key element. Myriad books, articles, videos, websites, and other media describe ways to resolve conflicts through communication techniques. Here are a dozen bits of advice adapted from varied sources that apply to adults and children of divorce:

1. Talk about differences and problems whenever possible, using a reasonable and calm tone of voice.
2. Avoid the "silent treatment"—nothing is gained by refusing to communicate.

3. Try to clarify reasons for the conflict without making accusations.
4. Reject name-calling and insults.
5. Resist statements with "should have," "could have," and "ought to have." What's done is done, so nothing is gained by belaboring past actions.
6. Be a nondefensive listener; let the other person express her or his feelings or viewpoints without interrupting.
7. Show respect for other's ideas; empathize.
8. Don't monopolize a conversation or discussion.
9. Disagree without being disagreeable; avoid communicating angrily or violently.
10. Try to accept situations that cannot be changed or are beyond a family member's control, such as mishaps from the past.
11. Be complimentary whenever possible and remember the words *please* and *thank you*.
12. Get help if communication breaks down and conflict escalates; find a mediator, someone who will help both sides look at differing views objectively.

To encourage conflict resolution, courts in some states may suggest a mediator for families experiencing breakups. Mediation is a voluntary process. In divorce

Did You Know?

Most people are aware that social networking and texting are part of teenagers' daily lives. They have grown up with electronic communication. Common Sense Media, a nonprofit organization that researches child and family issues, conducted a survey in 2012 of more than 1,000 students thirteen to seventeen years old, to determine how they view their digital lives. Thirteen percent of them "strongly" agreed that they would like to "unplug sometimes" while 30 percent "somewhat agreed" with that possibility. A majority of the teens think it is valuable to have one-on-one, look-me-in-the-eye conversations with their friends. According to the survey, "Some teens get frustrated by how attached their friends and parents are to their own devices. For example, 28% of those whose parents have a mobile device say they consider their parents 'addicted' to their gadgets, and 21% of all teens say they wish their parents spent less time with their cell phones and other devices." In another finding, 8 percent of the teenagers surveyed said that social networking helped their relationships with their parents while another 7 percent thought such connections were harmful.[d]

It Happened to Rebecca Walker

Rebecca Walker experienced parental divorce early in her life, and in her adult years connections and communication with her mother have been estranged. She is the daughter of 1983 Pulitzer Prize–winning author Alice Walker (*The Color Purple)* and white Jewish civil rights attorney Melvyn Leventhal. Alice Walker and Melvyn Leventhal met while working on a voter-registration drive in Mississippi, one of the most segregated areas of the South. They married and became the state's first legal biracial union.

Rebecca was born in Jackson, Mississippi, in 1969, but in 1974 the family moved to the New York City area. Rebecca's parents divorced when she was eight years old, and she wrote about the breakup in her *New York Times* bestselling book *Black, White, and Jewish: Autobiography of a Shifting Self* (2001). Although many readers and reviewers focus on the race and cultural issues presented in the book, the memoir describes common problems that a child of divorce encounters, such as traveling between homes.

After her parents' divorce, the ex-spouses decide that Rebecca should alternate every two years, living on the East Coast with her father and then the West Coast with mother. In Rebecca Walker's book, she noted, "I am more comfortable in airports than I am in either of the houses I call, with undeserved nostalgia, Home. I am more comfortable in airports than I was in any of the eight different schools where I learned all of the things I now cannot remember. . . . I remember coming and going, going and coming. That, for me, was home." Rebecca wondered if either of her parents considered that their daughter "might have some semblance of a normal relationship with friends and family members" if she didn't have to spend her "life zigzagging the country." Their decision, she added, meant that she "has to move, change schools, shift. My father returns to the life that was expected of him, marrying a nice Jewish girl he met as a kid in summer camp, and my mother falls for a Morehouse man, an old sweetheart from her Spelman days. For them there is a return to what is familiar, safe, expected. For me there is a turning away from all of those things."[e]

Shuttling between two very different homes and two very different cultures was one of the reasons Rebecca felt like a "shifting self." She did not know who she was and struggled with her biracial self as well as with being a child of divorce. In a 2007 interview with Sharon Krum of the *Guardian*, she noted, "I was torn apart by politics as a child . . . between Zionism and black nationalism, feminism and traditional family values, Judaism and the pagan feminine divine. I no longer see the necessity of having such strong ideological beliefs that could terminate or extinguish the idea of familial or even world peace."[f]

In spite of being "torn apart," Rebecca graduated cum laude from Yale University in 1992, and later cofounded Third Wave Foundation, a nonprofit organization whose purpose has been to help women get involved in activism and leadership. She became an avid feminist and bisexual, eventually settling in Berkeley, California, with recording artist Me'shell N'degeocello, who has a son, Solomon. Me'shell and Rebecca separated, but Rebecca has helped raise Solomon.

In 2004, Rebecca gave birth to a son, Tenzin, the child of partner Choyin Rangdrol (she calls him Glen), an African American Buddhist teacher. Rebecca Walker's book *Baby Love: Choosing Motherhood after a Lifetime of Ambivalence*, published in 2007, explains the difference between raising a stepson and a biological son.

settlements, a mediator is a go-between, an impartial person who negotiates regarding such issues as child custody for minors, support payments, and travel arrangements for children. He or she facilitates the process of negotiating, but does not take sides one way or the other. The mediator, for example, makes sure each person is given an uninterrupted time to speak, and asks questions to make communication clear. Ideally, a mediator helps the parties find a solution that works well for everyone involved.

PLANNING FOR A FUTURE MARRIAGE— OR NOT

....

"Like a bust-that-booty workout, marriage is hard labor, but it can be
exceptionally rewarding if the right amount of effort is put forth."
—teenager called mcramer55 in a 2011 essay on StageofLife.com.[1]

According to many online postings, teenagers and young adults often talk about marriage. Some are eager to get married; others are cautious about or not interested in a marital future. On a 2013 online forum, BachChatForum.com (which is no longer available), young people wrote about relationships and love, and responded to a question "Do teen marriages EVER last?" GetFresh wrote, "I think teens today who get married jump the gun too quickly. They regret their decision months in after their marriage. After a while, they realize the significant other they married just isn't the same person they thought they were."[2]

On the same forum, a woman in her twenties, Monique of Ontario, Canada, noted that a teen marriage might last, but that it is "not likely. I just think adolescence is such an important time for self-discovery and determining who you want to be. Therefore, choosing a life partner at such a vulnerable and transitional period in your life seems quite counter-productive to me."[3]

Akimbo, a female college student writing about marriage on another forum, declared, "It is so hard to become truly connected to someone despite all of the new technologies being invented. I don't want a watered down conversation or perpetual small talk. I want someone who really knows me—inside and out. Someone who can take me at face value and wants to spend the rest of his life with me. When I find that, then, I will say 'I do.'"[4]

Akimbo's comment was part of an essay she submitted for a contest on StageofLife.com, a website for people in all life stages. It is "both an online journal

. . . and free writing resource built around a blogging community." Each month the site poses a question on its blog and in 2011 asked its teen and college visitors, "What is the value of marriage?" According to the website, "Over 4,520 students from all 50 US states visited the marriage writing contest page." Of those who wrote an entry, "55% of the teenagers shared a positive view about marriage, 28% had a negative view, and 17% took a neutral, unbiased, or more academic approach. In less than 30 days, over 41,500 words were uploaded to stageoflife .com as students shared their opinions and feelings about marriage." Student opinions reflected the state of their parents' marriages. "If the parents' marriage was successful, then the student viewed marriage positively; if not, then the stu-

Most Americans—whatever their ethnic or cultural background— have a positive view of marriage.

dents often resented marriage." The majority of the essays submitted all revolved around one common thread: Marriage is serious. Religion was a major factor in ideas about "the sacrament of matrimony." In addition, most students declared that marriage—a successful marriage—involves both love and commitment.[5]

Effects of Divorce on Marriage Outlooks

Parental divorce and divorces of siblings and friends often affect young adult's future relationships and marriage. Some feel betrayed by parental divorce and have no confidence in having a romantic relationship. Others fear that their future marriage will be in jeopardy because of the pattern set by their parents. As one teenage girl calling herself CC3PEP on StageofLife.com explained,

> I admit my view of marriage is jaded. My father filed for divorce before I was even born and by the time I was six, I had seen the inside of more child custody courtrooms than most people see in their lifetime. Raised by a single mother, divorced parents is "the norm" for me. When I meet other teens, I automatically assume that their parents are divorced. And why shouldn't I? Half of all children will witness the divorce of their parents. Despite everything, I still believe in the power of marriage and family. Marriage is a sacred, holy union that should only be entered into after much serious thought.[6]

In another essay on StageofLife.com, ReadingKT wrote,

> If I were ever to get married I have some rules that I must follow. As the child of a divorce I may seem cynical at times but that's just the scar left behind from a bad marriage. I want to fall in love and live a fairytale life as much as the next girl (sometimes even more so) but I think before I act. And if someday I meet the guy of my dreams I need to have a serious discussion with myself about who this guy truly is and if I would want to spend my life with him. So here come the rules: Is this guy up to my standards? I have pretty high standards at that. Explaining all my standards would be a whole new essay, so I wont go into that now. To steal my heart in the first place he must have worked really hard. But is he really the guy that I thought he was? Later on in life would he resort to violence or cheat on me? I need to closely examine this man, ask around a bit and figure out if he is really the guy for me.[7]

Stephanie Kaloi, managing editor of OffbeatFamilies.com (which was discontinued in September 2013), is married to Sean. They are adults in their twenties and both are children of divorce. Stephanie explained that her parents split up, got back together, and split up again. She wrote, "There was an incredible amount of verbal abuse (to the point where I still don't handle yelling of any kind very well), and a few instances of physical violence that taint many of the good memories I have of growing up." In her view, her experiences along with her husband's "have helped our marriage be stronger than it might be if we had both never experienced divorce in the first place—we know what to watch for, and what to try to do and not do. We entered into our marriage knowing that there would be intense lows and periods of emotional anguish, but also knowing that we were both committed to working through those times and basking in the glow of the happy times together." She added,

> I love being married to Sean, but I do not for a single instance take my marriage for granted. Neither of us are under the impression that we're the only people in the entire world that we could be happy with, but we both also hope that we remain happy with one another for a very long time. It's safe to assume that if we're in love now we probably will be next month, and hopefully next year, and we both, at this point in our lives, want to be together. That is what matters, and that is what creates a happy home for us.[8]

Cohabitation as a Choice

A type of cohabitation called "bundling" is an ancient practice and came from Europe to American colonies. Some colonial preachers thought it appropriate while others condemned it. As Bron Ingoldsby, associate professor in the School of Family Life at Brigham Young University, explained,

> A courting couple would be in bed together, but with their clothes on. With fuel at a premium, it was often difficult to keep a house warm in the evenings. Since this is when a man would be visiting his betrothed in her home, they would bundle in her bed together in order to keep warm. A board might be placed in the middle to keep them separate, or the young lady could be put in a bundling bag or duffel-like chastity bag. The best protection against sin were the parents, who were usually in the same room with them. It may not have been good enough, however, as records indicate that up to one-third of couples engaged in premarital relations in spite of the public penalties, such as being fined and whipped, that often resulted.[9]

The practice of bundling faded, but is still part of some U.S. Amish communities where it is known as "bed courtship." However, Saloma Furlong, who broke away from her Ohio Amish community and authored *Why I Left the Amish: A Memoir* (2011), wrote, "The board disappeared somewhere along the line, so bed courtship is what remains. Naturally, the temptations are very great and not all couples abstain from sex before they are married, resulting in premarital pregnancies. . . . [T]his is embarrassing for the families involved, but most often the solution is for the couple to get married."[10]

Currently *cohabitation* is a term often used for unmarried, intimate couples sharing a household. Some call it "shacking up," but most people simply say it is "living together." Others call it "trial marriage." Still others, especially the religious, call it "living in sin."

Although cohabitation once referred to heterosexual couples only, it now includes any two partners whatever their sexual orientation. Same-sex couples choose cohabitation when their union is not legally recognized where they live. Cohabiting for some couples is the preferred arrangement because they do not want the legal and social commitments of marriage, and they can reduce their living expenses. However, many lawyers urge couples to create legal cohabiting agreements that spell out the responsibilities of each person. For example, the agreement can list the duties and rights concerning the relationship, such as the percentage each will pay toward the rent or home mortgage and how property will be divided in the event that a cohabiting couple breaks up or one of them dies. Some samples for such agreements are shown in Appendix A.

In most areas of the United States, cohabiting is accepted even if it is not particularly condoned. One person wrote online, "People should try living with a person for awhile first, as that is when true colors and habits form. If you can survive living together, you will be ok."[11]

Two of the most famous film celebrities who have cohabited for years are Angelina Jolie and Brad Pitt. Jolie once noted that at age fourteen she was allowed to live with her sixteen-year-old boyfriend in her mom's house. She has had no qualms about her children doing the same thing.

In a 2013 feature for *USA Today*, Amanda Marcotte wrote, "The old-school parental claim that their offspring should never have premarital sex under their roof is yielding to a more accepting attitude about their growing and grown children's sexuality. It makes sense that this attitude would extend beyond the 21-year-old living at home to the 16-year-old enmeshed in her first relationship."[12]

The U.S. Department of Health and Human Services (HHS) reported in 2008 that a growing proportion of youth approves of cohabitation before marriage and wants to delay getting married until later in life. However, "most teens express strong general support for marriage and believe it is better to get married than stay single. Among high school seniors, most say they feel well prepared for marriage and expect to get married one day." The HHS study also found teens' attitudes toward marriage differ by gender and family background characteristics. In general, teenage boys have more positive attitudes toward marriage than teenage girls do; however, boys are more likely than girls to want to delay marriage. Teens' attitudes toward marriage are also closely linked with their family structure, with support for marriage strongest among teens who are living with both of their biological parents. Support for marriage is stronger among teens living in rural areas than it is for those living in more urban area. Even so, most teens expect to get married regardless of where they live.[13]

The National Center for Health Statistics (NCHS) of the Centers for Disease Control and Prevention has also gathered data about cohabitation. The NCHS collected data from 2006 to 2010 through in-person interviews with 22,682 women and men aged fifteen to forty-four in the household population of the United States. Forty-eight percent of women interviewed cohabited with a male partner as a first union, compared with 34 percent of women in 1995. Between 1995 and 2006–2010, the percentage of women who cohabited as a first union increased for all Hispanic origin and race groups, except for Asian women. The report showed that 70 percent of women with less than a high school diploma were more likely to cohabit as a first union, compared with 47 percent of women with a bachelor's degree or higher. After three years of living together, 40 percent of the women surveyed married their partners, and 32 percent remained intact, while 27 percent ended their relationships. Cohabitation is a common family form in the United States, and serves both as a step toward marriage and as an alternative to marriage, the report noted.[14]

Every year the National Marriage Project and the Institute for American Values at the University of Virginia in Charlottesville issue a joint report called *The State of Our Unions*. The 2012 report noted that even though "high schoolers plan to marry one day and that having a good marriage is 'extremely important' to them" there is "a rapid rise in cohabitation prior to marriage and a dramatic increase in the number of children born outside of marriage. A growing number of couples, both young and old, now live together with no plans to marry eventually."[15]

Unmarried Teens with Children— a Present and Future Problem

Whether they plan to marry or not, teenagers with children are the subjects of numerous studies and news articles. One reason for such public interest is the fact that the U.S. teen birth rate is the highest of all industrialized countries, even though the teen birth rate has been declining since the 1950s. It declined 9 per-

? What Do You Think?

With all the pontificating about the future of marriage, questions arise about the "right" age to marry. Some experts insist that if marriages are delayed until couples are in their twenties or thirties, they have a better chance of being successful. Also, if there are children, the families are likely to be more stable than families that begin when couples are teenagers.

In an April 2013 article in *Deseret News* of Salt Lake City, Utah, Lois Collins asked readers if there is a right age to marry. A San Diego, California, reader responded, "When you marry doesn't matter at all—WHO you marry is what matters. To put it another way, if you are married to the perfect person, would it matter if you had gotten married at 19 or 29 or 39? No. Likewise, if you chose the wrong person, would waiting a few years have made that person suddenly the right one? No. The reason teenage marriage divorce rates are so high isn't because of age, it's because of poor judgment and low self-esteem."[a]

Another reader from Logan, Utah, wrote, "[H]ow do we define 'right'? Attractive to you, physically? It helps. Similar goals. Personalities that complement each other. And commitment to working things out, and staying married are also very important."

A Eugene, Oregon, reader commented, "Different strokes for different folks; some people can marry at nineteen and live happily and others marry in their thirties and struggle."

From Columbus, Ohio, came this response: "I think the reason for the higher risk in the late teens/early twenties has much to do with basic human development…. I and most people I know were very different people at 18 than we were at 25. Marrying before that age increases the likelihood each partner will develop into very different people, with radically different political and religious beliefs, among other things."

What *is* the "right" age to marry? What do you think?

cent from 2009 to 2010, reaching a historic low at 34.3 births per 1,000 women aged fifteen to nineteen; the rate dropped 44 percent from 1991 through 2010, according to the Centers for Disease Control's National Center for Health Statistics.

Nevertheless teens with children are of present and future concern because they are likely to be impoverished. Other concerns include an estimated $10.9

billion of taxpayer funds that are spent annually on teen childbearing.[16] The American Academy of Child and Adolescent Psychology (AACAP) noted in 2012: "Babies born in the U.S. to teenage mothers are at risk for long-term problems in many major areas of life, including school failure, poverty, and physical or mental illness. The teenage mothers themselves are also at risk for these problems."[17]

The AACAP pointed out as well that pregnant teens have varied emotional reactions to their pregnancies:

- Some may not want their babies.
- Others may view the creation of a child as an achievement and not recognize the serious responsibilities.
- Some may keep a child to please another family member.
- Some may want a baby to have someone to love, but not understand the amount of care the baby needs.
- Many pregnant teens experience depression.
- Many do not realize that their adorable baby can also be demanding and sometimes irritating.
- Some become overwhelmed by guilt, anxiety, and fears about the future.

In addition to such reactions, "Some teenage girls drop out of school to have their babies and don't return. In this way, pregnant teens lose the opportunity to learn skills necessary for employment and self-survival as adults. School classes in family life and sexual education, as well as clinics providing reproductive information and birth control to young people, can also help to prevent an unwanted pregnancy," the AACAP said.[18]

Off the Bookshelf

At the beginning of the novel *Pregnant Pause* (2011) by Han Nolan, the sixteen-year-old narrator Eleanor (Elly) Crowe of Maine reveals what the story is about: "I waited until I was five months pregnant to tell my parents. I guess I had sort of hoped the whole thing would go away. . . . The whole reason I didn't have an abortion, besides the fact that I didn't believe I needed one because I figured I'd miscarry, is because I hate, hate, hate doctors. And, okay, my parents would more likely kill me if I had had an abortion than if I were just pregnant, because that's very against their religion."[b]

As the tale evolves, Elly admits she has been no angel, has been a runaway and drug user and spent time in juvenile detention. Elly's missionary parents are extremely upset and insist that she accompany them to Kenya where they are involved in educational and church work, or stay with her older sister and her husband in California. But after long arguments Elly adamantly refuses to go to Kenya or California. She says she is going to marry her eighteen-year-old boyfriend, Lamont (Lam) Lathrop, who is a senior in high school.

The parents on both sides reluctantly agree that the teenagers should marry, and the missionaries head for Africa while the Lathrops go to a youth summer camp called Camp WeightAway, which they own and operate. Elly and Lam go with them because they will have a place to live—a cabin on the camp grounds; Elly will be a camp counselor and Lam a lifeguard and swim coach. Conditions at the camp create a lot of obstacles for pregnant Elly, not the least of which are the Lathrops, whom she sarcastically calls MIL and FIL for mother-in-law and father-in-law. The inlaws are highly critical of Elly, especially the MIL who sometimes acts like a bully and berates Elly for getting pregnant, obviously forgetting that her son was involved as well.

Elly's narration is full of sometimes spiteful, cynical, and/or humorous thoughts and comments. She also has compassionate moments for young campers who don't seem to fit in. At the same time, she is ambivalent about being a mom, and Lam is questioning his role as a father. And the two are not sure they should have married or even that they love each other. Meanwhile both families argue over who should have custody of the baby, who is eventually born by cesarean section and has Down syndrome. Then everyone wants Elly to place her baby, Emma Rose, for adoption. No one—not her mother and father, her sister, her in-laws, her so-called husband, her friends—wants the responsibility of a mentally disabled child. Elly feels totally abandoned. But at the end, there is an unexpected person willing to give Elly and Emma Rose a home and a job.

It Happened to Bristol Palin

At the age of seventeen, Bristol Palin of Wasilla, Alaska, was unmarried and pregnant—not an unusual circumstance for today's teenagers. But her pregnancy became national news because it was announced while her mother, former Alaska governor Sarah Palin, was campaigning as the Republican vice-presidential nominee in 2008. The former governor's political stances are well known—she has been against abortion and in favor of abstinence-only sex education.

Bristol and her high school boyfriend, Levi Johnston, planned to marry and twice set the date. But both times they called off the wedding. After their son, Tripp, was born in December 2008, Bristol as a single mom became active in teen pregnancy prevention, which seemed ironic to some observers since she had once noted that abstinence was unrealistic for teenagers. However, she hoped abstaining from sex would become an option for young people her age because that is the only infallible way to prevent pregnancy.

Since 2009, Bristol has been a spokesperson for the National Campaign to Prevent Teen and Unplanned Pregnancy and an ambassador for the Candie's Foundation, a nonprofit organization that conducts educational campaigns about the consequences of teen pregnancy. Because of her advocacy, *People* magazine featured Bristol in a 2009 photo spread and on the cover. However, critics were quick to speak out. Bonnie Fuller, editor-in-chief of HollywoodLife.com, wrote in a blog that the magazine's "photos, might as well be titled, 'I'm 18, a mom and HOT . . . and you can be too!' There's not one photo of an exhausted, haggard, harried, unkempt-looking Bristol, reeling under the enormous responsibilities of raising an infant, working part-time—which she is—and hoping to somehow continue her studies. Instead, Bristol appears tanned, rested and already fitting back into her skintight jeans."[c]

Bristol's public appearances since the birth of Tripp have included a brief role in one episode of *The Secret Life of the American Teenager* in 2010, interviews on many TV talk shows, several *Dancing with the Stars* competitions, and appearances in the reality show *Bristol Palin: Life's a Tripp*, documenting her life as a single mother. She has received lucrative payments for her appearances.

In 2012, Bristol became engaged to a pipeline worker Giacinto Paoletti; both were in their twenties. But she declared that she had no intention of having sexual relations with Giacinto until they were married. However, Bristol bought a house in Wasilla, and she and Giacinto moved into it together. At the time, she said her future plans included working for nonprofits to prevent teen pregnancy.[d]

Staying Single

From teenagers to people in their twenties and thirties to women and men over fifty years old, staying single is an option they choose. In other words they are divorced or widowed, or they have never married and do not plan to marry now or in the future. But it is no easy feat to remain single in a society that values marriage and pressures young women especially to find the "right" guy and be part of a couple. In fact, Kim Gamble, a single woman in her mid-thirties, reports on *MarieClaire.com* that her father sent her a subscription for the dating website eHarmony for her birthday. She was shocked because her father had always complimented her on her independence. Gamble writes, "Suddenly, it felt like his support was waning. The eHarmony message might as well have read, 'Guess what? Your dad is sick of pretending your lifestyle makes him comfortable. Can you get it together and get married already so he can relax? Is that really too much to ask?'"[19]

In many U.S. cultures and around the world the social expectation for women is to marry, have children, and care for the household. But that has been changing in the United States over the years as people choose singlehood: "Almost 50 percent of the 311 million people in the United States live alone," according to a *New York Times* 2012 report.[20]

In 2012, author Elizabeth Weil interviewed New York University's sociology professor Eric Klineberg about the U.S. trend of living alone. Klineberg is the author of *Going Solo: The Extraordinary Rise and Surprising Appeal of Living Alone* (2012). In the *New York Times* interview, he told Weil that "unlike 50 years ago, today we cycle in and out of different living arrangements: we live alone, then we live with a partner, we live alone again, we shack up with someone again. At certain points in modern lives, living alone is the more desirable state." Some analysts contend that people who prefer to live alone are self-centered, selfish, and antisocial. But Klineberg disagrees. In living alone, he sees positives such as "a way to gain freedom and experience." In his view, those who live solo still "care about other people. What's shifted is that we've learned we have to know how to take care of ourselves."[21]

Staying Married

When social psychologists, family researchers, journalists, and others interview people who have been married for decades, they frequently ask what the couples' secrets are. Along with maintaining a loving and intimate relationship, what other factors keep their marriage together? Commitment is a common reply. Supporting one another, communicating effectively, having a sense of humor, being friends, sharing interests, and having fun together are other responses. Long-term marriages also are facilitated when couples trust each other, are loyal, and agree about finances—have the same views about spending and saving.

Some long-married couples say they may argue, but then drop the controversial topic and turn their attention to something else. But what if they have heated arguments over their religious or political beliefs? Such disagreements can eventually cause partners to split, although that doesn't have to be the case. Consider TV pundits and political strategists James Carville, a staunch Democrat, and Mary Matalin, a staunch Republican. The long-married couple manage their political differences with humor and agreeing to disagree. In a 2009 interview published in the *Los Angeles Times*, the two responded to a question: "How can [you] two disagree so much and get along?" Their response:

Carville: I don't have a position on anything domestically. So I just say yes, and then go on and do it. I mean it. I would say the three ingredients to successful marriage is surrender, capitulation and retreat. If you've got those three things . . .

Matalin: Spoken like a true liberal. What a martyr. Faith, family and good wine. That's how we do it.[22]

Other celebrity couples who have been married long term make news when they celebrate their anniversaries. Those who have been married more than twenty years include Tom Hanks and Rita Wilson, Michael J. Fox and Tracy Pollan, Denzel and Pauletta Washington, John Travolta and Kelly Preston, Warren Beatty and Annette Benning, Iman and David Bowie, Bono and Ali Hewson, Jamie Lee Curtis and Christopher Guest, Kevin Bacon and Kyra Sedgwick, Danny DeVito and Rhea Perlman (who separated for five months in 2013 but reconciled). What keeps them together? No particular component, but according to a 2013 article in *Parade*, having fun and enjoying each other is one factor. Another is talking to one another a lot. Working at keeping the marriage together is still another aspect of celebrity intact unions.[23]

Karl Pillemer, professor of human development at Cornell University, writes about aging-related issues, including long-term marriage. In a 2013 article on *HuffingtonPost.com*, he pointed out that people commonly believe that in romantic relationships "opposites attract." But, he asked, do they live "happily ever after?" He answered his own question:

I've asked over 500 people married 40, 50 and more years what is most important for a long and happy marriage. To my surprise, their advice was nearly unanimous: Opposites may attract, but they don't usually make for

Watch This Flick!

My Big Fat Greek Wedding (2002), which was released on DVD in 2003, is a romantic comedy that dramatizes how Greek American Toula Portokalos (Nia Vardalos) plans for her future marriage. It is a story of trying to bring together two diverse cultures through a couple's marital union. Toula runs into complications because of her Greek family's intense objections to her choice for a husband.

In the film, Toula lives in a Greek community in Chicago and is considered a "spinster" because she is thirty and unmarried. She works in her father's restaurant, the Dancing Zorba. But she hopes to do something else with her life and eventually, with the help of her mother, takes computer classes and manages a travel agency owned by her aunt. During this time she meets Ian Miller (John Corbett), a high school English teacher who is not Greek and, horror of horrors, is Anglo Protestant. They date secretly but her family learns about Ian. Toula's father Gus (Michael Constantine), the patriarch, is incensed—crazed. He insists Toula should marry a nice Greek boy and have Greek babies.

But Toula and Ian are in love and decide to marry, although Toula at times is torn because of her father's objections. Ian for his part tries to find a way to get Gus to accept him into the family. A solution comes when Ian agrees to be baptized in the Greek Orthodox Church. That in effect makes him "Greek."

The story revolves around Gus learning to accept Ian and Ian learning how to fit into Toula's large Greek family, including Toula's mother, brother, and an aged grandmother who often wanders from the Portokalos home. The extended family— aunts, uncles, and cousin—seem ever-present as they appear in the restaurant, and at every festive occasion. Then there is the difficulty bringing Ian's conservative, rather "stuffy" parents in what to them is a confusing situation. When they are invited to the Portokalos home for a first meeting, the entire Portokalos clan is there. The scenes—the chaos, comedy, satire, and family interactions—are authentic, according to the film's star Nia Vardalos, who wrote the script based on memories of her own Greek American upbringing.

great and lasting marriages. Based on their long experiences both in and out of romantic relationships, the fundamental lesson is this: *You are much more likely to have a satisfying marriage for a lifetime when you and your mate are fundamentally similar* [his emphasis]. And if you're very different, the elders warn although that marriage can work, is likely to be much more difficult.[24]

Arranged Marriages

While most young people in the United States choose whom they will marry, some do not have that option. Their parents arrange their future marriage, a custom usually practiced by people of South Asian cultures—Hindu, Muslim, and Sikh communities in the United States. Ultra-Orthodox Jews also may arrange their children's marriages. Some of these unions are successful; others fall apart.

Lani Santo works with people in arranged marriages. Santo is executive director of Footsteps, a New York City organization founded in 2003 to help individuals in arranged marriages (particularly those in Ultra-Orthodox and Hasidic Jewish communities) who want to be part of secular society. She explained,

Many people are truly happy with the life plan laid before them and love the communal element of their everyday lives. If they don't feel a need to assert strong opinions, they can usually stay married. Others give in, rather than break up their families. Problems arise when someone is intellectually curious, has questions or is highly individualistic. If they question community values, have issues around their sexual identity, or have been abused or know someone who has been abused, they may need to speak out or leave.[25]

Omi Iqbal, a Pakistani American living in suburban Atlanta, Georgia, talked about arranged marriage with *Latitude News*. She said, "I was hoping I'd find Prince Charming on my own. But my parents always told me I'd have an arranged marriage. I accepted that, because that's what I was told. The concept of having a choice was alien to me." Her parents decided that Omi, age sixteen, should be engaged to a thirty-two-year-old man. They married when Omi was eighteen years old. According to the news story, "Omi says her husband was controlling, inconsiderate, and abusive to her son." She eventually separated from her husband and had to find a way to support herself and three children without any help from her father and mother, who blame her for the breakup.[26]

Many Americans believe that an arranged marriage is the same as a forced marriage, citing a U.S. State Department definition that declares a forced marriage is "one entered into without full consent and under duress where the individual has no right to choose a partner or ability to say no."[27] However, according to Hena Zuberi, editor-in-chief of MuslimMatters.com, arranged and forced marriages are two different entities. She wrote,

> Arranged marriages are the cultural norm for (many) Muslims across the world. Men and women who are ready to get married may meet their future spouse through family or friends. Since, generally, Muslims do not "date" in the popular Western cultural sense, many couples look to arranged marriages as a means to wedded bliss. The expectation is that the seed for love is planted and will continue to bloom after the marriage. Before any potential candidates are considered, families as a unit decide the values and characteristics that potential spouses should have so the couple have a satisfying life together.[28]

Heather M. Heiman, project manager of *Forced Marriage Initiative* and public policy attorney for the Tahirih Justice Center with headquarters in the Washington, D.C., area, noted that "the line between forced and arranged [marriage] is often fuzzy and straddles a host of related issues including child marriage, domestic abuse, human trafficking, and cultural and religious autonomy. . . . Forced marriage is an increasingly hidden issue in this country. But it isn't new. We have the term shotgun wedding. Where do you think that comes from?" (The term applies to a couple being forced at gunpoint to marry because of an unplanned pregnancy.) She explained that a Tahirih investigation released in 2012 found that "forced marriages occur everywhere, hitting people of all social classes and ethnic and religious backgrounds."[29]

Future of Marriage and Divorce

Academics write books about future marriages and divorces. People post blogs on the Internet about new types of relationships and family structures and whether they will exist in the future. Clergy in many religions discuss the future of marriage. In public debates, there are pro and con arguments about whether monogamy is really necessary and what will occur in the next decades for same-sex marriages, single-parent families, stepfamilies, cohabiting couples, teen marriages, and multiple marriages (and divorces). No one can predict exactly what the future holds, but some likely scenarios follow:

- Laws in some states that ban same-sex marriages and are being challenged in courts could once again be appealed to the U.S. Supreme Court.

- Same-sex marriages will become more common.
- Cohabitation will continue to be an option for some first unions.
- More marriages will be delayed until couples are in their twenties or thirties.
- Many groups will carry on programs to prevent divorce.
- Divorce pledges (contracts regarding property ownership if a married couple splits) may become common.
- As it does currently, economics will play an important role in whether people marry or divorce.

Perhaps the last word should come from young people who presented their opinions about future marriage and divorce. In posts on the former BachChatForum.com, they sometimes wrote about the subject. In June 2013 posts, for example, some were emphatic that they do not plan a future marriage. A contributor called athletictypist wrote,

I don't ever see [marriage] in my future. I enjoy the flexibility in my life. It may be selfish, but I'm not the type who likes to live for other people. I want to do what I want to do when I want to do it. In a relationship and especially a marriage, there are many rules that I know I would never follow. Also if you throw in kids, that's a whole other story. I don't want to be responsible for anyone but myself. It'd be unfair of me to make a commitment when I know I have no intention on keeping it. I never would want to intentionally hurt someone.[30]

Another contributor, AnnaU93, a twenty-year-old woman, declared that she does not "want to rush into things and I definitely want my partner to feel like divorce shouldn't be an option because if you are getting married you are getting into a huge commitment as well. I hope I meet someone with my values and morals and overall views on life in the near future!"[31]

Zeniquez, another woman who posted on BachChatForum.com, noted,

Right now I am single but I definitely desire to be married in the future. The challenge as usual, is always finding that right person that you would want to make a life long commitment to be with. Some persons may view marriage as a "mere formality" and assert that an unmarried couple may have just as awesome a relationship. In my opinion, I honestly view the institution of marriage as a truly beautiful thing which makes a relationship even more special. It totally takes it to a whole new level. I find that we often let past relationships bring us down and hinder us from trusting our future partners, and that is sometimes the reason why we are afraid to commit to marriage and take such a big step.[32]

One more contributor, EdenSB, a twenty-six-year-old male, wrote, "I don't want to marry any time soon, but I would like to at some point in the distant future. I'd have to really love that person though and would have had to live with them beforehand for a long time to make sure."[33]

So to paraphrase the lyrics of an old song: Love and marriage *do* go together. That is, if a person finds the right partner, at the right age, at the right place, at the right time, and for the right reasons. And a couple on the verge of marriage determines what "right" means.

Appendix: Sample Nonmarital Cohabitation Agreement

Articles describing the importance of protecting legal rights in cohabiting arrangements can be found on numerous websites such as http://www.us legalforms.com/cohabitation/ and http://www.ilrg.com/forms/cohab-agreement .html. These sites also provide forms for cohabiting agreements. The following is a sample adapted from various websites. (For additional protection, agreements should be witnessed or if questionable, presented to a legal representative for an opinion.)

Nonmarital Cohabitation Agreement
This Agreement is made by and between_____ (first party) and _____ (second party). The parties are residing with each other at_____ (address), have been doing so since_____ (date), and intend to continue living together in this arrangement. The parties each enter into this Agreement voluntarily. To define each party's property rights and liabilities during their joint residency, the parties agree:

1. The joint residency of the parties shall in no way cause the parties to be married, by common law or any other legal means.
2. This Agreement consists solely of the mutual promises herein contained during the course of the parties' joint residency.
3. Each party agrees to act with good faith and fair dealing toward the other in the management of their joint property and in all other aspects of this Agreement.
4. Jointly approved living expenses shall be apportioned between the parties as follows:
    The first party shall contribute _____ % per month; the second party shall contribute _____% per month.
5. Each party shall keep the following as their own separate property, which shall not be subject to division at the termination of this Agreement:
    a. Individual earnings, salary or wages acquired before or after the execution of this Agreement;

    b. Individual gifts, bequests, devises or inheritances acquired before or after the execution of this Agreement;

    c. All property, real or personal, owned by a party at the date of execution of this Agreement;

    d. All income or proceeds derived from the above properties.

6. All property acquired by the parties jointly with joint resources while this Agreement is in effect, shall be considered joint property of the parties with each party possessing the percentage of ownership described above in paragraph number 4.

7. If this Agreement or the joint residency is terminated, all jointly owned property shall be divided among the parties according to their pro rata share listed above in paragraph number 4.

8. This Agreement is effective on the date of execution and remains in effect until termination.

9. Either party may terminate this Agreement at any time by written notice to either party, or extinction of the joint residency by either party, or death of either party.

10. It is the intent of the parties that this Agreement be the complete agreement between the parties regarding their joint residency. This Agreement shall only be modified by a writing executed by both parties.

11. Should any provision of this Agreement be held invalid, void, or otherwise unenforceable, it is the intent of the parties that the remaining portions shall nevertheless continue in full force and effect.

12. This Agreement shall be governed by and in accordance with the laws of the State of _____.

Signed _____, 20____.

_____

Signature of First Party

_____

Signature of Second Party

_____

Signature of Witness

_____

Signature of Witness

Helpful Resources

Alcohol and Other Drug Abuse

Al-Anon and Alateen
Al-Anon Family Group Headquarters, Inc is a place to find support groups for family members of alcoholics.
1600 Corporate Landing Parkway
Virginia Beach, VA 23454-5617
Telephone: (757) 563-1600
www.al-anon.org/

Al-Anon Family Group Headquarters (Canada) Inc.
275 Slater Street, Suite 900
Ottawa ON K1P 5H9
(613) 723-8484

Alcoholics Victorious is a program of "Christians in Recovery."
P.O. Box 4422
Tequesta, FL 33469
alcoholicsvictorious.org/acoa.html

American Council for Drug Education is a program of Phoenix House, a non-profit provider of alcohol and drug abuse services in eleven states.
Addresses vary by state
(888) 286-5027
www.acde.org

Community Anti-Drug Coalitions of America has a mission to strengthen the capacity of community coalitions to create and maintain safe, healthy, and drug-free communities globally.
625 Slaters Lane Suite 300
Alexandria, VA 22314
(800) 542-2322
www.cadca.org

D.A.R.E. stands for Drug Abuse Resistance Education and is a program that helps youth gain the skills they need to avoid involvement in drugs, gangs, and violence.
P.O. Box 512090
Los Angeles, CA 90051-0090
(800) 223.3273 or (310) 215.0575
www.dare.com

National Association for Children of Alcoholics is a nonprofit organization working on behalf of children of alcohol and drug dependent parents.
10920 Connecticut Ave, Suite 100
Kensington, MD 20895
(888) 554-2627 or 301-468-0985
www.nacoa.org/

National Institute on Drug Abuse for Teens is a program of the National Institutes of Drug Abuse and educates adolescents ages eleven through fifteen (as well as their parents and teachers) on the science behind drug abuse.
National Institute on Drug Abuse
National Institutes of Health
6001 Executive Boulevard, Room 5213
Bethesda, MD 20892-9561
(800) 662-4357 or (301) 443-1124
www.teens.drugabuse.gov

Too Smart to Start is a public education initiative sponsored by the Substance Abuse and Mental Health Services Administration within the U.S. Department of Health and Human Services.
Substance Abuse and Mental Health Services Administration
Center for Substance Abuse Prevention/Too Smart to Start
1 Choke Cherry Road
Rockville, MD 20857
(301) 407-6798 or (866) 419-2514
www.toosmarttostart.samhsa.gov

Divorce

The Divorce Center is a nonprofit organization comprised of volunteer attorneys, mediators, psychotherapists, career counselors, mortgage professionals, and certified divorce financial advisers, whose mission is to make divorce civil and less traumatic, especially for the children.

Riverside Center
275 Grove St., Building 2, Suite 400
Newton, MA 02466
(888) 434-8787
www.divorcenter.org/

Lambda Legal is a national organization committed to achieving full recognition of the civil rights of lesbians, gay men, bisexuals, transgender people, and those with HIV.
120 Wall Street, 19th Floor
New York, NY 10005-3904
(212) 809-8585
www.lambdalegal.org/

National Association of Counsel for Children is an organization of individuals who provide legal and social work help in the areas of divorce, custody, abuse, neglect, termination of parental rights, foster care, adoption, and delinquency.
13123 E. 16th Avenue, B390
Aurora, CO 80045
(303) 864-5324 or (888) 828-6222
http://www.naccchildlaw.org/

National Center for Lesbian Rights is an organization that advances the civil and human rights of lesbian, gay, bisexual, and transgender people and their families through litigation, legislation, policy, and public education.
870 Market Street, Suite 370
San Francisco, CA 94102
(415) 392-6257
www.nclrights.org/

Suicide Prevention

American Foundation for Suicide Prevention is national not-for-profit organization dedicated to preventing suicide through research, education, and advocacy, and to reaching out to people with mental disorders and those impacted by suicide.
120 Wall Street
29th Floor
New York, NY 10005
(888) 333-2377 or (212) 363-3500
http://www.afsp.org/

National Organization for People of Color against Suicide addresses the issue of suicide prevention and intervention, specifically in communities of color; its primary focus and mission is to increase suicide education and awareness.
P.O. Box 75571
Washington, D.C. 20013
(866) 899-5317 or (202) 549-6039
http://www.nopcas.com/

SAVE stands for Suicide Awareness Voices of Education and is a national not-for-profit organization dedicated to suicide prevention through public awareness and educational programs.
8120 Penn Ave. S., Suite 470
Bloomington, MN 55431
(952) 946-7998
http://www.save.org/

Notes

Chapter 1

1. Creigh, "My Divorce Story," DivorceandTeens.weebly.com, n.d., http://divorceandteens .weebly.com/my-divorce-story2.html (accessed January 15, 2014).
2. Hope Yen, "United States Divorce Rate: 2009 Census Report Reveals Startling Marriage Trends," *HuffingtonPost.com*, August 25, 2011, http://www.huffingtonpost.com/2011/08/25/ united-states-divorce-rat_n_935938.html (accessed January 15, 2014).
3. Interview questions answered via e-mail to the author, June 22, 2013.
4. Katie, "Poem about Divorce," FamilyFriendPoems.com, June 2011, http://www.family friendpoems.com/poem/poem-about-divorce-through-the-eyes-of-a-child (accessed November 14, 2013).
5. Debbie B. Riley, "When Parents Divorce," AdoptiveFamilies.com, n.d., http://www .adoptivefamilies.com/articles.php?aid=1778/ (accessed October 18, 2013).
6. Jessica Bennett, "D Is for Divorce: *Sesame Street* Tackles Another Touchy Subject," *Time*, December 10, 2012, http://healthland.time.com/2012/12/10/d-is-for-divorce-sesame-street -tackles-another-touchy-topic/print/ (accessed January 15, 2014).
7. See *Little Children, Big Challenges: Divorce*, SesameStreet.org, n.d., http://www.sesamestreet .org/parents/topicsandactivities/toolkits/divorce (accessed February 7, 2013).
8. See http://www.cdc.gov/nchs/fastats/divorce.htm; also http://www.cdc.gov/nchs/nvss/ marriage_divorce_tables.htm (accessed January 16, 2014).
9. Alison Aughinbaugh, Omar Robles, and Hugette Sun, U.S. Bureau of Labor Statistics, "Marriage and Divorce: Patterns by Gender, Race, and Educational Attainment," *Monthly Labor Review*, October 2013, http://www.bls.gov/opub/mlr/2013/article/marriage-and-divorce -patterns-by-gender-race-and-educational-attainment.htm#top (accessed January 14, 2014).
10. Ashley Reich, "Divorce Rate by State: How Does Your State Stack Up?" *HuffingtonPost.com*, September 9, 2013, http://www.huffingtonpost.com/2013/09/05/divorce-rate_n_3869624 .html (accessed January 14, 2014).
11. Carma Haley, "Teens Discuss Marriage and Divorce," Family.com, n.d., http://family .go.com/parenting/pkg-teen/article-781286-teens-discuss-marriage-and-divorce-t/ (accessed February 14, 2013).
12. Amy Bushatz, "Military Divorce Rate Down Slightly in 2012," Military.com, January 23, 2013, http://www.military.com/daily-news/2013/01/23/military-divorce-rate-down-slightly -in-2012.html?comp=700001075741&rank=2 (accessed February 8, 2013).
13. Cathy Meyer, "Three Major Causes of Divorce," About.com, n.d., http://divorcesupport .about.com/od/isdivorcethesolution/a/Three-Major-Causes-Of-Divorce.htm (accessed February 8, 2013).
14. Jennifer F. Bender, "Is a Divorce Decree Supposed to Be Signed by the Petitioner & the Respondent?" LegalZoom.com, n.d., http://info.legalzoom.com/divorce-decree-supposed -signed-petitioner-respondent-21623.html (accessed February 9, 2013).

15. Sue Carlton, "Coming Together to Get a Divorce," *Tampa Bay Times*, September 21, 2013, p. 1B.

16. Belinda Luscombe, "Latchkey Parents," *Time*, September 26, 2011, http://www.time.com/time/magazine/article/0,9171,2093312,00.html (accessed February 13, 2013).

17. Bari Zell Weinberger, "Divorce and Devotion: How Does Religion Factor in Splits?" *HuffingtonPost.com*, August 3, 2012, http://www.huffingtonpost.com/bari-zell-weinberger-esq/divorce-and-devotion-is-f_b_1729395.html (accessed February 12, 2013).

18. United States Conference of Catholic Bishops, "Church Teachings Divorce," ForYourMarriage.org, n.d., http://foryourmarriage.org/catholic-marriage/church-teachings/divorce/ (accessed February 12, 2013).

19. Matt Vande Bunte, "Ethics and Religion Talk by Rabbi David Krishef: Jewish, Christian and Muslim Views on Divorce," *MLive.com* (blog), December 11, 2012, http://blog.mlive.com/grpress/opinion_impact/print.html?entry=/2012/12/ethics_and_religion_talk_jewis.html (accessed January 16, 2014).

20. Vande Bunte, "Ethics and Religion Talk."

21. Vande Bunte, "Ethics and Religion Talk."

22. The Book of Mormon, 2 Nephi 12:32.

23. Jayaram V., "Divorce in Hinduism," HinduWebsite.com, n.d., http://www.hinduwebsite.com/hinduism/h_divorce.asp (accessed February 12, 2013).

24. Amish America, "Can Amish Get Divorced," n.d., http://amishamerica.com/can-amish-get-divorced/ (accessed February 12, 2013).

25. Bahá'í Topics, "Marriage and Family Life," n.d., http://info.bahai.org/article-1-6-4-1.html (accessed October 20, 2013).

26. Anne Kass, "Religion Is a Worry for Kids in Divorce," AllLaw.com, n.d., http://www.alllaw.com/articles/family/child_custody/article34.asp (accessed January 16, 2014).

27. Anonymous, "Divorce: Child Custody and Religion," FindLaw.com, n.d., http://family.findlaw.com/child-custody/divorce-child-custody-and-religion.html (accessed February 15, 2013).

a. Bigmiki139, *Torn Apart*, uploaded June 21, 2009, http://www.youtube.com/watch?v=S8OUK_BrA10 (accessed October 19, 2013).

b. Evalyn G. Ursua, "Why the Philippines Needs a Divorce Law," PositivelyFilipino.com, February 1, 2013, http://positivelyfilipino.com/magazine/2013/2/why-the-philippines-needs-a-divorce-law (accessed June 20, 2013); Also see OMGFacts.com, "Divorce Is Still Illegal in Two Countries," n.d., http://www.omg-facts.com/Sex/Divorce-Is-Still-Illegal-In-Two-Countrie/41984 (accessed February 10, 2013).

Chapter 2

1. PBS.org, "Nelly Bly," n.d., http://www.pbs.org/wgbh/amex/world/peopleevents/pande01.html (accessed April 22, 2013).

2. See Bible Gateway, "Law Concerning Divorce," n.d., http://www.biblegateway.com/passage/?search=Deuteronomy+24&version=NKJV (accessed October 21, 2013); italics in the original.

3. Glenda Riley, *Divorce: An American Tradition* (Oxford and New York: Oxford University Press, 1991), 12.

4. Mary Ann Mason, "Divorce and Custody," *Encyclopedia of Children and Childhood in History and Society*, n.d., http://www.faqs.org/childhood/Co-Fa/Divorce-and-Custody.html (accessed March 26, 2013).

5. See http://www.coursehero.com/file/1283826/Hist-210-New-York-Run-Away-Wife-Ads/ (accessed January 10, 2014); also http://faculty.history.umd.edu/CLyons/Hist%20210%20New%20York%20Run%20Away%20Wife%20Ads.pdf (accessed January 10, 2014).

6. Elizabeth Cady Stanton, Susan B. Anthony, and Matilda Joslyn Gage, eds., "Emily Collins' Reminiscences," *History of Woman Suffrage*, Gutenberg.org, n.d., pp. 88–89, http://www.gutenberg.org/files/28020/28020-h/28020-h.htm (accessed March 27, 2013).

7. Eleanor H. Porter, *Mary Marie*, 1920 (Project Gutenberg e-book), http://www.gutenberg.org/cache/epub/11143/pg11143.html (accessed April 19, 2013).

8. Shirley Blackburn correspondence with the author, received April 1, 2013. Subsequent information about Blackburn's family comes from this correspondence.

9. See DivorceLawInfo.com, "California Divorce," n.d., http://www.divorcelawinfo.com/states/ca/california.htm (accessed April 14, 2013).

10. Glenda Riley, *Divorce: An American Tradition* (Oxford and New York: Oxford University Press, 1991), 164.

11. W. Bradford Wilcox, "The Evolution of Divorce," *National Affairs*, Fall 2009, pp. 81–82, http://www.nationalaffairs.com/publications/detail/the-evolution-of-divorce (accessed April 14, 2013).

12. Staal, *The Love They Lost: Living with the Legacy of Our Parents' Divorce* (New York: Delta/Random House, 2001), 56.

13. Staal, *The Love They Lost*, 2.

14. Elizabeth Marquardt, with a foreword by Judith Wallerstein, *Between Two Worlds: The Inner Lives of Children of Divorce* (New York: Crown Publishers, 2005), 31.

15. Marquardt, *Between Two Worlds*, 16.

a. Sue Macy, with foreword by Linda Ellerbee, *Bylines: A Photobiography of Nellie Bly* (Washington, D.C.: National Geographic Childrens Books, 2009), 15.

b. PBS.org, "Nelly Bly."

c. Bruce Bower, "Families in Flux," *ScienceNews.org*, November 29, 2012, http://www.sciencenews.org/view/feature/id/346695/description/Families_in_Flux (accessed April 14, 2013); print edition *Science News*, December 15, 2012, p. 16.

Chapter 3

1. Anonymous, "Divorce," *TeenInk.com*, April 29, 2013, http://www.teenink.com/nonfiction/personal_experience/article/433415/Divorce/ (accessed May 12, 2013).

2. DesolationRow, "Completely Blindsided," ExperienceProject.com, July 18, 2011, http://www.experienceproject.com/stories/Have-Divorced-Parents/1676117 (accessed April 25, 2013).

3. Blairwardolf, "Hating Divorce," ExperienceProject.com, November 26, 2012, http://www.experienceproject.com/stories/Have-Divorced-Parents/2753086 (accessed April 25, 2013).

4. Taylor1212, "I Never Thought It Could Happen to Me," ExperienceProject.com, February 12, 2013, http://www.experienceproject.com/stories/Have-Divorced-Parents/2951369 (accessed June 22, 2013).

5. Rareyes3, "Any Late Teens with Divorcing Parents?" ExperienceProject.com, June 3, 2011, http://www.experienceproject.com/groups/Have-Divorced-Parents/forum/ANY-LATE-TEENS-WITH-DIVORCING-PARENTS/40773 (accessed May 15, 2013).

6. Karen Fanning, "Dealing with Divorce: Esi Abercrombie's Mom and Dad Split Up Seven Years Ago, but the Demise of Her Parents' Marriage Hasn't Brought Her Down," *Scholastic Choices*, October 2011, p. 8.

7. Annie Carter, "Coping with Divorce: One Teen's Story," *YourTeenMag.com*, January 28, 2012, http://yourteenmag.com/2012/01/teenagersa-and-divorce/ (accessed May 1, 2013).

8. Lara G., "Views from a Child of Divorced Parents," *TeenInk.com*, n.d., http://www.teenink.com/nonfiction/all/article/9846/Views-From-A-Child-Of-Divorced-Parents/ (accessed May 5, 2013).

9. Joanne H., "Divorce," *TeenInk.com*, n.d., http://teenink.com/nonfiction/all/article/9212/Divorce/ (accessed May 12, 2013).

10. Joanna Moorhead, "Children and Divorce: 'I Just Want To Know Why They Broke Up,'" *TheGuardian.com*, August 31, 2013, http://www.theguardian.com/lifeandstyle/2013/aug/31/children-divorce-separated-documentary-olly-lambert (accessed November 22, 2013).

11. Max Sindell, *The Bright Side: Surviving Your Parents' Divorce* (Deerfield Beach, FL: Health Communications, 2007), xiii.

12. Laura Andrzejewski, correspondence with the author, July 12, 2013.

13. Joseph Nowinski, PhD, "Helping Children Survive Divorce: The Myth of the Mature Teen," *HuffingtonPost.com*, September 12, 2011, http://www.huffingtonpost.com/joseph-nowinski-phd/helping-children-survive-_2_b_947290.html (accessed April 24, 2013).

14. David Royko, *The Voices of Children of Divorce* (New York: St. Martin's Press, 2000), 3, 10.

15. Royko, *The Voices of Children of Divorce*, 27.

16. Susan Gregory Thomas, "The Divorce Generation," *Wall Street Journal*, July 9, 2011, http://online.wsj.com/article/SB10001424052702303544604576430341393583056.html (accessed July 2, 2013).

17. See the Coalition for Divorce Reform website, http://divorcereform.us/ (accessed May 2, 2013).

18. Chris Gersten, "Why the Parental Divorce Reduction Act," DivorceReform.us, June 30, 2011, http://divorcereform.us/why-the-parental-divorce-reduction-act/ (accessed May 2, 2013).

19. William J. Doherty and Leah Ward Sears, *Second Chances: A Proposal to Reduce Unnecessary Divorces* (New York: Institute for American Values, 2011), 9, http://www.americanvalues.org/pdfs/download.php?name=second-chances (accessed May 9, 2013).

20. See a news release about the study at http://www1.umn.edu/news/news-releases/2011/UR_CONTENT_316404.html (accessed May 8, 2013).

21. Doherty and Sears, *Second Chances*, 12.

22. Robert Franklin, "Should States Restrict Divorce for Spouses with Kids?" FathersandFamilies.org, August 22, 2011, http://www.fathersandfamilies.org/2011/08/22/should-states-restrict-divorce-for-spouses-with-kids/ (accessed May 3, 2013).

23. "When Divorce Is a Family Affair," Room for Debate, *New York Times*, February 13, 2013, http://www.nytimes.com/roomfordebate/2013/02/13/when-divorce-is-a-family-affair (accessed May 3, 2013).

24. O. Kay Henderson, "Bill Would Forbid Parents from Getting No-Fault Divorce," Radio-Iowa.com, March 4, 2013, http://www.radioiowa.com/2013/03/04/bill-would-forbid-parents-from-getting-no-fault-divorce/ (accessed May 7, 2013).

25. Henderson, "Bill Would Forbid Parents."

26. Erik Kane, "Justice Kennedy: DOMA Had to Go Because It "Humiliates Tens of Thousands of Children'" *MotherJones.com*, June 26, 2013, http://www.motherjones.com/print/228091 (accessed July 10, 2013).

27. See HowStuffWorks.com, "Should You Stay Together for the Kids?" n.d., http://health .howstuffworks.com/relationships/marriage/should-you-stay-together-for-the-kids.htm (accessed May 4, 2013).

28. Tammy Gold, "Should You Stay Together for the Kids?" FirstWivesWorld.com, April 23, 2013, https://www.firstwivesworld.com/index.php/experts/item/3717-should-you-stay -together-for-the-kids (accessed May 3, 2013).

29. Gold, "Should You Stay Together for the Kids?"

30. Rosalind Sedacca, "Divorce or Stay? Parents Must Put Kids First Either Way," *Huffington-Post.com*, April 3, 2013, http://www.huffingtonpost.com/rosalind-sedacca/divorce-or-stay -parents-m_b_2967125.html?view=print&comm_ref=false (accessed May 3, 2013).

31. Kelli B. Grant, "10 Things Your Marriage Counselor Won't Say," SmartMoney.com, August 21, 2012, http://www.smartmoney.com/plan/health-care/10-things-your-marriage -counselor-wont-say-1345237916645/#printMode (accessed May 7, 2013).

a. Alan J. Hawkins and Tamara A. Fackrell, *Should I Keep Trying to Work It Out: A Guidebook for Individuals and Couples at the Crossroads of Divorce (and Before)* (Salt Lake City, UT: Utah Commission on Marriage, 2009), 3.

b. See the discussion at http://www.collegenet.com/elect/app/app?service=external/ Forum&sp=31909 (accessed May 3, 2013).

Chapter 4

1. Avaz, "Dealing with Solitude," ExperienceProject.com, April 22, 2013, http://www .experienceproject.com/stories/Have-Divorced-Parents/3125556 (accessed April 25, 2013).

2. Carma Haley, "Teens Discuss Marriage and Divorce," Family.com, n.d., http://family .go.com/parenting/pkg-teen/article-781286-teens-discuss-marriage-and-divorce-t/ (accessed June 1, 2013).

3. Krystle Russin, "Kids Don't Like New Partner?" Divorce360.com, n.d., http://www. divorce360.com/divorce-articles/remarriage/step-children/kids-dont-like-new-partner .aspx?artid=413 (accessed April 26, 2013).

4. Daniel Pikar, "Identifying Children's Stress-Responses to Divorce," *Sonoma County Medicine Magazine: Parenting*, Summer 2003, http://www.scma.org/magazine/articles/print. asp?articleid=302 (accessed June 2, 2013).

5. Reuters, "Children of Divorce Score Worse in Math, Social Skills," *ABS-CBNnews.com*, June 2, 2011, http://www.abs-cbnnews.com/lifestyle/06/02/11/children-divorce-score-worse-math-social-skills (accessed November 15, 2013).

6. University of Toronto Media Room, "Children of Divorced Parents More Likely to Start Smoking," University of Toronto Media Room, March 14, 2013, http://media.utoronto.ca/ media-releases/children-of-divorced-parents-more-likely-to-start-smoking/ (accessed November 15, 2013).

7. Sandi Greene, "When Your Parents Divorce," FocusontheFamily.com, 2002, http://www. focusonthefamily.com/lifechallenges/relationship_challenges/divorce/when_your_parents_divorce.aspx (accessed June 29, 2013).

8. Bethany Jordan, "My Parent's Divorce," *AZTeenMagazine.com*, April 2007, http://www .azteenmagazine.com/real-life.php?article=90 (accessed May 22, 2013).

9. CathinFrance, "Divorce: Think the Kids Will Be Fine If You Divorce? Think Again," Suite101.com, July 18, 2011, http://suite101.com/article/divorce-think-the-kids-will-be -fine-if-you-divorce-think-again-a380037 (accessed August 25, 2013).

10. CathinFrance, "Divorce."

11. K. L. West, "What I Learned from My Parents' Divorce," Yahoo! Voices, June 8, 2012, http://voices.yahoo.com/what-learned-parents-divorce-11431934.html?cat=41 (accessed June 7, 2013).

12. DesireeInWonderland, "I Learned How to Deal with It," ExperienceProject.com, March 26, 2013, http://www.experienceproject.com/stories/Have-Divorced-Parents/3059401 (accessed April 25, 2013).

13. Tyler Maffesoli (with parent's permission), correspondence with the author, June 3, 2013.

14. Megan Reilly, "Parent Problems? Ask a Girl," *New Moon Girls*, January–February 2013, p. 16.

15. Rob Callahan, "The Seven Stages of Grief for Divorce," LiveStrong.com, May 23, 2010 (updated by Alison Williams, October 29, 2013), http://www.livestrong.com/article/129455 -seven-stages-grief-divorce/ (accessed May 26, 2013).

16. NerfFoushee, "The Disappointment of Divorce," *TeenInk.com*, May 3, 2013, http:// www.teenink.com/nonfiction/personal_experience/article/192125/The-Dissapointment-of -Divorce/ (accessed May 27, 2013).

17. _ThrowAway_Account__, "As a Teenager with Divorced Parents, I Need a Moment to Let Out My Feelings," Reddit.com, April 20, 2013, http://www.reddit.com/r/self/comments/1cs5gm/ as_a_teenager_with_divorced_parents_i_need_a/ (accessed May 26, 2013).

18. Catherine Pearson, "Teen Depression: How One Girl Coped after Her Parents' Divorce," *HuffingtonPost.com*, May 31, 2013, http://www.huffingtonpost.com/2013/05/31/teen -depression-after-divorce_n_3361195.html (accessed June 2, 2013).

19. M. V. Lee Badgett and Jody L. Herman, *Patterns of Relationship Recognition by Same-Sex Couples in the United States*, Williams Institute, November 2011, http://www.google.com/ url?sa=t&rct=j&q=&esrc=s&source=web&cd=2&ved=0CEAQFjAB&url=http%3A%2F %2Fwilliamsinstitute.law.ucla.edu%2Fwp-content%2Fuploads%2FMarriage-Dissolution -FINAL.pdf&ei=HIDQUePZCYXQ8QT57YGoDA&usg=AFQjCNE6d-cfpiMaYblxOMAy 0Fu1e9rBzQ&sig2=3J5VSMyicV3smANjZOiLrw (accessed June 30, 2013).

20. Alan J. Hawkins and Tamara A. Fackrell, *Should I Keep Trying to Work It Out: A Guidebook for Individuals and Couples at the Crossroads of Divorce (and Before)* (Salt Lake City, UT: Utah Commission on Marriage, 2009), 41.

21. See Divorce Statistics, http://www.divorcestatistics.org/ (accessed July 19, 2013).

22. Leslie Sheline, correspondence with the author, July 18, 2013. Subsequent comments by Leslie come from this correspondence.

23. Pam.Bunnell, "How Does Parental Divorce Affect Adult Children's View of Love and Marriage?" Yahoo! Answers, n.d., http://answers.yahoo.com/activity?show=0353707a2e204471a ce4dd360a12d57aaa (accessed July 22, 2013).

24. Geoff Williams, "Second Divorces Multiply the Cost and Pain," Reuters.com, July 12, 2012, http://www.reuters.com/article/2012/07/12/us-divorce-multiple-costs-idUS BRE86B1A120120712 (accessed July 19, 2013).

25. Kevin Friedland, "A Teenager Reflects on Divorce," DivorceWizards.com, n.d., http://www .divorcewizards.com/A-Teenager-Reflects-on-Divorce.html (accessed April 30, 2013).

26. Friedland, "A Teenager Reflects on Divorce."

a. Noel Brinkerhoff, "Arkansas Leads Nation in Multiple Divorces," AllGov.com, October 21, 2009, http://www.allgov.com/news/controversies/arkansas-leads-nation-in-multiple -divorces?news=839733 (accessed November 12, 2013).

b. Trudi Strain Trueit, *Surviving Divorce: Teens Talk about What Hurts and What Helps* (New York: Scholastic/Franklin Watts, 2007), 63.

c. Trueit, *Surviving Divorce*, 17.

d. Trueit, *Surviving Divorce*, 64.

Chapter 5

1. Anonymous male (known as 17780), "Daughter Won't See Father after Divorce," MedHelp .org, June 18, 2011, http://www.medhelp.org/posts/Parenting-Teens-12-17/Daughter-wont -see-father-after-divorce/show/787058 (accessed January 17, 2014).

2. Lonesome_george, "As a Teenager with Divorced Parents, I Need a Moment to Let Out My Feelings," Reddit.com, April 20, 2013, http://www.reddit.com/r/self/comments/1cs5gm/ as_a_teenager_with_divorced_parents_i_need_a/ (accessed June 3, 2013).

3. Leigh Blickley, "Justin Timberlake Still Scarred from His Parents' Divorce: 'I Have a Lot of Issues,'" HollywoodLife.com, July 29, 2011, http://hollywoodlife.com/2011/07/29/justin -timberlake-parents-divorce-jessica-biel/ (accessed July 1, 2013).

4. Nicole and Lionel Richie interview on *Oprah*, 2006, http://nicolerichiefan.com/interview .html (accessed July 1, 2013)

5. Alex Winehouse, "'I Wanted My Parents to Divorce' Johnny Depp Admits," Entertainment-Wise.com, October 28, 2011, http://www.entertainmentwise.com/news/64500/I-Wanted -My-Parents-To-Divorce-Johnny-Depp-Admits (accessed July 1, 2013).

6. Michael Norman, "Brooke Hogan Talks Parents' Divorce, New CD," *Cleveland.com* (blog), August 5, 2009, http://blog.cleveland.com/ent_impact_music/print.html?entry=/2009/08/ brooke_hogan_talks_parents_div.html (accessed July 1, 2013).

7. Alyssa Pry and Gail Deutsch, "Mom: 'I'm a Terrific Divorced Dad': Noncustodial Moms Increase, Despite Social Pressure," *ABCNews.com*, June 14, 2013, http://abcnews.go.com/ US/mom-im-terrific-divorced-dad-noncustodial-moms-increase/story?id=19403924#. UcRP89jQvFw (accessed June 20, 2013).

8. Sam Margulies, "Some Thoughts on Blame in Divorce," *Psychology Today*, July 1, 2008, http://www.psychologytoday.com/blog/divorce-grownups/200807/some-thoughts-blame-in -divorce (accessed June 9, 2013).

9. Lisa Arends, "The Blame Game," *HuffingtonPost.com*, March 12, 2013, http://www.huffington post.com/lisa-arends/the-blame-game_5_b_2809856.html (accessed June 14, 2013).

10. MTV UK, "Justin Bieber Wants 'Somebody to Love,'" June 11, 2010, http://www.mtv.co.uk/ news/justin-bieber/225750-justin-bieber (accessed June 16, 2013).

11. Hailee Smith, correspondence with the author, May 13, 2013.

12. CrackyGirl, "I Hate Them," ExperienceProject.com, May 13, 2013, http://www .experienceproject.com/stories/Cant-Stand-My-Parents-Fighting/3172413 (accessed June 11, 2013).

13. Anita E. Kelly, "Why Parents of Girls Divorce More," *Psychology Today*, August 29, 2010, http://www.psychologytoday.com/blog/insight/201008/why-parents-girls-divorce-more (accessed June 12, 2013).

14. Eva Chen, "*Modern Family*'s Ariel Winter Tells Her Story," *TeenVogue.com*, March 2013, http://www.teenvogue.com/entertainment/tv/2013-03/ariel-winter-modern-family (accessed October 14, 2013).

15. Hollie McKay, "Child Stars in Crisis: Divorcing One's Parents Can Lead to Success, or Disaster," *FoxNews.com*, November 14, 2012, http://www.foxnews.com/entertainment/2012/11/14/child-stars-in-crisis-why-and-how-divorce-their-parents/ (accessed June 15, 2013).

16. Interview questions answered via e-mail to the author, June 22, 2013.

17. Chaim Steinberger, "Father, What Father? Parental Alienation and Its Effect on Children," New York State Bar Association *Family Law Review*, Spring 2006, p. 10.

18. Steinberger, "Father, What Father?" 12.

19. Natie, "Things My Mother Told Me," ExperienceProject.com, May 30, 2013, http://www.experienceproject.com/stories/Have-Divorced-Parents/3210958 (accessed January 17, 2014).

20. Kathy Mitchell and Marcy Sugar, "Teen Needs Help Dealing with Divorce and Remarriage," Annie's Mailbox, September 2011, http://www.creators.com/advice/annies-mailbox/teen-needs-help-dealing-with-divorce-and-remarriage.html (accessed January 17, 2014).

21. Virginia State Bar, "Children & Divorce," updated April 24, 2013, http://www.vsb.org/site/publications/children-divorce/ (accessed June 21, 2013).

a. David Hiltbrand, "Miley Cyrus Braced for Disney Stardom," *U-TSanDiego.com*, May 20, 2006, http://www.utsandiego.com/uniontrib/20060520/news_1c20hannah.html (accessed June 13, 2013).

b. See http://www.afcc-nj.org/bill_of_rights.html (accessed June 18, 2013).

c. Michael Logan, "*Divorce Court* Makes Judgment Call with New Format," *TVGuide.com*, May 18, 2011, http://www.tvguide.com/News/Divorce-Court-Toler-1033240.aspx (accessed January 17, 2014).

Chapter 6

1. David Royko, *Voices of Children of Divorce* (New York: St. Martin's Griffin, 1999), 49.

2. Royko, *Voices of Children of Divorce*, 49–64.

3. Tanith Carey, "Torn between Warring Parents," *Mail Online*, December 5, 2012, http://www.dailymail.co.uk/femail/article-2243693/Torn-warring-parents-How-woman-carries-emotional-scars-caught-middle-parents-bitter-divorce.html (accessed June 28, 2013).

4. Sandi Greene, "Caught in the Middle," FocusontheFamily.ca, 2008, http://www.focusonthefamily.ca/parenting/adult-kids/caught-in-the-middle (accessed June 18, 2013).

5. LonexWolf, "I Wish Every Person Considering a Divorce Could Read This First," ExperienceProject.com, December 11, 2011, http://www.experienceproject.com/stories/Have-Divorced-Parents/1936285 (accessed April 25, 2013).

6. Batteredsoul, "I Am a Financial Argument," ExperienceProject.com, June 11, 2012, http://www.experienceproject.com/stories/Have-Divorced-Parents/2339261 (accessed April 25, 2013).

7. Alan J. Hawkins and Tamara A. Fackrell, "What Are the Possible Consequences of Divorce for Children?" in *Should I Keep Trying to Work It Out*, chapter 5 (Logan, Utah: Utah State University Cooperative Extension, 2009), 78.

8. Hailee Smith, correspondence with the author, May 13, 2013.

9. Lisa Buie, "Soft Fur Soothes the Court Jitters," *Tampa Bay Times/Pasco Times*, December 8, 2013, p. PSC 1, 5.

10. Nolo, "Child Custody FAQ," n.d., http://www.nolo.com/legal-encyclopedia/child-custody -faq-29054.html (accessed July 10, 2013).

11. Ruth Bettleheim, "In Whose Best Interests?" *NYTimes.com*, May 19, 2012, http://www .nytimes.com/2012/05/20/opinion/sunday/child-custody-in-whose-best-interests.html?_r=0 (accessed July 11, 2013).

12. Lisa Helfend Myer, "Divorce and the Child with Special Needs," *HuffingtonPost.com*, March 10, 2011, http://www.huffingtonpost.com/lisa-helfend-meyer/divorce-and-the-child -wit_b_833639.html?view=screen (accessed July 13, 2013).

13. Judith Messina, "Gay Divorce: It May Not Be as Easy as the Marriage," *NBCNews .com*, October 16, 2013, http://www.nbcnews.com/business/gay-divorce-it-may-not-be-easy -marriage-8C11400904 (accessed October 18, 2013).

14. *Times* editors, "Protecting Rights of All Parents," *Tampa Bay Times*, November 9, 2013, p. 14A.

15. See Same-Sex Marriage Map at http://www.governing.com/gov-data/same-sex-marriage -civil-unions-doma-laws-by-state.html (accessed January 19, 2014).

16. See Grandparents.com, "Grandparents Rights: State by State," n.d., http://www.grand parents.com/family-and-relationships/grandparents-rights/grandparent-rights-united-states (accessed July 8, 2013). Also see answers to the post "How Have the Issues Judged under Family Law Changed over Time?" at http://www.enotes.com/family-law-reference/grand parents-rights (accessed July 8, 2013).

17. For more on *Kendall v. Kendall* see http://caselaw.findlaw.com/ma-supreme-judicial -court/1089362.html and also http://scholar.google.com/scholar_case?case=16880672587888 326102&hl=en&as_sdt=2&as_vis=1&oi=scholarr (accessed July 7, 2013).

18. See FindLaw.com, "Divorce: Child Custody and Religion," n.d., http://family.findlaw.com/ child-custody/divorce-child-custody-and-religion.html (accessed July 7, 2013).

19. Naomi Schaefer Riley, "Interfaith Unions: A Mixed Blessing," *New York Times*, April 6, 2013, http://www.nytimes.com/2013/04/06/opinion/interfaith-marriages-a-mixed-blessing .html (accessed July 7, 2013).

20. Ann Kass, "Religion Is a Worry for Kids in Divorce," AllLaw.com, n.d., http://www.alllaw .com/articles/family/child_custody/article34.asp (accessed January 17, 2014).

21. Sarah Fenske, "Judge Bars Man from Taking His Kids to Mormon Services," *Phoenix NewTimes.com*, April 30, 2009, http://www.phoenixnewtimes.com/2009-04-30/news/ richard-franco-discovered-that-the-government-can-interfere-with-a-man-s-freedom-of -religion-in-divorce-court/ (accessed July 7, 2013).

22. Susan L. Brown and I-Fen Lin, *The Gray Divorce Revolution: Middle-Aged and Older Adults 1990-2009* (Bowling Green, OH: National Center for Family & Marriage Research: March 2012), 3.

23. Chuck Barney, "Divorce Is a Big Deal Even for Adult Kids," *SeattleTimes.com*, July 7, 2011, http://seattletimes.com/html/living/2015514692_divorce08.html (accessed July 18, 2013).

24. Barney, "Divorce Is a Big Deal."

a. See, for example, http://www.supportinasplit.com/know-the-limits-of-friendship-during -divorce/ (accessed June 29, 2013); also http://teens.familieschange.ca/caught-middle (ac cessed July 8, 2013).

b. See USA Youth Survey, http://www.gordonpoll.com/youthsurvey/March09/about_survey.asp (accessed July 8, 2013).

c. See responses at http://www.gordonpoll.com/youthsurvey/March09/text.asp?poll=16 (accessed July 8, 2013).

Chapter 7

1. Morgan Thomas, "Coping with Divorce: Teenage Daughter's Response," *YourTeenMag.com*, January 28, 2012, http://yourteenmag.com/2012/01/divorce-and-teenagers/ (accessed August 19, 2013).

2. Batteredsoul, "I Am a Financial Argument," ExperienceProject.com, June 11, 2012, http://www.experienceproject.com/stories/Have-Divorced-Parents/2339261 (accessed April 25, 2013).

3. Justbreathe90, "Advice," A Community for Adult Children of Divorce, December 22, 2012, http://adultsofdivorce.livejournal.com/.

4. Mallie, "What Happens to Me If My Parents Get a Divorce?" AsktheJudge.info, July 3, 2009, http://www.askthejudge.info/what-happens-if-my-parents-divorce/ (accessed July 16, 2013).

5. See http://www.divorceinfo.com/chadolescents.htm (accessed January 17, 2014).

6. Susan Silverberg Koerner, Marcella Korn, Renée Peltz Dennison, and Sara Witthoft, "Future Money-Related Worries among Adolescents after Divorce," *Journal of Adolescent Research*, May 2011, abstract.

7. Kathryn Tuggle, "Teaching Gap: 83% of Teens Don't Know How to Manage Money," FoxBusiness.com, July 17, 2012, http://www.foxbusiness.com/personal-finance/2012/07/17/teaching-gap-83-teens-dont-know-how-to-manage-money/ (accessed July 14, 2013).

8. *Daily Mail* reporter, "Till Debt Do Us Part? How Money Issues Cause More Arguments Than Children or Chores—and Often End in Divorce," *DailyMail.co.uk*, June 6, 2012, http://www.dailymail.co.uk/femail/article-2155480/Till-debt-How-money-issues-cause-arguments-children-chores—end-divorce.html (accessed July 15, 2013).

9. Sarah Bulgatz, "What One Teen Can Teach Us about Money," Schwab.com, May 24, 2011, http://www.aboutschwab.com/blog/what_one_teen_can_teach_us_about_money (accessed January 17, 2014).

10. Teresa Dixon Murray, "Teens Hungry to Learn about Managing Money Because They're Not Learning It at Home," *Cleveland.com*, April 2, 2012, http://www.cleveland.com/business/index.ssf/2012/04/teens_hungry_to_learn_about_pe.html (accessed January 17, 2014).

11. John Pelletier, *National Report Card on State Efforts to Improve Financial Literacy in High Schools*, Summer 2013, p. 1, http://www.champlain.edu/centers-of-excellence/center-for-financial-literacy/report-making-the-grade (accessed January 17, 2014).

12. U.S. Department of Health and Human Services Office of Child Support Enforcement, *Child Support Handbook*, n.d., p. 2.

13. U.S. Department of Health and Human Services Office of Child Support Enforcement, *Child Support Handbook*, 7.

14. Stephanie Stahl, *The Love They Lost: Living with the Legacy of Our Parents' Divorce* (New York: Delacorte Press, 2000), 88–93.

15. Edward Kruk, "Father Absence, Father Deficit, Father Hunger," *Psychology Today*, May 23, 2012, http://www.psychologytoday.com/blog/co-parenting-after-divorce/201205/father-absence-father-deficit-father-hunger (accessed July 30, 2013).

16. See U.S. Census Bureau, "Poverty," Census.gov, n.d., http://www.census.gov/hhes/www/poverty/ (accessed August 4, 2013).

17. U.S. Census Bureau, "Income, Poverty and Health Insurance Coverage in the United States: 2012" (news release), Census.gov, September 17, 2013, http://www.census.gov/newsroom/releases/archives/income_wealth/cb13-165.html (accessed October 19, 2013).

18. See the Welfare Information website at http://www.welfareinfo.org/ (accessed August 4, 2013).

19. Tony Lopez, "Teens Getting Jobs to Help Their Families Make Ends Meet," *Sacramento .cbslocal.com*, February 28, 2012, http://sacramento.cbslocal.com/2012/02/28/teens-getting-jobs-to-help-their-families-make-ends-meet/ (accessed August 2, 2013).

20. John Bacon, "Fast-Food Workers Strike, Protest for Higher Pay," *USA Today*, December 5, 2013, http://www.usatoday.com/story/money/business/2013/12/05/fast-food-strike-wages/3877023/ (accessed January 18, 2014).

21. See U.S. Department of Labor, "Know the Rules," YouthRules! n.d., http://www.youthrules.dol.gov/know-the-limits/ (accessed July 29, 2013).

22. See U.S. Department of Labor, "Agricultural Jobs," YouthRules! n.d., http://www.youthrules.dol.gov/know-the-limits/agriculture/index.htm (accessed July 30, 2013).

23. Alliance for Excellence in Education, *The High Cost of High School Dropouts: What the Nation Pays for Inadequate High Schools* (issue brief), November 2011, p. 1, http://www.all4ed.org/publication_material/issue_policy_briefs (accessed August 2, 2013).

24. Alliance for Excellence in Education, *The High Cost of High School Dropouts*, 1.

25. See the SkillsUSA website at http://www.skillsusa.org/about/facts.shtml (accessed August 3, 2013).

---

a. Josh Smith, "Top 10 Money Myths Held by Teens and How to Change Them," DailyFinance .com, September 9, 2009, http://www.dailyfinance.com/2009/09/08/top-10-money-myths-held-by-teens-and-how-to-change-them/ (accessed July 23, 2013).

b. Abigail Dalton, "What My Parents' Divorce Taught Me about Money," TheDailyMuse.com, September 3, 2012, http://www.thedailymuse.com/money/what-my-parents-divorce-taught-me-about-money/ (accessed July 14, 2013).

c. Mark Mather, "U.S. Children in Single-Mother Families," PRB.org, May 2010, http://www.prb.org/pdf10/single-motherfamilies.pdf (accessed August 4, 2013).

d. Laura Shin, "How She Lives on Minimum Wage: One McDonald's Worker's Budget," *Forbes .com*, July 19, 2013, http://www.forbes.com/sites/laurashin/2013/07/19/how-she-lives-on-minimum-wage-one-mcdonalds-workers-budget/ (accessed August 5, 2013).

e. Allen Zadoff, *Since You Left Me* (New York: Egmont USA, 2012), 27.

Chapter 8

1. "Emmy's Story—Rebel with a Cause," *NIE Rocks* (blog), October 27, 2010, http://nierocks.areavoices.com/2010/10/27/emmys-story-rebel-with-a-cause/ (accessed November 12, 2013).

2. "Emmy's Story."

3. "Emmy's Story."

4. *My Journey My Journal*, "My Story," FamilyinDivorce.com, n.d., http://www.familyindivorce.com/ (accessed August 18, 2013).

5. Daniel Pikar, "Identifying Children's Stress-Responses to Divorce," *Sonoma County Medicine Magazine: Parenting*, Summer 2003, http://www.scma.org/magazine/articles/print .asp?articleid=302 (accessed June 2, 2013).

6. The National Center on Addiction and Substance Abuse at Columbia University (CASA), *Adolescent Substance Use: America's #1 Public Health Problem* (New York: Author, June 2011), 87.

7. CASA, *Adolescent Substance Use*, 95.

8. National Institute on Drug Abuse, "Monitoring the Future Survey, Overview of Findings 2012," updated December 2012, http://www.drugabuse.gov/related-topics/trends-statistics/ monitoring-future/monitoring-future-survey-overview-findings-2012 (accessed November 12, 2013).

9. CASA, *Adolescent Substance Use*, 78.

10. Mayo Clinic staff, "Teen Depression," MayoClinic.com, November 7, 2012, http://www .mayoclinic.com/health/teen-depression/DS01188 (accessed June 3, 2013).

11. The Pew Charitable Trusts, *Collateral Costs: Incarceration's Effect on Economic Mobility* (Washington, D.C.: Author, 2010), 4.

12. Substance Abuse and Mental Health Services Administration, "Report Shows 7.5 Million Children Live with a Parent with an Alcohol Use Disorder" (news release), SAMHSA.gov, February 16, 2012, http://www.samhsa.gov/newsroom/advisories/1202151415.aspx (accessed January 18, 2014).

13. Child Welfare Information Gateway, *Parental Drug Use as Child Abuse* (Washington, D.C.: U.S. Department of Health and Human Services, Children's Bureau, 2012), https://www .childwelfare.gov/systemwide/laws_policies/statutes/drugexposed.cfm (accessed August 13, 2013).

14. Izaskun E. Larrañeta, "State's Own Miss USA Erin Brady Sets New Standard," *TheDay.com*, July 5, 2013, http://www.theday.com/apps/pbcs.dll/article?AID=/20130705/ NWS01/307059950/1070/ (accessed January 18, 2014).

15. Larrañeta, "State's Own Miss USA Erin Brady Sets New Standard." See also Daniel Bates, "The Utterly Uplifting Story of the Miss USA Winner Who Overcame Mother's 'Messy' Divorce to Alcoholic Father by Working 12 Hour Waitress Shifts to Pay for College to Get Honors Degree in Finance," *Mail Online*, June 18, 2013, http://www.dailymail.co.uk/ news/article-2344011/Erin-Brady-The-utterly-uplifting-story-Miss-USA-winner-overcame -troubled-home-alcoholic-father-working-12-hour-waitressing-shifts-pay-college-honors (accessed January 18, 2014).

16. Dana Hee, "About Dana Hee," *Gold Medal Motivation* (blog), n.d., http://goldmedal motivation.me/about/ (accessed August 12, 2013).

17. CASA, *Behind Bars II: Substance Abuse and America's Prison Population* (New York: Author, February 2010), 4, http://www.casacolumbia.org/addiction-research/reports/substance -abuse-prison-system-2010 (accessed August 13, 2013).

18. Erik Ortiz, "*Sesame Street* Introduces First-Ever Muppet with a Parent in Prison," *NYDailyNews.com*, June 19, 2013, http://www.nydailynews.com/entertainment/tv-movies/ sesame-street-introduces-muppet-dad-jail-article-1.1376845 (accessed August 15, 2013).

19. Council on Crime and Justice, *Children of Incarcerated Parents*, January 2006, p. 16, http:// www.crimeandjustice.org/councilinfo.cfm?pID=33 (accessed August 15, 2013).

20. Council on Crime and Justice, *Children of Incarcerated Parents*, 22–23.

21. Colette Kimball, "Adolescents with Incarcerated Parents," *Prevention Researcher*, January 8, 2009, http://blog.tpronline.org/?p=227 (accessed January 18, 2014).

a. Charles R. Cross, *Heavier Than Heaven: A Biography of Kurt Cobain* (New York: Hyperion, 2002), 25.

b. The Biography Channel website, "Kurt Cobain," 2013, http://www.biography.com/people/kurt-cobain-9542179 (accessed August 8, 2013).

c. See the questions and answers at http://teens.drugabuse.gov/drug-facts/real-questions-real-teens (accessed August 8, 2013).

d. U.S. Centers for Disease Control and Prevention, "Suicide Prevention," August 2012, http://www.cdc.gov/violenceprevention/pub/youth_suicide.html (accessed June 1, 2013).

e. Chase Block, "Coping with Family Tragedies: Divorce, Addiction & Suicide," Intervene, August 10, 2010, http://intervene.drugfree.org/2010/08/coping-with-family-tragedies-divorce-addiction-suicide/ (accessed August 9, 2013).

f. Chase Block, "Chasing Happiness" (press kit), n.d., http://chaseblock.presskit247.com/ (accessed August 11, 2013).

g. Chase Block, *Chasing Happiness: One Boy's Guide to Helping Other Kids Cope with Divorce, Parental Addictions and Death* (West Conshohocken, PA: Infinity Publishing, 2009), 97.

h. See http://www.youtube.com/user/undroppable.

Chapter 9

1. Anonymous correspondence with the author, August 12, 2013.

2. Creigh, "What Divorce Can Teach You," Divorceandteens.weebly.com, n.d., http://divorceandteens.weebly.com/the-silver-lining.html (accessed January 20, 2014).

3. Annie Carter, "Coping with Divorce: One Teen's Story," *YourTeenMag.com*, January 28, 2012, http://yourteenmag.com/2012/01/teenagersa-and-divorce/ (accessed January 18, 2014).

4. Richard Niolon, "Children of Divorce and Adjustment," PsychPage.com, September 19, 2010, http://www.psychpage.com/family/childrenadjust.html (accessed August 17, 2013).

5. Abigail Dalton, "What My Parents' Divorce Taught Me about Money," TheDailyMuse.com, September 3, 2012, http://www.thedailymuse.com/money/what-my-parents-divorce-taught-me-about-money/ (accessed January 18, 2014).

6. WebMD, "Anorexia Nervosa Health Center," n.d., http://www.webmd.com/mental-health/anorexia-nervosa/anorexia-nervosa-topic-overview (accessed August 23, 2013).

7. Ohio State University Extension, "Teens and Divorce: What Hurts and What Helps?" 2002, http://ohioline.osu.edu/flm02/FS11.html (accessed August 18, 2013).

8. Michelle New, "Dealing with Divorce," KidsHealth.org, reviewed August 2010, http://kidshealth.org/teen/your_mind/Parents/divorce.html# (accessed August 26, 2013).

9. Jann Gumbiner, "Divorce Hurts Children, Even Grown Ones," *Psychology Today*, October 31, 2011, http://www.psychologytoday.com/blog/the-teenage-mind/201110/divorce-hurts-children-even-grown-ones (accessed January 18, 2014).

10. Laurenashley, "What Happened When My Dad Walked Away after the Divorce," *BlogHer.com*, December 1, 2011, http://www.blogher.com/father-mine-even-though-youve-never-really-been-mine (accessed August 26, 2013).

11. Laurenashley, "What Happened When My Dad Walked Away."

12. Denise Witmer, "Teen Very Angry over Divorce" (with comment by Kim King), About.com, March 9, 2010, http://parentingteens.about.com/b/2010/03/09/teen-very-angry-over-divorce.htm (accessed February 15, 2013).

13. Drewmat, "Adult Children of Divorce, What Happened, What Are Your Feelings and How Are You Coping?" Reddit.com, February 22, 2013, http://www.reddit.com/r/AskReddit/comments/191tct/adult_children_of_divorce_what_happened_what_are/ (accessed June 3, 2013).

14. Donna F. Ferber, "Adult Children of Divorce—Dealing with Your Parents' Pain," Donna Ferber.com, February 23, 2013, http://donnaferber.com/2013/02/adult-children-of-divorce-are-you-parenting-your-parent/ (accessed July 2, 2013).

15. Kasey Edwards, "Adult Children of Divorce," *HuffingtonPost.com*, March 15, 2013, http://www.huffingtonpost.com/kasey-edwards/adult-children-of-divorce_1_b_2806544.html (accessed June 3, 2013).

16. Erik Kersting, "The Effects of Divorce on Adult Children," *The Pointer* (University of Wisconsin–Stevens Point), n.d., http://www.uwsp.edu/pointeronline/Pages/articles/The-Effects-of-Divorce-on-Adult-Children.aspx (accessed January 18, 2014).

17. M. Gary Neuman, *The Long Way Home: The Powerful 4-Step Plan for Adult Children of Divorce* (Hoboken, NJ: John Wiley & Sons, 2013), 14.

18. Lisa Laumann-Billings, and Robert E. Emery, "Distress among Young Adults from Divorced Families," *Journal of Family Psychology*, December 2000, abstract.

19. Hal Arkowitz and Scott O. Lilienfeld, "Is Divorce Bad for Children?" *Scientific American*, March 19, 2013, http://www.scientificamerican.com/article.cfm?id=is-divorce-bad-for-children (accessed May 27, 2013).

20. Arkowitz and Lilienfeld, "Is Divorce Bad for Children?"

21. E. Mavis Hetherington and John Kelly, *For Better or For Worse: Divorce Reconsidered* (New York and London: W.W. Norton, 2002), 3.

22. Judith Wallerstein, "What Children of Divorce Do and Don't Learn," *HuffingtonPost.com*, December 7, 2011, http://www.huffingtonpost.com/judith-wallerstein/what-children-of-divorce-_b_1132953.html (accessed July 21, 2013)

23. Leslie Sheline, correspondence with the author, July 18, 2013.

24. Susan L. Pollet and Melissa Lombreglia, "A Nationwide Survey of Mandatory Parent Education," *Family Court Review*, April 2008, p. 385.

a. Anonymous correspondence with the author, August 12, 2013.

b. Lila Margulies, "Banana Splits—Middle and Upper School Adolescents," BananaSplits ResourceCenter.org, n.d., http://www.bananasplitsresourcecenter.org/act-adol.html (August 21, 2013).

Chapter 10

1. Sonya and Sean (hosts), "Divorce and Stepfamilies: Breaking Apart, Coming Together," episode transcript from *In the Mix*, PBS.com, n.d., http://www.pbs.org/inthemix/shows/show_divorce.html (accessed November 12, 2013).

2. Hailee Smith, e-mail correspondence with the author, May 13, 2013.

3. Sonya and Sean, "Divorce and Stepfamilies."

4. Sabrina Mercado, "Effects of Divorce Send Teens Shuttling between Parents," *Mosaic*, n.d., http://www.bazeley.net/mosaic/news/archives/life/effects_of_divorce_send_teens_shuttling_between_parents.html (accessed September 18, 2013).

5. Chase Block, *Chasing Happiness: One Boy's Guide to Helping Other Kids Cope with Divorce, Parental Addictions and Death* (West Conshohocken, PA: Infinity Publishing, 2009), 48.

6. Block, *Chasing Happiness*, 48.

7. Block, *Chasing Happiness*, 49, 51.

8. Tayce Taylor, "The Reality of Divorced Parents during the Holidays," *HuffingtonPost.com*, December 24, 2012, http://www.huffingtonpost.com/tayce-taylor/the-reality-of-divorced -p_b_2357383.html (accessed November 28, 2013).

9. Kate Mannarino, "Divorced Teens Struggle to Deal with Holiday Stress," *Lance*, November 20, 2013, http://lhslance.org/2013/features/divorced-parents-struggle-to-deal-with-holiday -stress/ (accessed November 28, 2013).

10. Carol Morello, "Blended Families More Common, but the 'Step' In 'Stepmom' Still Carries a Stigma," *WashintonPost.com*, January 19, 2011, http://www.washingtonpost.com/wp-dyn/ content/article/2011/01/19/AR2011011902589_pf.html (accessed September 3, 2013).

11. Sonya and Sean, "Divorce and Stepfamilies."

12. Sonya and Sean, "Divorce and Stepfamilies."

13. Anonymous interview, June 17, 2010.

14. Terry Gaspard and Tracy Clifford, "Let's Talk about Stepfamilies," Movingpastdivorce.com, December 2011, http://movingpastdivorce.com/2011/12/lets-talk-about-stepfamilies/ (accessed September 6, 2013).

15. Gaspard and Clifford, "Let's Talk about Stepfamilies."

16. Melanie Ford, "I Like My Stepmom. Am I Weird?" BonusFamilies.com, n.d., http://www. bonusfamilies.com/articles/index.php?id=17# (accessed September 7, 2013).

17. Ford, "I Like My Stepmom."

18. Alex Randall, "Dealing with My Parents' Divorce," BonusFamilies.com, n.d., http://www .bonusfamilies.com/articles/index.php?id=205 (accessed September 10, 2013).

19. Avaz, "Dealing with Solitude," ExperienceProject.com, April 22, 2013, http://www .experienceproject.com/stories/Have-Divorced-Parents/3125556 (accessed September 18, 2013).

20. Deanna Linville and Maya O'Neil, "Same-Sex Parents and Their Children," AAMFT .org, n.d., http://www.aamft.org/imis15/content/consumer_updates/Same-sex_Parents_and _Their_Children.aspx (accessed January 19, 2014).

21. Jeannette Lofas, "The Stepfamily Must Become a Team to Survive," StepFamily.org, n.d., http://www.stepfamily.org/article.html (accessed September 4, 2013).

22. Virginia Rutter, "Lessons from Stepfamilies," *Psychology Today*, May 1, 1994, last reviewed June 19, 2012, http://psychologytoday.com/articles/pto-19940501-000019.html (accessed September 6, 2013).

23. American Psychological Association (APA), "Making Stepfamilies Work," APA.org, n.d., http://www.apa.org/helpcenter/stepfamily.aspx (accessed September 6, 2013).

24. APA, "Making Stepfamilies Work."

a. Graham Salisbury, *Lord of the Deep* (New York: Dell Laurel-Leaf/Random House, 2001), 11.

b. Max Sindell, "Max Sindell's Biography," RedRoom.com, n.d. http://redroom.com/member/ max-sindell/bio (accessed September 3, 2013).

c. Max Sindell, *The Bright Side: Surviving Your Parents' Divorce* (Deerfield Beach, FL: Health Communications, 2007), x.

d. Julissa Cruz, *Remarriage Rate in the U.S. 2010*, National Center for Family & Marriage Research, n.d., http://www.bgsu.edu/content/dam/BGSU/college-of-arts-and-sciences/NCFMR/documents/FP/FP-12-14.pdf (accessed September 1, 2013).

e. Pew Research Center, "A Portrait of Stepfamilies," January 13, 2011, http://www.pewsocialtrends.org/2011/01/13/a-portrait-of-stepfamilies/ (accessed September 1, 2013).

f. See 1 Samuel 1:4-8 in the New International Version of the Bible.

Chapter 11

1. Allycia-Ashely M., "My Struggle," ResponsibleDivorce.com, 2003, http://responsibledivorce.com/teens/allycia.htm (accessed September 16, 2013).

2. Teresa Opdycke, "When Parents of a Teen Divorce," FamilyLobby.com, n.d., http://articles.familylobby.com/291-when-parents-of-a-teen-divorce.htm (accessed September 23, 2013).

3. Terry Gaspard, "Fathers and Daughters: Staying Connected after Divorce," MarriageandSeparation.com, May 22, 2013, http://www.marriageandseparation.com/profiles/blogs/fathers-and-daughters-staying-connected-after-divorce (accessed September 23, 2013).

4. Terry Gaspard, "Mothers and Daughters: A Crucial Connection after Divorce," *Huffington Post.com*, August 29, 2013, http://www.huffingtonpost.com/terry-gaspard-msw-licsw/mother-daughter-relationship-divorce_b_3833285.html (accessed September 23, 2013).

5. Charles B., "The Challenges," ResponsibleDivorce.com, 2003, http://responsibledivorce.com/teens/charles.htm (accessed September 16, 2013).

6. Yolanda H., "Life with a Single Parent," ResponsibleDivorce.com, 2003, http://responsibledivorce.com/teens/yolanda.htm (accessed September 16, 2013).

7. Allycia-Ashely, "My Struggle."

8. Penn State University, "Divorce May Widen Distance between Teens, Fathers" (news release), *Penn State News*, January 9, 2008, last updated April 1, 2010, http://news.psu.edu/story/191509/2008/01/09/divorce-may-widen-distance-between-teens-fathers (accessed September 27, 2013).

9. Linda Nielson, *Between Fathers and Daughters: Enriching and Rebuilding Your Adult Relationship* (Nashville, TN: Cumberland House Publishing, 2008), 11.

10. Jean McBride, "Long Distance Parenting: Staying in Touch When Miles Separate You and Your Children," DivorceHelpforParents.com, n.d., http://www.divorcehelpforparents.com/long-distance-parenting.html (accessed September 28, 2013).

11. Max Sindell, *The Bright Side: Surviving Your Parents' Divorce* (Deerfield Beach, FL: Health Communications, 2007), 82.

12. Griffin Mitchell, "Surviving Divorce of Your Parents," *Teen Life* (*Press Democrat* blog), January 20, 2011, http://teenlife.blogs.pressdemocrat.com/10915/surviving-divorce-of-your-parents/ (accessed September 19, 2013).

13. Phantomyoda13, "I Am Miserable, Please Help," DailyStrength.org, November 24, 2012, http://www.dailystrength.org/c/Children-Of-Divorced-Parents/advice/15265213-i-am-miserable-please-help (accessed August 26, 2013).

14. Roni Caryn Rabin, "What Cellphone Calls Say about Parent-Teenager Relations," *Well* (*New York Times* blog), July 1, 2011, http://well.blogs.nytimes.com/2011/07/01/what-cellphone-calls-say-about-parent-teenager-relations/?pagewanted=print (accessed September 19, 2013).

15. Ted Rubin, "Parents Coping with Divorce: One Father's Story," *YourTeenMag.com*, January 28, 2012, http://yourteenmag.com/2012/01/divorce-parents-teenagers/ (accessed September 23, 2013).

16. Julia Bodeeb, "A Grateful Teenager? Bring Out Their Soft Side with a Letter Writing Project," ed. Wendy Finn, BrightHubEducation.com, updated January 20, 2012, http://www.brighthubeducation.com/high-school-english-lessons/46486-writing-thank-you-letters-for-parents/ (accessed September 21, 2013).

17. Jennifer Wolf, "8 Words to Include in a Birthday or 'Just Because' Letter to a Child," About.com, n.d., http://singleparents.about.com/od/familyrelationships/tp/letter_to_child.htm (accessed September 21, 2013).

18. Anonymous, comment in e-mail to the author, October 1, 2013.

---

a. Karen Buscemi, *Split in Two: Keeping It Together When Your Parents Live Apart* (San Francisco, CA: Zest Books, 2009), 15.

b. Buscemi, *Split in Two*, 45.

c. Sarah Dessen, *that Summer* (New York: Speak/Penguin Group, 1996), 10.

d. Common Sense Media, *Social Media, Social Life: How Teens View Their Digital Lives*, Summer 2012, pp. 22, 25, http://www.commonsensemedia.org/sites/default/files/research/socialmediasociallife-final-061812.pdf (accessed September 29, 2013).

e. Rebecca Walker, *Black, White, and Jewish: Autobiography of a Shifting Self* (New York: Riverhead Books, 2001), 3, 116–17.

f. Sharon Krum, "'Can I Survive Having a Baby? Will I Lose Myself . . . ?'" *TheGuardian.com*, May 25, 2007, http://www.theguardian.com/lifeandstyle/2007/may/26/familyandrelationships.family2 (accessed September 30, 2013).

Chapter 12

1. Mcramer55, "Marriage: Stay Strong," StageofLife.com, February 3, 2011, http://www.stageoflife.com/Default.aspx?tabid=72&g=posts&t=2052 (accessed October 2, 2013).

2. Monique, GetFresh, "Do Teen Marriages EVER Last?" BachChatForum.com, September 13, 2013, http://www.bachchatforum.com/search/22992/?q=teen+marriage&t=post&o=date (accessed October 15, 2013).

3. Monique, GetFresh, "Do Teen Marriages EVER Last?"

4. Akimbo, "Marriage: The Adhesive That Loses Stickiness," StageofLife.com, February 10, 2011, http://www.stageoflife.com/Default.aspx?tabid=79&g=posts&m=3412 (accessed October 3, 2013).

5. StageofLife.com, "Value of Marriage: How Teens Feel about Real World Issues," March 29, 2011, http://www.stageoflife.com/marriage.aspx (accessed January 19, 2014).

6. CC3PEP, "Marriage: Thinking Beyond the Vows," StageofLife.com, http://www.stageoflife.com/Default.aspx?tabid=72&g=posts&t=2271 (accessed April 1, 2014).

7. ReadingKT, "Marriage: My Rules," StageofLife.com, February 3, 2011, http://www.stageoflife.com/Default.aspx?tabid=72&g=posts&t=2047 (accessed October 3, 2013).

8. Stephanie Kaloi, "Why I'm Happy My Parents Divorced," OffbeatFamilies.com, August 2010, http://offbeatfamilies.com/2010/08/divorce (accessed October 7, 2013).

9. Bron B. Ingoldsby, "Bundling," Family.jrank.org, n.d., http://family.jrank.org/pages/186/Bundling.html (accessed October 9, 2013).

10. Saloma Furlong, "Traditional Amish Courtship Practices," *About Amish* (blog), December 27, 2009, http://aboutamish.blogspot.com/2009/12/traditional-amish-courtship-practices.html (accessed October 9, 2013).

11. Alycat32, "Do Teen Marriages EVER Last?" BachChatForum.com, September 13, 2013, http://www.bachchatforum.com/search/22992/?q=teen+marriage&t=post&o=date (accessed October 7, 2013).

12. Amanda Marcotte, "Teens and Sex in Dad's House," *USAToday.com*, August 14, 2013, http://www.usatoday.com/story/opinion/2013/08/14/teen-sex-angelina-jolie-column/2657775/ (accessed October 13, 2013).

13. Robert G. Wood, Sarah Avellar, and Brian Goesling, *Pathways to Adulthood and Marriage: Teenagers' Attitudes, Expectations, and Relationship* (Washington, D.C.: U.S. Department of Health and Human Services, October 2008), http://aspe.hhs.gov/hsp/08/pathways2adulthood/ch3.shtml (accessed October 3, 2013).

14. Casey E. Copen, Kimberly Daniels, and William D. Mosher, *First Premarital Cohabitation in the United States: 2006–2010 National Survey of Family Growth* (Hyattsville, MD: National Center for Health Statistics, 2013), 1, 7.

15. Elizabeth Marquardt, David Blankenhorn, Robert I. Lerman, Linda Malone-Colón, and W. Bradford Wilcox, "The President's Marriage Agenda for the Forgotten Sixty Percent," in *The State of Our Unions* (Charlottesville, VA: National Marriage Project and Institute for American Values, 2012), 1.

16. Brady E. Hamilton and Stephanie J. Ventura, "Birth Rates for U.S. Teenagers Reach Historic Lows for All Age and Ethnic Groups," National Center for Health Statistics data brief no. 89 (Hyattsville, MD: National Center for Health Statistics, 2012).

17. American Academy of Child & Adolescent Psychiatry (AACAP), "When Children Have Children," Facts for Families Pages, May 2012, http://www.aacap.org/AACAP/Families_and_Youth/Facts_for_Families/Facts_for_Families_Pages/When_Children_Have_Children_31.aspx (accessed October 11, 2013).

18. AACAP, "When Children Have Children."

19. Kim Gamble, "Love and the Single Girl/My Matchmaker Dad," *MarieClaire.com*, May 30, 2012, http://www.marieclaire.com/sex-love/single-girl-trend-2 (accessed October 12, 2013).

20. *NYTimes.com*, "America: Single, and Loving It," February 12, 2012, http://www.nytimes.com/2012/02/12/fashion/America-Single-and-Loving-It.html?_r=0 (accessed October 12, 2013).

21. *NYTimes.com*, "America."

22. Andrew Malcolm, "Dear Abby: How Do Mary Matalin and James Carville Stay Married without Homicide?" *Top of the Ticket* (*Los Angeles Times* blog), December 27, 2009, http://latimesblogs.latimes.com/washington/2009/12/mary-matalin-james-carville-marriage.html (accessed February 10, 2013).

23. Vi-An Nguyen, "15 Long-Lasting Celebrity Marriages," *Parade.com*, April 30, 2013, http://www.parade.com/9927/viannguyen/15-long-lasting-celebrity-marriages/ (accessed October 13, 2013).

24. Karl A. Pillemer, "'Opposites Attract' Or 'Birds Of A Feather'—What's Best for a Long Marriage?" *HuffingtonPost.com*, January 31, 2013, http://www.huffingtonpost.com/karl-a-pillemer-phd/marriage-counseling-opposites-attract_b_2557391.html (accessed October 14, 2013).

25. Eleanor J. Bader, "Arranged Marriage Is a US Issue," *Truth-Out.org*, April 20, 2013, http://truth-out.org/news/item/15845-arranged-marriage-is-a-us-issue (accessed January 19, 2014).

26. *Latitude News* staff, "Arranged Marriages, American Style," *LatitudeNews.com*, n.d., http://www.latitudenews.com/story/arranged-marriages-american-style/ (accessed January 19, 2014).

27. U.S. Department of State, *Trafficking in Persons Report*, 10th ed., June 2010, p. 15, www.state.gov/documents/organization/142979.pdf (accessed November 11, 2013).

28. Hena Zuberi, "Arranged Marriage Is Not Forced Marriage," MuslimMatters.org, December 22, 2011, http://muslimmatters.org/2011/12/22/arranged-marriage-is-not-forced-marriage/ (accessed November 11, 2013).

29. Bader, "Arranged Marriage Is a US Issue."

30. Athletictypist, BachChatForum.com, June 23, 2013, http://bachchatforum.com/threads/how-old-were-you-when-you-married.75/#post-4862 (accessed January 19, 2014).

31. AnnaU93, BachChatForum.com, June 22, 2013, http://bachchatforum.com/threads/how-old-were-you-when-you-married.75/#post-4862 (accessed January 19, 2014).

32. Zeniquez, BachChatForum.com, June 4, 2013, http://bachchatforum.com/threads/do-you-wish-to-marry.190/ (accessed January 19, 2014).

33. EdenSB, BachChatForum.com, June 5, 2013, http://bachchatforum.com/threads/do-you-wish-to-marry.190/ (accessed January 19, 2014).

a. "Comments about 'Right Age to Marry? Lots to Consider, but after Teens, Age Is Not Most Important Factor, Experts Say," *Deseret News*, http://www.deseretnews.com/user/comments/765626529/Right-age-to-marry-Lots-to-consider-but-after-teens-age-is-not-most-important-factor-experts-say.html (accessed October 9, 2013). Subsequent reader responses in this section are taken from this source.

b. Han Nolan, *Pregnant Pause* (New York: Harcourt/Houghton Mifflin Harcourt, 2011), 1–2.

c. Bonnie Fuller, "Bristol Palin's *People* Magazine Cover Is a Total Promotion for Teen Pregnancy!" *HuffingtonPost.com*, May 21, 2009, http://www.huffingtonpost.com/bonnie-fuller/bristol-palins-empeopleem_b_206244.html?view=screen (accessed October 7, 2013).

d. *In Touch Weekly*, "Bristol Palin: This Time I'm Not Having Sex Until Marriage," *In Touch Weekly.com*, June 2012, http://www.intouchweekly.com/entertainment/news/bristol-palin-time-im-not-having-sex-until-marriage (accessed January 19, 2014).

Selected Bibliography

Berman, Claire. *Adult Children of Divorce Speak Out* (New York: Simon & Schuster, 1991).

Block, Chase. *Chasing Happiness: One Boy's Guide to Helping Other Kids Cope with Divorce, Parental Addictions and Death* (West Conshohocken, PA: Infinity Publishing, 2009).

Brown, Susan L., and I-Fen Lin. *The Gray Divorce Revolution: Middle-Aged and Older Adults* (Bowling Green, Ohio: National Center for Family & Marriage Research: *1990-2009*, March 2012).

Buscemi, Karen. *Split in Two: Keeping It Together When Your Parents Live Apart* (San Francisco, CA: Zest Books, 2009).

Coontz, Stephanie. *The Way We Really Are: Coming to Terms with America's Changing Families* (New York: Basic Books/Harper Collins, 1997).

Copen, Casey E., Kimberly Daniels, and William D. Mosher. *First Premarital Cohabitation in the United States: 2006–2010 National Survey of Family Growth* (Hyattsville, MD: National Center for Health Statistics, 2013).

Hawkins, Alan J., and Tamara A. Fackrell. *Should I Keep Trying to Work It Out: A Guidebook for Individuals and Couples at the Crossroads of Divorce (and Before)* (Salt Lake City: Utah Commission on Marriage, 2009).

Hetherington, E. Mavis, and John Kelly. *For Better or For Worse: Divorce Reconsidered* (New York and London: W.W. Norton, 2002).

Langwith, Jacqueline, ed. *Divorce: Introducing Issues with Opposing Viewpoints* (Farmington Hills, MI: Greenhaven Press, 2012).

Marquardt, Elizabeth. *Between Two Worlds: The Inner Lives of Children of Divorce* (New York: Crown Publishers, 2005).

Marquardt, Elizabeth, David Blankenhorn, Robert I. Lerman, Linda Malone-Colón, and W. Bradford Wilcox. *The State of Our Unions* (Charlottesville, VA: National Marriage Project and Institute for American Values, 2012).

Neuman, M. Gary. *The Long Way Home: The Powerful 4-Step Plan for Adult Children of Divorce* (Hoboken, NJ: John Wiley & Sons, 2013).

Papernow, Patricia. *Surviving and Thriving in Stepfamily Relationships: What Works and What Doesn't* (New York: Routledge, 2013).

Riley, Glenda. *Divorce: An American Tradition* (Oxford and New York: Oxford University Press, 1991).

Royko, David. *Voices of Children of Divorce* (New York: St. Martin's Press, 2000).

Sindell, Max. *The Bright Side: Surviving Your Parents' Divorce* (Deerfield Beach, FL: Health Communications, 2007).

Staal, Stephanie. *The Love They Lost: Living with the Legacy of Our Parents' Divorce* (New York: Delta/Random House, 2001).

Thomas, Susan Gregory. *In Spite of Everything: A Memoir* (New York: Random House, 2011).

Trueit, Trudi Strain. *Surviving Divorce: Teens Talk about What Hurts and What Helps* (New York: Scholastic/Franklin Watts, 2007).

Walker, Rebecca. *Black, White: Autobiography of a Shifting Self* (New York: Riverhead Books, 2001).

Wallerstein, Judith, Julia M. Lewis, and Sandra Blakeslee. *The Unexpected Legacy of Divorce: The 25 Year Landmark Study* (New York: Hyperion Books, 2001).

Woo, Ilyon. *The Great American Divorce: A Nineteenth-Century Mother's Extraordinary Fight against Her Husband, the Shakers, and Her Times* (New York: Atlantic Monthly Press, 2010).

Worthen, Tom, ed. *Broken Hearts . . . Healing: Young Poets Speak Out on Divorce* (Logan, UT: Poet Tree Press, 2001).

Index

AAMFT. See American Association for Marriage and Family Therapy
abuse, 2, 9–10, 30, 36, 41, 54, 66, 79, 83, 109, 166, 176, 199nc; domestic, 21, 25, 68, 177; emotional, 68; self, 108; substance, 68, 108, 112–13, 116–17
adoption, 3–4, 83, 116, 142, 171, 185
Afghanistan, 7
AFSP. See American Foundation for Suicide Prevention
alimony, 55, 72, 96
Alliance for Excellent Education, 103
American Association for Marriage and Family Therapy (AAMFT), 142, 201n20
American Civil War, 23
American Foundation for Suicide Prevention (AFSP), 114, 185
American Psychological Association (APA), 148, 201n23–24
American Revolution, 18
Andrzejewski, Laura, 34, 190n12
APA. See American Psychological Association
artificial insemination, 52

Banana Splits (organization), 127–28, 200nb
Barrymore, Drew, 68
Blackburn, Shirley, 25–26, 189n8
Block, Chase, 114–15, 199ne–g, 201n5, 207
Bly, Nellie, 17, 20, 189na–b
brainwashing, 70. See also parental alienation

CASA. See National Center on Addiction and Substance Abuse
Catholic(s), 8, 12, 14, 17, 83–84, 86, 188n18
CDC. See United States Centers for Disease Control and Prevention
CDR. See Coalition for Divorce Reform
Child-Centered Divorce Network, 42; child custody, 9–10, 82, 86–88, 116, 123, 142, 150, 162, 185; arrangements, 11, 57, 62, 72, 79–80, 88, 125, 134; battles, 20–22, 29, 35, 68, 81, 144, 162, 165, 171; joint, 11, 84, 86, 88, 96, 146; legal, 20, 83, 188n26–27, 189n14, 195n10–11, 195n18, 195n20
child labor, 23; laws, 68. See also U.S. Department of Labor
child support, 55, 70, 92, 96–97, 99, 102, 196n12–13
Church of England (Anglican Church), 17
Church of the Latter-day Saints. See Mormon(s)
Clinton, Bill, 100
Coalition for Divorce Reform (CDR), 36, 190n17
Cobain, Kurt, 111, 114, 199na–b
cocaine, 107, 112
cohabit/cohabitation, 166–68, 178, 181, 204n14
Council on Crime and Justice, 19, 198n19–20
counselor(s), 11, 51, 59, 69, 76, 113, 127, 130, 148, 171; divorce, 127, 159, 184; marriage, 33, 35, 40–41, 44–45, 56, 191n31

Culkin, Macaulay, 68
Cyrus, Miley, 67, 194na

Dalton, Abigail, 98–99, 123, 127nb, 199n5
Defense of Marriage Act (DOMA), 41, 81
dissolution of marriage, 9, 14, 17, 26, 28
Divorce Court, 5, 73–74, 194nc, 195n21
DoL. See U.S. Department of Labor
DOMA. See Defense of Marriage Act
domestic violence, 36, 41, 86, 118
Dr. Phil, 5
dysfunctional family/household, 30, 43, 111, 116

eating disorders, 113, 123
elope(abandon), 18–19
emancipation of minor children, 66, 68

financial literacy, 95, 196n11
First Amendment to the United States Constitution, 15, 84–85

Gibbons, Jim, 5
Gingrich, Newt, 5
Giuliani, Rudi, 5
Goldwater, Barry, 4
good divorce, 30
Gore, Al, 5
Great Depression, 29, 100
Guardian ad Litem, 82

heroin, 107, 110, 112
HHS. See U.S. Department of Health and Human Services
high school dropouts, 103–4, 118, 197n23–24. See also Undroppable
hippies, 27

"ideal" family, 26, 145
illicit drugs, 108–10
in loco parentis (in place of parents), 83
Iraq, 7
irreconcilable differences, 10, 28, 67, 159

Junior Achievement, 104

Kennedy, John F., 27
Kennedy, Robert, 27
King, Martin Luther Jr., 27
Kramer vs. Kramer, 29

Little Children, Big Challenges, 6, 117, 187n7

Maffesoli, Tyler, 50, 192n13
marijuana, 68, 110
Massachusetts Bay Colony, 17–18
mediator(s), 35, 40, 160, 162, 184
methamphetamine (meth), 107, 116
Millay, Edna St. Vincent, 23
minimum wage, 66, 101–2, 197nd
Money Matters program, 94
Mormon(s), 13, 83, 85–86, 188n22, 195n21
Mum and Dad Are Splitting Up, 34

National Center on Addiction and Substance Abuse (CASA), 108–10, 117, 198n6–7, 198n9, 19817
National Institute on Drug Use (NIDU), 110
NIDU. See National Institute on Drug Use
no-fault divorce, 10, 28, 39, 63, 190n24

Palin, Bristol, 171–72, 205nc–d
parent education, 133–34, 200n24
parental alienation, 69–70, 194n17
Parental Divorce Reduction Act (PDRA), 37, 39, 41
petitioner, 9, 187n14
Porter, Eleanor H., 24
Protestant, 17, 175
psychotherapist(s), 41, 47, 130–31, 184
Pulitzer Prize, 23, 161

Reagan, Ronald, 4, 28, 88–89
reconciliation, 12, 37–38

rehabilitation, 114
Rockefeller, Nelson, 4
runaway(s), 18, 107, 170

same-sex couples, 40–41, 52–53, 81,
    142–43, 167, 177–78, 192n19, 195n15,
    201n20
Sanford, Mark, 4
SCA. *See* Second Chances Act
Scholastic Choices, 33, 190n6
Second Chances Act (SCA), 38
Sesame Street, 5, 117, 187n6, 198n18
Shakers, 21–22
Sheline, Leslie, 53, 133, 192n22,
    200n23
Sindell, Max, 34, 144, 153, 190n11,
    201nb–c, 202n11, 208
Smith, Hailee, 64, 77, 135, 193n11,
    194n8, 200n2
SNAP. *See* Supplemental Nutrition
    Assistance Program
social media, 110, 118, 152, 157, 203nd
special-needs children, 80, 195n12
Squid and the Whale, The, 57
suffrage, 23, 189n6
Supplemental Nutrition Assistance
    Program (SNAP), 100

TANF. *See* Temporary Assistance for
    Needy Families
Teen Ink, 33, 51

Temporary Assistance for Needy Families
    (TANF), 100
therapist(s), 44, 47, 52, 139, 159;
    family, 44, 80, 127, 138, 152. See also
    psychotherapist(s)
therapy, 37–38, 44, 52, 113; using dogs in,
    79
Torn Apart, 3

U.S. Bureau of Labor Statistics, 6, 187n9
U.S. Census Bureau, 56, 99–100, 142,
    187n2, 197n16–17
U.S. Centers for Disease Control and
    Prevention (CDC), 6, 80, 113, 187n8,
    199nd
U.S. Department of Health and Human
    Services (HHS), 96, 116, 167, 184,
    196n1213, 198n13, 204n13
U.S. Department of Labor (DoL), 102,
    197n21–22
Undroppable, 118, 199nh. *See also* high
    school dropouts

visitation rights, 82–83
volunteering, 105, 127

Walker, Rebecca, 161–62, 203ne, 208
Winter, Ariel, 68
World War II, 7, 29

YouTube, 3, 34, 37, 118, 188na, 199nh

About the Author

With over 120 books published, **Kathlyn Gay** finds her life enriched by writing nonfiction works focusing on social and environmental issues, culture, and history. She also has written books about science, communication, sports, and other topics. She notes, "Because of the extensive research required when writing nonfiction, the learning opportunities abound." In addition, she feels rewarded by being able to collaborate on some book projects with family members who are scattered across the United States.

Some of Kathlyn's works have received starred reviews in *Booklist* and have been selected as Books for the Teen Age by the New York Public Library, awarded Outstanding Book by the National Council for Social Studies and National Science Teachers' Association, selected for "notable books for young people" by the American Library Association, and listed on *Voya's* Nonfiction Honor List. *School Library Journal* declares Gay's books are "well-organized, thoughtful presentations." A Kirkus reviewer writes that her books contain "lively, effective quotes." "Well researched, supported by facts" is a *Booklist* description.

A full-time freelance author, Kathlyn has also published hundreds of magazine features, stories, and plays, and she has written and contributed to encyclopedias, teachers' manuals, and textbooks. She is the author of a number of titles in the It Happened to Me series: *Epilepsy* (2002, with Sean McGarrahan), *Cultural Diversity* (2003), *Volunteering* (2004), *Religion and Spirituality in America* (2006), *The Military and Teens* (2008), *Body Image and Appearance* (2009), *Living Green* (2012), and *Bigotry and Intolerance* (2013).